1887

EDITORIAL WILD OATS

EDITORIAL WILD OATS

*Edward Ward Carmack
and Tennessee Politics*

WILLIAM R. MAJORS

The Poynter Institute
For Media Studies

ISBN 0-86554-133-7

Editorial Wild Oats
Copyright ©1984
Mercer University Press
All rights reserved
Printed in the United States of America

All books published by Mercer University Press
are produced on acid-free paper that exceeds the minimum standards
set by the National Historical Publications and Records Commission.

Library of Congress Cataloging in Publication Data:
Majors, William R., 1929-
Editorial wild oats.
Bibliography: p. 185
Includes index.
1. Carmack, Edward Ward, 1858-1908.
2. Legislators—Tennessee—Biography.
3. United States. Congress. House—Biography.
4. Journalists—Tennessee—Biography.
5. Tennessee—Politics and government—1865-1950.
I. Title.
E664.C28M34 1984   976.8'05'0924 [B]   84-10870
ISBN 0-86554-133-7 (alk. paper)

CONTENTS

FOREWORD ix
PREFACE xiii
ACKNOWLEDGEMENTS xix

1
MAKING OF THE MAN 1

2
APPRENTICESHIP 17

3
THE DAILY AMERICAN 35

4
THE COMMERCIAL APPEAL 51

5
SILVER AND POLITICS 69

6
CONGRESS 87

7
A CAT FIGHT 105

8
PROHIBITION AND POLITICS 123

9
MARTYRDOM 139

10
THE LEGACY 159

PICTORIAL ARCHIVES 169

BIBLIOGRAPHICAL ESSAY 185

INDEX 191

DEDICATION

In Memory of
C. L. Majors
Margaret Majors

FOREWORD

Edward Ward Carmack (1858-1908) has waited a long time for a scholarly biographer. A brilliant journalist, a spellbinding orator, and a powerful figure in Tennessee politics, Carmack made a vivid impression upon his contemporaries. His reputation in the early twentieth century transcended his own state, spread through the South, and momentarily achieved national scope. He was unmistakably and almost stereotypically a Southerner: dashing and romantic, proud and fearless, and passionately devoted to Southern traditions and values. He was also defensive, self-righteous, quick to anger, and sometimes vindictive. He was, as his biographer writes, a dynamic and flamboyant editor and politician who left his mark on the history of his state and region.

Professor William R. Majors, an authority on the modern political history of Tennessee and the author of a valuable political biography of a more recent Tennessean, Governor Gordon Browning,[1] has devoted the past few years to the research for and the writing of this book on Edward Ward Carmack. He has illuminated Carmack's career as a journalist and politician and has added to our understanding of the turn-of-the-century social and cultural milieu in which the Tennessean lived and worked. Read-

---

[1] William R. Majors, *The End of Arcadia: Gordon Browning and Tennessee Politics* (Memphis: Memphis State University Press, 1982).

ers will not find very much in this study about the inner man or his private life—in part, one suspects, because of the relative lack of personal correspondence at the author's disposal. The result is preeminently a public life. Even so, we learn a good deal about the makeup of this extraordinary man. Mr. Majors demonstrates a sensitive comprehension of his subject's family background, formative experiences, regional heritage, personality, and character traits.

Carmack's career was divided between—one might better say conjoined by—journalism and politics. The Tennessean wrote for or edited a succession of newspapers, including several of the state's leading journals. "Every Southern paper," Thomas D. Clark observed in *The Southern Country Editor* (1948), "reflected the personality of its editor." This was certainly true in the case of Tennessee's Carmack. He was an aggressive, crusading, unrelenting journalist, who wrote with a caustic pen and was unexcelled in his use of the penetrating gibe and the sarcastic rejoinder. His bitter and highly personal journalism led him into many controversies, one of which resulted in an abortive duel and another in his tragic death at the age of fifty. Following Carmack's death, the Memphis *Commercial Appeal* called attention to his admirable qualities, but also remarked that "his pen was too often steeped in bitterness and in the heat of controversy he said things that we are sure his goodness of heart caused him to regret when calm reflection resulted in deliberate judgment."

The Tennessee journalist was an inveterate champion of the Democratic party, and Mr. Majors's treatment of his editorial experience emphasizes his partisanship as a Democrat and as a party factionalist. The newspapers of that time, as the author shows, were intensely political; they played a vital part in the factional politics of the dominant party in the Southern states. One of the contributions of this study is the light it sheds on the role of the press in state and regional politics during this period.

Carmack's political career is the second major focus of this biography. In the 1890s the Tennessee editor's political influence grew rapidly, and he eventually emerged as the leader of one wing of the state's Democratic party. Mr. Majors follows the intricacies of Tennessee politics in the late nineteenth and early twentieth centuries with a sure hand, and he deftly locates Carmack in the shifting context of the Volunteer State's factional party politics.

Although Carmack was a conservative and was long identified with the Bourbon faction of the Democratic party, there was an element of reformism in his politics. In Congress, his renown as an orator was enhanced, speaking out in support of tariff reform, antitrust action, and the free coinage of silver. He condemned American imperialism at the turn of the century in language as rhetorical as that of William Jennings Bryan, and he lashed out at many of Theodore Roosevelt's foreign policies. In state politics he became, ironically, an ally of reformers and a hero of Democratic insurgents. One scholar has suggested that after he died, Carmack became "a symbol of public and political virtue, the defender of good, and a martyr for prohibition."[2]

The Tennessean was typical of "the dynamic and aggressive journalists of the nineteenth and early twentieth centuries who became popular political leaders," a breed that disappeared "with the advent of the electronic media and with changes in the structure and organization of print journalism." Carmack's "true place in Tennessee history," Mr. Majors concludes, is not as a symbol of virtue nor as a leader who brought about the end of the liquor traffic, but rather as "an interpreter of cultural patterns" who both reinforced traditional values and helped prepare the way for social change. His thinking and behavior reflected the South's defensiveness, conservatism, and tendency toward violence. He contributed to the mythology that surrounded the Old South, to the shining vision of the Lost Cause, and to the deeply held belief in Southern virtue. Yet Carmack was also an advocate of sectional reconciliation, and he eventually accepted and worked for a measure of economic and social reform, including free silver and statewide prohibition.

The cultural themes that most absorbed Carmack were those related to the heroic and romantic South. The most dramatic expression of that interest was Carmack's "Pledge to the South," delivered in the United States House of Representatives in 1898. That famous peroration endeared him to a host of Southerners. The Tennessee congressman spoke, he declared on that occasion, "for my native South. It is a land . . . scarred and riven by the plowshare of war and billowed with the graves of her dead, but [also] a land of legend, a land of song, a land of hallowed and heroic memories." Carmack's death in 1908 at the hands of a political foe provided dra-

---

[2]Joe Michael Shahan, "Reform and Politics in Tennessee: 1906-1914" (Ph.D. dissertation, Vanderbilt University, 1981) 178.

matic evidence of the extreme individualism, personal sensitivity, and resort to violence that still ran strong in Southern politics and journalism.

Despite the fact that this animated and compelling man was a forceful presence in the minds of his contemporaries, few Tennesseans today know much about him, and fewer still know why he is a significant figure in their state's history. I am sure that other readers will join me in applauding Professor Majors for rescuing Edward Ward Carmack from this long historical neglect and for giving us a balanced account of his career and a persuasive interpretation of his political and cultural role.

Nashville, Tennessee
February 1984

Dewey W. Grantham

PREFACE

Humorist Mark Twain was a versatile writer, journalist, lecturer, satirist, and social critic. One of his more obscure works is a collection of satirical essays published early in the twentieth century under the title, *Editorial Wild Oats*. Literary critics suggest that the essays are exaggerated versions of Twain's own experiences in journalism. One of the essays that I found particularly intriguing is entitled "Journalism in Tennessee."[1]

This essay is the story of a fictional journalist who was advised by a physician that a move to a Southern climate would improve his health. Accordingly, he secured a position as an associate editor on a small-town newspaper in Tennessee, the *Morning-Glory and Johnson County Warwhoop*. Upon reporting for duty, he discovered that the chief editor was an aggressive journalist who wrote vicious editorials abusing fellow journalists and other prominent citizens. The new associate was soon made painfully aware that the victims retaliated violently. On two occasions, angry, gun-wielding editors appeared at the newspaper office and shot at the chief. Then someone dropped a grenade down the chimney that shattered the stove. The chief received only minor scratches, but the new associate was struck by several wayward bullets and flying fragments of the stove. Shortly, "An in-

---

[1] Mark Twain, *Editorial Wild Oats* (New York: Harper and Brothers, Publishers, 1905). "Journalism in Tennessee" may have been written as early as 1871.

furiated mob" descended upon the newspaper office. The result was "a scene of riot and carnage" in which the new associate received a severe beating. The melee ended after a time, and the chief said to his new assistant: "You'll like this place when you get used to it." The associate replied: "I'll have to get you to excuse me. . . . I came South for my health; I will go back on the same errand, and suddenly. Tennesseean [sic] journalism is too stirring for me."

The message in Twain's satire is obvious: journalism could be a violent profession in Tennessee; editors wrote vituperative editorials, and the victims were often violent in response. Although grossly exaggerated, there was an element of truth in Twain's essay. There were indeed instances of violence in the history of journalism in Tennessee, including shooting affairs. It would be wrong, however, to assume that violence was peculiar to journalism in Tennessee, or that the Volunteer State press was more aggressive than the press in the rest of the nation. On the contrary, newspapers in the state mirrored the patterns and trends of journalism across the nation. The American style of journalism was aggressive and outspoken; even vicious editorials were characteristic from the beginning. Indeed, during the years between the Revolution and the Civil War when the modern newspaper emerged, journals were established as partisan political organs and editors wrote inflammatory editorials, for which they were occasionally physically assaulted or had their presses wrecked. But violence was not the only similarity between the press in Tennessee and the rest of the country.

Journalism in Tennessee, as across the nation, expanded rapidly in the post-Civil War years. More efficient presses and typesetting machines were introduced and cheap wood-pulp paper replaced the more expensive rag paper. This reduced the cost of publishing, and the result was a proliferation of newspapers accompanied by an increase in readership. New city dailies and small-town and county weeklies sprang up all over the country. It was not uncommon to have two or more competing morning dailies and two or more evening dailies in Tennessee's cities. Almost every small town and county had at least one weekly newspaper. While many journals remained a one-man operation, the financial requirements of publishing a city daily were beyond the resources of most individuals.

Major urban daily newspapers were thus owned by syndicates as corporate enterprises or as an investment with the expectation of a reasonable return on the investment. However, profit was not an exclusive motive for founding and publishing newspapers. While there was still an element of romance and adventure in journalism, the press served as an important outlet for partisan political and economic propaganda. In addition, certain vested interests had motives for investing in newspapers. The more publicly visible business enterprises such as railroads sought to control or influence the editorial policy of journals. Because of the type of service offered, railroads were targets of popular discontents. Railroad management, therefore, sought to establish a positive public image through a favorable press. This was achieved in several ways. Railroad advertising was an important source of revenue for newspapers, and editors would occasionally demonstrate their appreciation with favorable editorials, for which they were rewarded with free boarding passes and market tips. The desire for influence led one Tennessee railroad to outright ownership when in 1882 the Louisville and Nashville Railroad became the proprietor of the Nashville *Daily American*. An instance such as this was the exception rather than the rule. Railroad management, generally, was content with less direct control either by providing capital to sympathetic individuals in order that they may purchase a newspaper or by having one of the firm's executives sit on the board of directors.

Journalism became a highly competitive business in the years following the Civil War. Although machinery and cheaper paper had reduced costs and readership had increased, advertising remained the principal source of revenue. Because advertisers were attracted by large circulations, the contest for readership was highly competitive. Many adopted the sensational style of Joseph Pulitzer who set the pattern for modern journalism in his stewardship of the *New York World*. The techniques of sensational journalism included an aggressive news policy with detailed treatment of crime, sex scandals, and disasters, the sponsoring of stunts, crusades, and a variety of promotions, plus copious illustrations.

Some even adopted the style of "yellow journalism" made famous by publisher William Randolph Hearst. Yellow journalism was a more blatant and dishonest sensationalism that featured large scareheads screaming excitement, faked pictures, impostures, and various kinds of frauds. Not all publishers in Tennessee or across the nation adopted the sensational style; indeed, many remained both conservative and successful. But it caused others to follow the pattern set by Pulitzer. Such style was, however, a matter of degree, for sensational journalism was a tendency, not having a precise pattern, and some Tennessee publishers indulged in sensationalism only on occasion. By the 1880s the sensational style was common in the Volunteer

State. Headlines were often bold, imaginative, and exciting, being purposely designed to attract readers. Six or more subheads followed, partially summarizing the story which was often long, quite detailed, and sometimes excessive.

Journals that practiced some degree of sensationalism also tended to be blatantly partisan in political reporting. During a political campaign, for example, reports would be slanted in favor of the candidate that the newspaper supported. On a speaking tour, he would be "magnificently received" by a "large and enthusiastic crowd." The opponent was elsewhere being received by a "sullen and unresponsive" group.

The conservative press in Tennessee and the sensational newspapers differed in style, but both tended to have one thing in common: editors engaged in what might be called the rhetoric of excess on the editorial page. Like Twain's fictional journalist, editors penned outspoken, hardhitting, and inflammatory editorials. Often they were so bold and vigorous in character assassinations that they bordered on slander and libel. Partisan newspapers always singled out the opposition party—its principles, policies, practices, and its leaders—for censure. An editorial in the *Nashville Democrat* in November 1888 is illustrative. The editor suggested that "the people of Tennessee must never let one important fact escape them—the republican party in this state is rotten from root to branch and in its very nature can be nothing else. What can be hoped from a party whose . . . masses are made up of chicken thieves, burglars, drunken bums and the most ignorant and degraded hoodlums on earth?" At the same time the party that was endorsed received praise for true patriotism, principles, and wise leadership.

Some of the most truculent language used by editorial writers was reserved for their counterparts on other newspapers, both in the city or across the state. Editors regularly took issue with colleagues who held contrary political and economic views, debating each other in editorial columns. The maverick editor of the Louisville *Courier-Journal*, Henry Watterson, was a favorite target of Tennessee journalists, and a number of long-range debates took place. Most discussions, however, were with locally competing editors. Some were of short duration, lasting only a few days, while others lasted for weeks or even months, finally becoming feuds. The language could become so volatile that abused editors resorted to threats of violence, challenges to duels, and even actual violence.

Editorial debates tended to be esoteric in nature, being written less for public consumption than as internal contests among peers. It was a challenge to pen a good editorial, or even better, a good rebuttal to one written by a competitor. Points seemingly were scored by a well-written editorial as judged by peers; the public was a mere observer of the game. In any case, reputations within the journalistic fraternity were made on the editorial page. Because of the competitive and partisan nature of newspapers, journalism in Tennessee was not always a profitable enterprise.

In the latter half of the nineteenth century, Tennessee journalism exhibited a pattern of instability. Its history is a crazy quilt of the founding of new papers, of failures, mergers, takeovers, and of frequent changes in management and editorships. Some failed within a few months, some lingered a year or two. Those that survived experienced mergers, takeovers, and name changes. In Nashville, for example, at least nine newspapers were established between 1865 and 1890 but in effect only two survived. Some simply died while others were bought out by competitors; there were seven mergers. One of the most successful newspapers in that city was the *Daily American*, but it bought out, or was merged with, several competitors and experienced four name changes during those years. Moreover, between 1880 and 1895, the *Daily American* was owned by eleven distinct syndicates. Despite the lack of stability, the press in the late nineteenth and early twentieth centuries was an institution in Tennessee, as in the nation, providing news, information, and entertainment, interpreting news and information, and transmitting culture. Accordingly, print journalism had a good deal of influence in molding public opinion.

Scholarly research in the social sciences postulates that only in very rare circumstances is the press, or the mass media, able to change well-established cultural values, beliefs, and norms. In short, the public responds to and interprets news and information selectively. On the other hand, the press does influence the adoption of new styles, fads, manners, and technological innovations. More important, journalism can set the issues by deciding what is news and providing this information selectively. The ability of the press to shape public opinion in the late nineteenth and early twentieth centuries depended in large measure on the leadership of the journalistic profession.

The history of American journalism during this era is replete with the names of famous publishers and editors: Horace Greeley, James Gordon Bennett, Whitelaw Reid, Edwin Lawrence Godkin, Joseph Pulitzer, William Randolph Hearst, and more. These men were leaders in their field, but they were also public figures, influential in politics, and each had a personal following. Tennessee had its share of locally well-known and influential publishers and editors. One of the state's most successful journalists was Edward Ward Carmack. As much as anyone, he made sensational journalism a common pattern in Tennessee. As an editor, he reinforced the values and beliefs of Bourbon conservatism, but he also set the issues on the social agenda. Dynamic and flamboyant, Carmack had his own personal following that enabled him to secure an elective political office, but he was at his best as an editorial writer. Skilled in the use of satire, sarcasm, and vitriol, Carmack was always at the center of controversy, often of his own making. The victims of his editorial barbs sometimes felt compelled to retaliate. Violence or threats of violence were a part of his life. Although to a much lesser degree, his experiences were those depicted in Mark Twain's satire. The only missing element in Twain's description of journalism in Tennessee was the ultimate tragedy—violent death.

ACKNOWLEDGEMENTS

A good many individuals provided assistance in a variety of ways throughout the course of researching and writing this study. The most significant contribution was a grant by the National Endowment for the Humanities to attend a summer seminar at the University of North Carolina at Chapel Hill. It provided the support and time to do a great majority of the research and to examine the papers of Edward Ward Carmack that are in the Southern Historical Collection at the University of North Carolina. I owe a debt of gratitude to George Brown Tindall for inviting me to attend the seminar. Thanks go to the other members of the seminar who provided encouragement and especially to Richard Hughes, John Lupold, and Adrienne Bond for suggesting sources, and to Douglas McReynolds for calling my attention to Mark Twain's essay, "Journalism in Tennessee." The staffs at the library and at the Southern Historical Collection at the University of North Carolina and at the Tennessee State Library and Archives efficiently supplied materials for research. Special thanks go to Robert E. Corlew and Robert L. Taylor for reading an earlier draft and making useful suggestions for improving the manuscript. Gary Freeze and Stanley Pearson helped in procuring and processing photographs and Becky Eldridge typed the manuscript. Finally, I am grateful to my most severe reader and critic, my wife Lynelle, for incisive comments about content and style.

1

MAKING OF THE MAN

The citizens of Culleoka, a quiet Middle Tennessee village located a few miles south of Columbia in Maury County, were proud of the little school in their community. They boasted that the schoolmaster, William Robert Webb, was the best teacher in the state. A native of North Carolina and a wounded veteran of the Civil War, Webb had migrated to Tennessee in 1870 and was soon employed as principal of the Culleoka Institute. Under his leadership, the school prospered and quickly won such a reputation that it attracted pupils from across the state and beyond.

Curriculum at Culleoka Institute stressed the classical courses—literature, composition, mathematics, history, and the Greek and Latin languages. Excellence in the classroom was required; sloppy work was not tolerated. Discipline was strict and punishment for violation of school rules was swift and sure. Webb was also an innovative schoolmaster; he allowed his pupils to establish their own individual study habits and permitted them to organize and control their own scholastic societies and athletic teams. More important, Webb revealed a deep caring and concern for those under his tutelage and most responded with respect for the schoolmaster. They referred to him affectionately as "Sawney."[1]

---

[1]Laurence McMillan, *The Schoolmaker: Sawney Webb and the Bell Buckle Story* (Chapel Hill: University of North Carolina Press, 1971) xi-xvii, 5-82; see also W. R. Webb (Sawney Webb's son) to J. D. Anderson, 1 January 1937, Box 14, Folder 7, James Douglas Anderson

Despite the rigorous scholastic requirements, the pupils at Culleoka Institute also had time for play. There was time for team games, swimming, or simply roaming the fields and forests around the village. Life at the school was ordinarily quiet and peaceful as the pupils went about the serious business of their studies. Except for high jinks and mischief by normally active and fun-loving boys, the tranquility at the school was seldom broken by controversy. So in the spring of 1876 when the pupils erupted in anger over the severe discipline applied to one of their peers, it was startling. They were outraged by the suspension from school of one of the most popular boys, the winsome, seventeen-year-old Edward Ward Carmack, "Ned." Indeed, the boys at Culleoka Institute were so close to open revolt that the schoolmaster felt compelled to dismiss classes and declared a holiday in order to ease tension and maintain discipline.

The issue that led to the suspension developed soon after a young man by the name of Joshua Harrison enrolled. Already ordained as a Methodist minister, Harrison was somewhat older than the other pupils; he wore a long black tailcoat, had a deep voice, and was stern and solemn in manner. Harrison was soon the butt of ridicule because of his pious demeanor. Not long after his arrival, he began holding a revival, preaching to convert the "sinners" among the boys at the school. Webb made no attempt to stop the revival and, in fact, gave it his tacit approval. A devout Christian himself, he hoped that the religious experience would give his "boys direction and purpose in their lives." However, some of the pupils began to lampoon Harrison with a counter revival, a "revival of sinners."[2]

Stung by the ridicule, the young minister appealed to the schoolmaster for relief. Upon investigation, Webb confirmed his suspicion that Ned Carmack was the ringleader. The boy was a leader of his peers and mischievous; he was also the schoolmaster's most brilliant pupil and was like a son to him. Webb confronted Ned, told him to quit holding his meetings, and pleaded with him to stop ridiculing Harrison. The boy gave his word that

---

Papers, Tennessee Historical Society's Collection, Tennessee State Library and Archives, Nashville. William R. "Sawney" Webb eventually became a legend. In 1886, he moved from Culleoka to Bell Buckle, Tennessee, and founded a school that is still active today. It captured the public's attention because it produced a number of leaders in the various professions. In January 1913, the Tennessee General Assembly honored Webb by electing him to a temporary vacancy in the United States Senate.

[2]McMillan, *The Schoolmaker*, 81-82.

he would hold no more meetings, but would not promise to cease making fun of the minister. His control of the school challenged, Webb felt that he had no choice but to discipline young Ned; "he could not allow this brilliant headstrong youth to wag the school." He suspended the lad for the duration of the revival, about two weeks. The suspension quickly became an issue among the boys. Ned's friends and followers, no doubt with his encouragement, reacted "with resentment and anger," forcing the dismissal of classes. Moreover, much to the distress of the schoolmaster, Ned Carmack took his suspension as expulsion, or so he declared, and refused to return to the institute at the end of the two weeks. Ned implied that he had been persecuted by Webb. The young man's refusal to return pained the schoolmaster, for he was deeply fond of the lad, later following Carmack's career "like a doting father." In reality, Ned Carmack's response to the suspension was contrived.[3]

The controversy at Culleoka Institute reveals a good deal about the young man who became a brilliant journalist, a popular politician, the leader of crusades, the martyr for the cause of prohibition in Tennessee, and the man who provoked his own destruction with behavior similar to his response to the suspension. At a tender age, Edward Ward Carmack demonstrated the charismatic qualities of a natural leader and a mastery of the use of ridicule, sarcasm, and invectiveness. He learned through experience how to create controversy over issues of little moment and how to draw attention to himself by placing himself at the center of the storm. He learned to employ a tactic sometimes used by successful leaders: winning recognition by making it appear that he was being persecuted in defense of a cause or of a distressed minority. The incident of the suspension revealed that Carmack possessed not only this ability, but also had the personality and character traits of stubbornness, contentiousness, restlessness, mental rigidity, and impatience with restraint. It would be impossible to identify precisely what caused these traits, though undoubtedly the environment in which he was raised was a factor—he had had a fatherless childhood that spanned the crises of the Civil War and Reconstruction. However, upon closer examination, these recalcitrant traits were perhaps the heritage of his Scot ancestors.

---

[3]Ibid.

The Scots were one of the largest of the European national groups to settle in the British North American colonies. Beginning in the seventeenth century, thousands immigrated and settled in every colony. The migration became a steady flow and the hardy Scots, moving relentlessly westward with each new generation, helped people areas such as Tennessee. Courageous, the Scots were ideal pioneers on the inhospitable frontier—they were known by the same traits that characterized Carmack. All stereotypes contain a good deal of exaggeration, yet there is always an element of truth that lends credibility to them. Ascribing Edward Ward Carmack's character and personality to his heritage would no doubt be simple mythification. Nevertheless, his progenitors were predominantly, if not exclusively, of Scot origin.

There was little of distinction in the Carmack line. Like most American families, theirs was a record containing both successes and failures. Compiled in 1828, their history identified a few who were in the professions, some who were successful in politics, some in the crafts, and a few modest war heroes. There were also "lazy braggarts" and drunkards. Marriage infused the Carmack family with a number of strains, and the family history cited the McMillan line as contributing to the honor and glory of the Carmacks. Yet, the McMillans do not appear to have achieved any greater stature. The most prominent infusion came from the Stephenson family. Edward Ward Carmack's paternal grandmother was Nancy Agnes Smith, a Stephenson progeny. This family was among the Scot settlers in South Carolina where a number achieved positions of social and political leadership. In the pattern of migration, the Stephenson offsprings moved west across the mountains into Tennessee. It was here that Nancy Smith met and married Cornelius Carmack. But this union did not lead to dramatic change in the social status accorded the Carmacks. The family remained neither gentry nor peasantry, but was part of what has been called the hardy yeomanry that populated North America.[4]

Edward Ward Carmack's great-great grandfather was the family's original Cornelius Carmack, the son of John and Elizabeth Carmack. Although it is possible that Cornelius Carmack was born in Scotland, it is more likely that he was born in Maryland about 1750. He apparently served

---

[4]Family history in Franc M. Carmack Diaries, vol. 2, Southern Historical Collection, University of North Carolina Library, Chapel Hill.

during the American Revolution, after which he then married and settled in Washington County, Virginia. Cornelius raised a large family and saw most of his children migrate to Tennessee, as he did in his later years to live with one of his sons. Another son, Joseph, settled first in Sumner County and then in Robertson. Joseph's son, also named Cornelius, was Edward Ward Carmack's grandfather. Cornelius served as a corporal in the Seminole War in 1818, farmed, taught school, married Miss Smith, and settled in Lauderdale County in northwest Alabama in the early 1820s. While there, he occupied several militia positions, was a justice of the peace, and once was a member of the Alabama legislature. In 1841, a restless Cornelius moved a few miles west to Tishomingo County, Mississippi. He became active in the politics of that state and was attending a convention in Jackson, called in 1851 to consider secession, when he fell ill with typhoid fever and died. To the union of Cornelius and Nancy Smith Carmack were born five children, three boys and two girls, one of whom died in infancy. The third son, born in Lauderdale County in 1832, was christened Francis McMillan Carmack. Franc, as he was called, was the father of Tennessee's editor-politician, Edward Ward Carmack.[5]

Intelligent and quick to learn, Franc Carmack was a precocious child. Being of some substance, Cornelius Carmack was able to provide educational opportunities for his progeny and in 1848, at the age of sixteen, Franc was enrolled in Franklin College in Franklin, Tennessee. His older brother, Edward Ward, graduated that year from Franklin, returning to Mississippi to establish Euclid Hill Academy in the community of Jacinto near his father's home. Franc finished his course at Franklin College in three years, graduating in October 1851 at the age of nineteen at the head of his class. He returned to Mississippi and taught briefly with his brother at Euclid Hill Academy, but at some point in 1852 he returned to Franklin College as a teacher. The following year he taught at a school in Robertson County, Tennessee. Although the dates are not known, during this time he had become engaged to marry Elvira Kate Holding of Lewisburg in Marshall County. Nothing is known of the background of Kate Holding except that she was listed in the census of 1850 as a fifteen-year-old member of a Marshall County household headed by a Vaden S. Stevens.[6] Possibly she was an or-

---

[5]Ibid.

[6]Ibid.; Byron and Barbara Sistler, transcribers, *1850 Census of Tennessee* (Evanston: Byron Sistler and Associates, 1976) 8:26.

phan, but in any case her guardian was able to send her to school at Minerva College, a female academy near Franklin College, and it was here that she and Franc Carmack became acquainted. They were married in October of 1853 and to this union was born three children—a daughter Agnes, and two sons, Samuel Cornelius and Edward Ward.

In 1854, Franc Carmack was appointed professor of ancient languages at Franklin College. He also became a minister in the Christian, or Campbellite, Church. At some point in the previous five years Franc had been converted to that denomination, having been raised a devout Methodist. There is a legend that Cornelius never forgave his son for this departure from the faith. But as there is no evidence that he disinherited his son, it is uncertain that his father even had knowledge of the conversion. It is quite possible that he died before Franc was converted to the Christian Church.

Franc Carmack remained at Franklin College until 1858 when he accepted a position at Bledsoe Female Academy in Sumner County. It was here at Castalian Springs that Edward Ward Carmack was born on 5 November that same year. He was not destined to have a normal childhood or to be raised in the house of his father, for Franc Carmack was in declining health by 1858. It is said that he had been severely injured when a horse kicked him in the chest and the injury grew progressively worse. It seems likely, however, that he suffered from tuberculosis. Whatever the problem, his lungs began to hemorrhage as early as 1855 and his health deteriorated as he suffered from persistent and increasingly violent coughing spells. He gave up teaching in 1860 and was, in his own words, a "confirmed invalid." In a desperate effort to regain his health, Franc and Kate journeyed south to Selma, Alabama, in hopes that the warmer climate would be beneficial. After several months, there was no improvement, and Franc Carmack accepted the inevitable. He visited briefly in Jacinto, Mississippi, before returning to Sumner County to await death. It came in the summer of 1861.[7]

Thus was Kate Carmack left a widow with three small children to raise and with few resources. Franc Carmack had not acquired material goods and had left no estate. Indeed, he had not been able to support his family

---

[7]Franc M. Carmack Diaries, vol. 2. See also Robert E. Hooper, *Crying in the Wilderness: A Biography of David Lipscomb* (Nashville: David Lipscomb College, 1979) 312; Paul Franklin Bumpus, *Carmack: The Edward Ward Carmack Story* (Franklin: Paul Franklin Bumpus, 1977) 1-2; Kenneth McKellar, *Tennessee Senators As Seen By One of Their Successors* (Kingsport: Southern Publishers, Inc., 1942) 461-62.

for more than a year prior to his death. But Kate's situation was not hopeless, for she could look to family for help. In the manner common to extended families in agrarian communities, family took care of its own, and Kate and her children moved to Jacinto to live with her husband's people. If the times had been normal, this would have been sufficient to provide the material, if not the emotional, needs of Kate Carmack's children. But the times were not normal. Like so many other Southern families, the Carmacks were directly affected by the upheaval of secession and Civil War that broke out in 1861.

Jacinto is located in the northeastern corner of Mississippi, an area that saw a good deal of military activity and some heavy fighting. Young Edward Ward Carmack was not old enough to understand the nature of the conflict, but some of the activities of war must have been within his memory. He certainly observed marching armies, both Blue and Grey, and he surely saw foraging soldiers taking livestock and produce, if not other portable property. He must have seen the tragic results of battle with the inevitable casualties, and it is likely that he heard the sounds of battle.[8] Although he could not comprehend the events, he could sense the feelings and attitudes of his kin toward the conflict.

Carmack's family, like most Southerners, were convinced of the justness of the South's cause and were optimistic in the beginning. As time passed, however, optimism was replaced by anger at defeat, bitterness toward foraging armies, humiliation at occupation, and frustration at the inability to do anything about the situation. As his teenage years spanned the Reconstruction era, he was more readily able to absorb the Southern hostility toward the Northern Radicals and their program to restore the Southern states to the Union. Young Ned Carmack was less than three years old when his father died and thus had little, if any, memory of Franc Carmack. Yet his father left a legacy that contributed a good deal to the making of Edward Ward Carmack as an adult. Franc Carmack had kept a journal and, near the end of his life when he realized that death was close at hand, he began to write for his children with the expectation that they would read his messages as soon as they were old enough. In an eloquent passage, dated 4 July 1861, he justified the cause of secession:

---

[8]Jacinto is barely twenty miles south of Shiloh, Tennessee, the location of one of the bloodiest battles of the war, and even closer to Corinth, Mississippi, where another battle occurred.

> This day eighty-five years ago was born our national independence, and the foundations laid of one of the first nations of the earth. Glorious, almost beyond historic parallel, was the career of the United States of America, until Fanaticism . . . grasped the reins of power, and Liberty and Equality were ruthlessly driven from their seats in the once fair, fair fabric of our national government. How changed the scene! Behold today, instead of a prosperous and happy People, bound together by the ties of kindred and interest . . . a divided and hostile people [are] in arms against each other; whilst in the City of Washington—the once proud capital of a united people—sits a sectional Congress, deliberating, in all probability, upon the ways and means of prosecuting the most wicked, the most unhuman war, perhaps, that the world ever saw! O, my bleeding Country, is there no help for Thee? Must fanaticism and intolerance continue to trample upon the palladium of our liberties of the sacred constitution bequeathed to us by our Fathers—or force it to seek refuge in a more congenial clime, where it may find brave and patriotic hearts to do and dare in its defense? Such seems to be the potent of the passing hour.

The following day, he wrote: "My heart bleeds at the thought of the divisions of the glorious heritage transmitted by our Fathers, of the desecration of our national Constitution, and the perversion of the original objects of our government. I have advocated and now as acquiesce in, the dissolution of the union, only as a matter of necessity—the less of two evils."[9] Those words alone were not enough to influence young Ned Carmack, but they reinforced attitudes conveyed by his living kin and together they conditioned his thinking. In his adult years he expressed the firm conviction that the South's cause had been righteous and that secession had been just.

After the war, in 1865 or possibly 1866, Kate Carmack returned to Tennessee and moved her family back to Sumner County. The reason for the move is not clear, but she very likely returned to raise her children in her religion. Like her husband, Kate was a devoted member of the Christian Church, and no doubt she felt isolated at Jacinto and wanted to be with others in her faith, especially David Lipscomb, a family friend. Lipscomb was a prominent Christian minister who founded the Nashville Bible School, an institution later renamed in his honor. Franc Carmack and Lipscomb had been classmates at Franklin College where they became fast

---

[9]Franc M. Carmack Diaries, vol. 2.

friends. Both entered the ministry about the same time. They also worked together in church organizational and educational efforts in the Middle Tennessee area. David Lipscomb's father, Granville, baptized Edward Ward and possibly the other children. When he came to the realization that he was dying, Franc asked his friend to attend the spiritual guidance of his family. After Kate's return to Sumner County, Lipscomb did indeed try to live up to the responsibility, but with far less success with young Ned than he desired.[10]

Life in Sumner County was no easier than in Jacinto. The post-Civil War years were difficult throughout the South, but perhaps more so for the widow and her small brood. Under the circumstances, it was expected that young Ned would help provide his keep, so he went to work at an early age. While still a small boy, he plowed fields for twenty-five cents a day as well as performing other farm labor. He once worked as a laborer in a brickyard, and possibly had other forms of employment during these years. Almost every biographical reference to Carmack emphasizes that he was a poor boy who had to work unusually hard to help his mother. In his adult years, Carmack occasionally referred to the poverty of his youth and sometimes described the winter that the driven snow sifted through holes in the roof and patched windowpanes onto his bed.[11] However, the emphasis on youthful poverty and Carmack's references to it tended to be exaggerated and self-serving. The times were indeed difficult, and everyone had to work hard just to survive. Small boys in most families performed heavy labor; even those from relatively affluent families in this rural and agrarian environment were expected to help with the work. In this respect, Ned Carmack's childhood was normal. Moreover, he had an advantage denied most boys of his generation: he had access to as good an education as was available. His heritage was certainly sufficient to motivate him to take advantage of every opportunity to learn and achieve. In Jacinto, he lived with an uncle who directed an academy, and his mother, a teacher, who undoubtedly provided direct instruction in the basics of an education. He had access to what books were available.

---

[10]Hooper, *Crying in the Wilderness*, 40, 51, 58, 60, 69, 312.

[11]Bumpus, *Carmack*, 2; McKellar, *Tennessee Senators*, 462; Hugh Walker, "Carmack-Cooper: Editor's Murder Shocked State," *The Tennessean*, 19 April 1981.

Precocious, young Carmack demonstrated a desire to learn and he read voraciously. By the age of thirteen, he had exhausted the available educational resources, and Kate Carmack was forced to turn elsewhere. That is when she learned of the existence of the unique school at Culleoka, a village a few miles from her hometown, Lewisburg. Kate Carmack enrolled her son in Webb's school in 1872.

Sawney Webb quickly recognized that he had an exceptionally bright pupil in Ned. The young man proved to be gifted in literature and composition, and developed such a facility of expression that he excelled in public speaking and debate. The slender red-haired youth with a dimple in both his nose and chin was also cheerful, outgoing, and well liked by his peers. He was also a bit mischievous. Webb's biographer described one incident:

> At commencement time in May of 1873, Culleoka was swarming with visitors. Laughter greeted a vital, red-headed fatherless youth named Ned Carmack who led a "choir of boys" with combs and tissue paper in a hilarious rendition of "Rye Straw." Professor Webb uneasily consented to the "profane" performance in the church sanctuary. Ned appealed to him. Ned was original. Ned was a handful. "He was the greenest boy that ever hit this school, with the exception of his hair and that was the reddest, but he wouldn't stay green, he caught on."[12]

For some reason, Carmack left the tutelage of Webb at the end of the school year in the spring of either 1873 or 1874. It is not known where he went or what he did. Possibly he returned to Jacinto and attended his uncle's Euclid Hill Academy. In any event, he was back with Webb in the fall of 1875 and a Columbia newspaper reported the event: "Ned Carmack, a former pupil of the Webb Brothers returned to school last week, after an absence of about eighteen months. Ned is warmly welcomed by his many friends, who are glad to have him with them again." The youth's return to the Culleoka school was even more meaningful to the schoolmaster. According to Webb's biographer, "Ned Carmack's arrival was like a triumphal homecoming. The school, in fact, was like a home to him. . . . This fatherless youth was someone special to him [Webb]. . . . Sawney was convinced that Ned was a genius. He watched the youth devour volume after volume of English and

---

[12]McMillan, *The Schoolmaker*, 73-74.

classical literature under the wise tutelage of Brother John. He marveled at Ned's sharp wit and rollicking energies."[13]

In spite of the accolades, Ned Carmack was a problem. When his mischievous nature forced Webb to suspend him in the spring of 1876, followed by Ned's failure to return to school, both the schoolmaster and his mother were deeply hurt. She realized that she had an unusually bright son and had high hopes for his future. She appealed to Webb:

> I rec'd a letter from Ned this morning bringing to me the sad news of his disgrace. . . . I feel it is due you, as those who would have been friends to my fatherless boy to say something, I scarcely know what. Ned said that you required him to go home. Poor boy, he has no home, and no money to come to me, and I none to send him. . . . He has always held you both in such high esteem that I thought you could have more influence over him than anyone else. For a sorrowing mother's sake try him once more if you can.[14]

Ned Carmack was indeed a trial to his mother. His antics at school, his mischievousness, and his rebellious and independent nature distressed Kate Carmack. Her greatest dream was for her brilliant son to enter the ministry of her church, and she tried every way to turn him in that direction. David Lipscomb also tried to persuade the youth to turn his talents to a spiritual calling, but to no avail. At one time, possibly when he was suspended from Webb's school, Ned Carmack came close to accepting the call. Lipscomb's biographer declared that "he was to have met David Lipscomb with every intention of beginning a life of preaching, but the meeting did not materialize."[15] His failure to enter the ministry left his mother sorely disappointed.

Not yet eighteen years of age, Ned Carmack faced the world with no material possessions and few prospects. But in the manner of youth, the personable and handsome lad looked to the future with confidence. He was intelligent and articulate in both the written and spoken word, talents that opened doors and provided opportunities. The details of his activities for

---

[13]Columbia *Herald and Mail*, 29 October 1875; McMillan, *The Schoolmaker*, 80. Webb's chief assistant was his brother, John Maurice Webb.

[14]McMillan, *The Schoolmaker*, 81-82.

[15]Hooper, *Crying in the Wilderness*, 312.

several years are not clear. It appears, however, that he took up residence in Columbia soon after leaving the Culleoka Institute and worked in a library for a while. He was soon studying law with an unknown patron and in 1879, at the age of twenty-one, he was admitted to practice as an attorney. One biographical statement declared that Carmack had to struggle as a young lawyer, referring to his first years of practice as the "starving time." Although he did not step into a lucrative practice, it is probable that he joined his benefactor. Moreover, his talents were quickly recognized and Ned Carmack was soon well established in Columbia.[16]

Carmack's advancement was rapid. Two years after admission to the bar, he was made city attorney of Columbia, a position often presented to promising young attorneys. A year later, the popular lawyer was elected justice of the peace and magistrate of the Maury County court. As the local legislative bodies for Tennessee, county courts were not known as great deliberative bodies nor were they often called upon to debate great issues. Yet even here, Carmack was able to seize an issue and capture the public's attention.

A request by the chancery court for funds for new furnishings annoyed the Maury County court. After an angry debate, the young squire in all seriousness, but perhaps facetiously, moved that the chancery court be abolished and the motion carried by a wide margin. The action could not stand a constitutional test, but Carmack had gained publicity. His reputation grew, and in 1884 he was elected representative from Maury and Williamson Counties to Tennessee's General Assembly. His one term in the legislature was undistinguished, but again he revealed his talent for creating publicity. He challenged the method long used to select nominees for the state's constitutional offices. The General Assembly is required to elect the secretary of state, treasurer, and comptroller, and it was the practice of the parties to nominate candidates in caucus. When the legislature convened in January 1885, Carmack introduced a resolution before the Democrats calling for the abolition of this method. The resolution failed, but the freshman lawmaker again drew attention to himself. Only once in that session did he make remarks on the floor of the House of Representatives, but he made a name for himself nonetheless.

---

[16]Bumpus, *Carmack*, 3.

His legislative record preceding him, the political novice was offered an opportunity to become a member of the fourth estate. Whether he deliberately sought to become a journalist cannot be known, but his ability to write obviously inclined him in that direction. He must have realized, too, that successful publishers and editors were able to sway and incite public opinion, and that the names of prominent journalists were as much, if not more, the subject of household conversation as were those of the leading politicians. It was, therefore, natural that, given his talents and craving for leadership, he gravitated to an avocation that had the potential for prestige and power. Whatever his motives, at some point in the mid 1880s, he became an editorial writer for one of the Columbia newspapers. Whereas it is possible that he wrote for the larger *Herald and Mail*, it is more likely that it was the *Maury Democrat*, a paper founded in 1882 principally by J. T. Williamson and J. L. Bullock as an organ of the "Sky Blue" faction of the Democratic party. In any case, Carmack earned a considerable reputation as a writer. The result was an offer in 1886 to join the editorial staff of the Nashville *Daily American* and to pursue a career in journalism.[17]

Edward Ward Carmack was twenty-seven years of age and still a bachelor when he went to Nashville. Standing six feet tall, weighing about 180 pounds, and with a head of flowing red hair, he was both handsome and distinguished looking. Charming, talented, and ambitious, he was one of the most eligible men in Columbia and many of the available young women must have looked upon him as a desirable catch. Being compulsive and so committed to a life in public affairs, Carmack was almost married to his work. He had little time for affairs of the heart or for leisure-time activity. Yet he realized that he needed a wife. Because the move to Nashville did not require that Carmack give up his domicile in Columbia, he returned to that city to look for a spouse. His choice was Elizabeth Cobey Dunnington.

Cobey Dunnington was the daughter of the late Frank Cobey Dunnington, a prominent lawyer and a leading citizen of the community. It was said that F. C. Dunnington had learned the printing trade as a mere lad and was an editor by the time he was fifteen. He became editor of the Nashville *Union and American* a few years before the Civil War, served on the staff of

---

[17]Ibid. Only a few issues of the Columbia *Herald* and *Herald and Mail* and none of the *Maury Democrat* between 1878 and 1889 are extant and, therefore, no surviving copies of Carmack's early editorial writings.

General Nathan Bedford Forrest during that conflict, and helped to reestablish the Nashville paper soon after the war was over. From one of the leading families, the twenty-nine-year-old Cobey was an excellent choice for a wife. Just when the courtship began or when they became engaged is unknown, but the marriage was solemnized by the Reverend C. M. Grey in Columbia on 29 April 1890 at St. Peter's Episcopal Church where Cobey was a communicant. It was a large wedding and one of the big events of the social season. The ceremony began with seven little girls from the bride's Sunday school class marching up the aisle. Next came six bridesmaids and six attendants followed by the maid of honor and the best man. Cobey Dunnington "entered the church leaning on the arm of her mother," Ellen Ewing Dunnington. Cobey's "dress was of heavy Duchesse satin, studded with pearls, embroidered with white and dashed with gold. She carried a white prayer book and all the maids were gowned in pink. The bride and groom later received under an umbrella of flowers."

The couple left immediately on an extended trip. As Carmack found it difficult to completely leave his work, he and his bride went on a honeymoon that combined work with pleasure. They first traveled to Charleston, South Carolina, where he attended a convention of journalists before sailing up the Atlantic coast to New York City. Upon returning to Columbia, the newlyweds took up residence with Cobey's mother in the Dunnington house on West Market Street (now West Seventh). The house remained Carmack's home even when he had legal residence elsewhere.[18]

Ned and Cobey Carmack were apart much of the time. She stayed in Columbia, often for weeks at a time, after he accepted an editorial position in Memphis; she did not accompany him to Washington when he went to Congress. Carmack's letters to his wife expressed unhappiness at being apart and occasionally chiding her for not writing. Once when he was in Washington, he wrote: "I haven't been hearing from you very often since I got here and I hope you will do better in the future." Nevertheless, the couple seems to have been devoted to each other. To this union was born one child, a boy, christened Edward Ward Carmack, Jr. Seeking to follow in his

---

[18]Nashville *Daily American*, 30 April 1890; Jill Garrett, *St. Peter's Episcopal Church, Columbia, Tennessee* (Columbia: privately printed, 1979) 27. The Dunnington residence now houses a funeral home.

father's footsteps, the son was also a journalist and a politician, but being something of an eccentric, he was not able to equal the success of the elder Carmack in either.[19]

---

[19]Carmack to Cobey Carmack, 2 December 1899, Box 1, Folder 7, scattered correspondence, The Edward Ward Carmack Papers, Southern Historical Collection, University of North Carolina Library, Chapel Hill.

2

APPRENTICESHIP

In 1886, Edward Ward Carmack became an editorial writer for one of the most successful newspapers in Tennessee's capital city during the latter half of the nineteenth century, the Nashville *Daily American*. The origin of this newspaper can be traced to the founding of the *Nashville Union* in 1835 and the *Nashville American* that began publishing in 1848. The two newspapers merged in 1853 under the name *Nashville Union and American*. Publication of all papers in Nashville was suspended during the Civil War, and it was 1865 before the *Union and American* resumed printing. After several ownerships, mergers, and consolidations, the journal assumed the name, *Daily American*, in 1875. Like most of its contemporaries, it was a political organ. The partisanship of that newspaper, as with other journals, reflected the confusing nature of Tennessee's political patterns during the post-Civil War era.

The Democrats emerged as the dominant political party in the Volunteer State, a power that lasted throughout the post-Civil War generation. Although in the minority statewide, Republicans controlled East Tennessee and had significant pockets of strength elsewhere. The Democrats were wracked continuously by internecine conflict as various groups within the party divided over a variety of issues. The Republicans, providing a vigorous opposition, were a constant threat to the hegemony of the

Democracy. Indeed, on one occasion, a split among Democrats enabled Republicans to elect a governor.

Scholars have long attempted to explain political party divisiveness in Tennessee in terms of factionalism. Daniel Merritt Robison identified three factions within the post-Civil War Democratic party: Whig industrialists, the old state-rights Bourbons, and small farmers.[1] This simplistic classification has been challenged by Roger L. Hart, who suggests that the factions lacked cohesion and discipline. He identifies the Democratic party as being composed of ever-shifting alliance systems of local and regional factions fighting for power and spoils.[2] The Democrats, in fact, contained a variety of persuasions that ranged from the very conservative planter-aristocracy to old Whig industrialists, who espoused the doctrine of the New South, with various colorations in between. In short, there were no neat, consistent categories such as those identified by Robison. As a result, the Democratic party was in a continuous uproar over both substantive and philosophical issues such as state debt, tariff protection, and federal paternalism and state rights.

In the 1880s, however, the party was controlled by an alliance system called the Bourbon, or "regular," Democrats. Their symbolic leader was Tennessee's secession governor, Senator Isham Green Harris. Many of the Bourbons were advocates of industrialization, but generally opposed tariff protection and federal paternalism in any form. On the outside, trying to win control of the party, were the advocates of the New South creed, some of whom favored tariff protection and federal aid to education. In a real sense, however, the conflict was a struggle between the "ins" and the "outs" in the party. The editorial policies of Tennessee's newspapers reflected the wide variation of political coloration within the Democratic party. Some journals spoke for the Bourbons, some for the New South, and others for the variations in between. The Nashville *Daily American* was, in 1886, an organ of the "regular" wing of the Democracy, a posture in harmony with Carmack's political inclinations.

In January 1886, a syndicate headed by Colonel Duncan Brown Cooper obtained control of the *Daily American*. A native of Maury County,

---

[1]Daniel Merritt Robison, *Bob Taylor and the Agrarian Revolt in Tennessee* (Chapel Hill: University of North Carolina Press, 1935).

[2]Roger L. Hart, *Redeemers, Bourbons, and Populists: Tennessee 1870-1896* (Baton Rouge: Louisiana State University Press, 1975) 224-35.

Duncan Cooper was of Scot ancestry, the scion of the landed aristocracy, and a family of Whiggish inclinations. He was related to Governor John C. Brown, and his wife was a cousin of Tennessee's President James Knox Polk. One of Duncan Cooper's brothers was a justice of the state Supreme Court and another served a term as a United States senator. After the Civil War broke out, Cooper enlisted in the Confederate army at the age of seventeen. His war record is incomplete, but it seems that he became the commander of a unit known as "Cooper's Cavalry," founded in the fall of 1862. This troop came under the command of General Nathan Bedford Forrest in 1864, but it is questionable whether Cooper was still with the outfit because at some point during that year he was taken prisoner. There is also some doubt whether he was actually promoted to lieutenant colonel before his capture; nevertheless, he used the title of colonel the rest of his life.

After the war Cooper mined in Mexico, helped build railroads in Honduras, and upon his return to the United States, assisted in the construction of the Washington Monument. By the 1870s Cooper was back in Tennessee, a resident of Columbia, and involved in Democratic party politics. He represented Maury and Williamson Counties in the state House of Representatives (1881-1883) and later served in the Senate representing Davidson County. Cooper was a prime example of the difficulty in identifying consistent categories within the party. During a bitter debate over the state debt at the Democratic state convention in 1872, he was a leader of a group of bolters—the "Sky Blues"—in protest to a proposal to scale down the debt. That action placed Cooper in sympathy with Whig industrialists, but he was a consistent opponent of tariff protection, a position that allied him with the more conservative elements of the Democratic party. In 1886, he was known as a "regular" Democrat. Shrewd and cunning, Cooper was a pragmatic politician rather than an ideologist. He also preferred to operate behind the scenes, manipulating others rather than appearing on stage himself. Perhaps that is another reason why his interests turned toward journalism.[3]

There is a legend that Duncan Cooper gained control of the *Daily American* by winning a high-stakes, all-night poker game. Another, less

---

[3]Ibid., 61, 63, 69, 225; William Waller, ed., *Nashville, 1900-1910* (Nashville: Vanderbilt University Press, 1972) 91-93; Hugh Walker, "Carmack-Cooper: Editor's Murder Shocked State," *The Tennessean*, 19 April 1981.

frequently repeated legend tells that he lost it in a like manner. The legends ignore the question of when these gambling events took place. There is no evidence that either confirms or denies the tales, but Cooper's personality suggests that the transfer of ownership could have happened at the poker table. It is a fact that Cooper gained and lost that newspaper on several separate occasions. He was adventuresome—some called it wanderlust—with a casual and indifferent attitude toward wealth. He won and lost fortunes in a cavalier manner, adding to his reputation as a confirmed gambler.

Another legend has Colonel Cooper perplexed over his new acquisition because he knew little about journalism or how to run a newspaper. Someone told him about Carmack, and the Columbia journalist was brought in to assist Cooper. However, he and Carmack had been well acquainted with each other for quite some time, as their residences in Columbia had overlapped. Another story tells of Carmack arriving in Nashville to assume his duties on the *Daily American* clad in homespun clothing, looking like a country bumpkin, and had to be told that he needed a better wardrobe. The tale is apocryphal. If indeed Carmack arrived that way, he either deliberately tried to create an image or else he had no interest in clothing at that point in his life. Actually Columbia, Tennessee, was a rather sophisticated community that had more than its share of aristocrats. It is unlikely that any man who had a law practice there, had served in positions of community leadership, and had represented the county in the legislature would have been wearing homespun. One thing is certain: when Cooper offered Carmack a position as an editorial writer, the ambitious attorney accepted without hesitation.

One of the major editorial themes emphasized by Carmack's new employer was party harmony. The *Daily American* regularly called for unity within the Democracy as the only way to prevent the party that pursued oppressive policies, the Republicans, from gaining control of the state. The *Daily American* urged its readers to give loyal support to "regular" Democratic leaders who followed true principles and policies. Independent Democrats and other party renegades were criticized, sometimes quite sharply, for allegedly causing discord. In 1886, the most convenient target for attack was the *Nashville Union*, which was edited by Arthur St. Clair Colyar. Although known as a Democratic organ, the *Union* endorsed economic policies that the Bourbons thought repugnant. Colyar, for example, was staunchly protectionist and argued editorially that a tariff was just and necessary for a prosperous economy. The *Daily American*, on the other hand, declared that a protective tariff was one of the "most iniquitous engines of robbery and oppression ever devised" and the *Union* was condemned for supporting such a policy.

The *Union* and *Daily American* also clashed over a proposal for the federal government to aid education in the states. In 1883, Senator Henry William Blair of New Hampshire introduced a measure in Congress that would distribute surplus funds to the states according to the level of illiteracy in order to promote education. Because of a high level of illiteracy, Tennessee, like the rest of the South, would receive a good deal of money. The Blair bill did not pass in 1883, but remained as a live issue in 1886. Colyar's *Union* argued that aid to education would stimulate growth and economic development in Tennessee. The *Daily American*, however, found the Blair proposal objectionable. It declared that the measure was not only a threatening federal invasion of the rights of states, but that it would be tied to the tariff which was an undesirable source of revenue.[4]

The position taken by the *Daily American* in the gubernatorial campaign in 1886 reflected the newspaper's concern with party harmony. Prior to the Democratic state convention in August, the journal did not endorse a gubernatorial candidate. Although the proprietor of the *Daily American* may possibly have preferred someone else, the journal endorsed the eventual nominee, Robert Love Taylor, but with a noticeable lack of enthusiasm. As the canvass progressed, the paper quickly warmed to the candidate. By October, the *Daily American* was enthusiastically lauding Bob Taylor as a most outstanding Democrat and the perfect candidate for governor. News reports of the campaign were slanted. One of the features of the race was a series of debates between Taylor and the Republican candidate, his own brother Alfred Alexander Taylor. In reporting the joint discussions, the *Daily American* usually suggested that Bob outshone Alf and that his receptions and cheers were louder and more enthusiastic. When Bob Taylor emerged the victor in the election in November, the paper's expressions of joy were unrestrained. But the honeymoon between the two was short.

The *Daily American* soon broke with Governor Taylor over the issue of federal aid to education. During the gubernatorial campaign, Taylor had successfully evaded the issue, but soon after he became governor, he spoke out in favor of the Blair bill. In a message to the General Assembly, he de-

---

[4]Nashville *Daily American*, 1886, passim.

clared that "the masses of the people of this state were anxiously turning their eyes to the Federal Government for" assistance in educating their youth. The *Daily American* was incredulous. Taylor had committed heresy and treason to both the South and the Democratic party. The paper stated that it was sorry to have to take issue with the governor, but the Blair bill was not favored by a majority of Tennesseans or of the Democratic party. Democrats, the *Daily American* said, were not "beggars" anxious for federal handouts.[5] The Nashville journal did not drop the subject after one scathing editorial. Federal aid to education was an emotional issue, and Governor Taylor had aroused the ire of the more conservative Bourbon Democrats by endorsing the Blair proposal. Over the following weeks, the *Daily American* regularly censured the governor for deviating from what was described as the proper position for all loyal Democrats and Southerners.[6] The attacks on Taylor might have continued indefinitely had not a change in the ownership of the *Daily American* occurred in May 1887. Because the new proprietors held sharply differing political and economic views, Carmack was soon forced to join the ranks of the unemployed.

On 13 May, the *Daily American* carried the terse announcement that "with this issue the control and management of the American passes into other hands."[7] The details of the change were not made public, nor is it known whether Duncan Cooper willingly relinquished control of the newspaper. In any event, the journal was merged with the *Nashville Union*, but retained the name, *Daily American*. G. M. Fogg became president and A. S. Colyar was named editor-in-chief. Colyar also received stock and second-mortgage bonds in the new enterprise.[8] The change in editorial policy that followed the change in ownership could not have been more profound. The new editor, Tennessee's most eloquent exponent of the New South creed, was both colorful and controversial.

Colyar was born in East Tennessee in 1818, but grew up in Winchester in Franklin County. In the pre-Civil War years, he was an attorney, saw suc-

---

[5]Ibid., 13 February 1887.

[6]Ibid., February-May 1887, passim.

[7]Ibid., 13 May 1887.

[8]William Waller, ed., *Nashville in the 1890s* (Nashville: Vanderbilt University Press, 1970) 79; *History of Nashville, Tenn.* (Nashville: H. W. Crew, 1890) 361.

cess in business ventures, and was a leader in the Whig party. As a staunch Unionist, he had worked tirelessly for the cause of the Constitutional Union party's presidential candidate, John Bell, in the crucial campaign of 1860. However, when Tennessee seceded in 1861, Colyar went with his state, later serving in the Confederate Congress as a gadfly to President Jefferson Davis. After the war, he had returned to Tennessee to resume his business activities, one of which was the successful reorganization of the Tennessee Coal and Railroad Company. He had also become involved in politics, but had had little success in securing an elective office for himself. Like so many Southern Whigs, Colyar had converted to the Democratic party as an exponent of industrialization. This brought him into conflict with the Bourbons whom he referred to as those "damn brigadiers." Colyar had turned to journalism in 1882 when he had acquired control of the *Daily American*. Giving up that newspaper in 1885, he helped found the *Nashville Union*, the journal that merged with the *Daily American* in May 1887. As a journalist, Colyar was of the same mold as Joseph Pulitzer; his style was colorful and tended to be sensational. He also pressed the doctrine of the New South with vigor.[9]

The year on the staff of the *Daily American* was a rewarding experience for Carmack. It gave him an opportunity to learn the operations of an urban daily newspaper. Precisely when he became a member of the staff is not known, nor is it clear the extent of his influence on editorial and news policy. There is evidence, however, that he played a role in the evolution of the newspaper's style. In the first weeks after Duncan Cooper obtained control, the journalistic style remained conservative. But in the spring of 1886, the newspaper began to change. Headlines and stories tended more toward the sensational and editorials became more vigorous. At one point in the fall, the *Daily American* ventured into "yellow journalism" when the newspaper insisted that it had proof that some East Tennessee Republicans had tried to assassinate Robert L. Taylor. The newspaper adopted the style that Carmack used later to become a successful editor himself. In any case, a statement by the retiring editor of the *Daily American* suggests that Carmack had been given a good deal of responsibility. He declared that he "gratefully ac-

---

[9]Sarah McCanless Howell, "The Editorials of Arthur S. Colyar, Nashville Prophet of the New South," *Tennessee Historical Quarterly* 27 (Fall 1968): 262-76; Clyde L. Ball, "The Public Career of Colonel A. S. Colyar, 1870-1877," *Tennessee Historical Quarterly* 12 (March, June, September 1953): 23-47, 106-28, 213-38.

knowledges . . . [the help of] Mr. E. W. Carmack, who has done the great volume of the editorial writing."[10] Regardless of his influence on the newspaper, he had established himself in the community as a writer and a first-rate journalist. Nonetheless, Colyar's control of the newspaper placed a Bourbon Democrat at a disadvantage. Carmack could not have remained on the *Daily American* long even if that had been his desire. Whether he left voluntarily or was discharged is unknown, but he was without a position soon after the merger.

The combining of the *Union* and *Daily American* left Nashville with only one other newspaper, the evening *Nashville Banner*, published by a railroad executive, Edward Bushrod Stahlman. Although the evening paper declared itself to be independent, it spoke for the conservative business interests of Nashville. This left Tennessee's capital city without a journal to voice the Bourbon sentiments, which represented a very large segment, if not a majority, of the population. By the 1880s, newspapers had become big business, and founding and operating one required a sizable investment. Yet there was still enough romance and adventure in journalism—as well as a willingness to back a political cause—for some to take the risk. It was inevitable, perhaps, that some individuals of means, especially those opposed to Colyar's Whiggish sentiments, would establish a new journal. Who financed the venture is not known, but in March 1888, a new newspaper, the *Nashville Democrat*, appeared with Edward Ward Carmack as editor-in-chief.

Politically, the *Democrat* declared itself to be an organ of what it called the true Democracy in Tennessee and stressed the need for unity in the party. Editorials expressed strong opposition to the Blair bill as well as the protective tariff. It supported the renomination and reelection to the presidency of antiprotectionist Democrat Grover Cleveland. In the state, Governor Robert L. Taylor faced a bitter struggle for renomination. Although it is likely that Carmack privately opposed Taylor's bid, the newspaper did not openly challenge the incumbent, and when he eventually won renomination, the newspaper endorsed him without reservation in the name of harmony. In contrast, the Republican party was fair game for attack at any time under any circumstance. Republicans were assailed for a variety of reasons, but especially for relying upon the black vote. Carmack declared that blacks

---

[10]Nashville *Daily American*, 13 May 1887.

were merely the tools of Republicans to win office, and that their occasional black candidate was proffered merely to attract black votes. "The Republican leaders," he wrote, "when they put a 'nigger' on the tail of their ticket have not the slightest idea of voting for or electing him. They simply bait the hook with a 'nigger' to catch niggers."[11] Carmack believed that Republicans, in combination with the black vote, constituted a threat to Democratic hegemony in Tennessee.

Although the *Democrat* may have voiced the sentiments of most Democrats in Nashville and the surrounding area, it was not a financial success. Inadequately capitalized, the physical plant was of poor quality, the type and presses were old and almost worn out. Privately, Editor Carmack complained about occasional press breakdowns.[12] Publicly, he exuded enthusiasm about the success of the *Democrat*. In the manner of sensational journalists, Carmack practiced braggadocio and blatant self-praise. Beginning in May, the *Democrat* printed daily a block on the editorial page that claimed that the journal "now has a larger city circulation than any other morning paper published in Nashville." In September, Carmack penned a long editorial in which he boasted of the newspaper's success. Its circulation was growing, he wrote, and its style was crisp and clear like New York City's and other Northern papers.[13] But the *Democrat* was a financially troubled newspaper and could survive only with the best of leadership. Carmack had the ability to provide the leadership. With a natural talent for showmanship, he knew how to create interest that would in turn attract both subscribers and advertisers. He certainly provided readers with excitement during the summer of 1888.

Nashville readers were entertained by a lively newspaper war between the *Democrat* and the *Daily American*, and a personal feud between Carmack and Colyar. Carmack took the initiative. For example, he accused his competition of practicing intemperate journalism. In an editorial under the title of "Vicious Journalism," he declared that "The province of a respectable newspaper, as we understand it, is to furnish a correct history of each day. . . . One of the most vicious and pernicious features of a certain class

---

[11]*Nashville Democrat*, 6 August 1888.

[12]Letter scrap, Box 4, Folder 47, The Edward Ward Carmack Papers, Southern Historical Collection, University of North Carolina Library, Chapel Hill.

[13]*Nashville Democrat*, May-November 1888.

of journals . . . is the habit of publishing alleged interviews or startling pieces of news on such authority as 'It was rumored last night,' 'It is said,' 'It is currently reported.' " In contrast, he concluded, "The DEMOCRAT does not deal in rumors." On another occasion, he accused his competition with a "sensational attempt . . . to create a panic on the subject of yellow fever." Fortunately, he said, the attempt fell flat.[14]

Most reader interest was generated by Carmack's vicious personal assault on Editor Colyar. Shortly after assuming his duties on the *Daily American*, Colyar tried to reassure the paper's readers that the journal would be a loyal Democratic organ. He also made it clear that the new editorial policy would espouse tariff protection. He then expressed sympathy with the proposal to distribute surplus federal funds to the states for educational purposes if those funds were "freed from Federal control." On the tariff, however, he soon began to modify his protectionist stance, admitting that import duties needed to be revised downward. Eventually he called for a tariff for revenue only and a reduction down to the needs of government, but not so low that American labor could not successfully compete with European labor.[15]

Colyar's connection with Nashville's industrial interests was sufficient to make him a prime target of the Bourbon editor of the *Democrat*, but his new position on the tariff left him especially vulnerable. Carmack went gleefully on the attack. In an editorial entitled "Let Us Have The Truth," he laid down a challenge. "We have heard a great deal from the Nashville American, the recognized organ of the Tennessee Coal, Iron and Railroad Company, about . . . the present tariff which it grudgingly admits needs to be reformed." At the same time, however, it advocated that "the tariff should always be kept high enough to cover any increased cost of production on account of higher rate of wages in this country." Carmack insisted that "THE DEMOCRAT wishes to be perfectly fair about the matter, but it also intends that the people shall not be deceived by the hypocrisy of those who are eternally clamoring for a tariff to protect labor." He concluded with a "distinct challenge to the American, as the known representative of the Tennessee Coal, Iron & Railroad Company," to tell the truth about the cost of labor and the cost of production. The organ of that enterprise could do

---

[14]Ibid., 6, 25 September 1888.

[15]Nashville *Daily American*, May 1887-August 1888, passim.

so by merely opening the books of the company. "We make the challenge and dare it to accept the issue." The day following that editorial, Carmack chastised Colyar for using what he called vile language in a war of words with free-trade advocate Henry Watterson of the Louisville *Courier-Journal*. He observed, tongue in cheek, that "The Nashville American . . . uses some very harsh and bitter epithets concerning the distinguished Henry Watterson. When a 'great newspaper' falls to cursing like a drab, a scullion, you may know that it has been bit on a very tender spot."[16]

On a more serious note, Carmack charged Colyar with disloyalty to the Democratic party. He insisted that although the *Daily American* espoused to be a Democratic organ, its petty and foolish carping in regard to party leadership and policies only hurt the party. The problem with the *American* was "its eternal and unquenchable desire for a row with Democrats." The newspaper was "one of a number of alleged democratic papers which is in reality engaged in knifing the democratic party." Carmack further suggested that the editor of the *Daily American* cooperated with Republicans, that some of the proprietors of that newspaper were Republicans, and that the journal and its editor had thrown all of its weight against the Democratic nominees in the county elections in August 1888 in favor of what he termed "the American's mule ticket." Colyar denied the charge and, in fact, claimed credit for the *Daily American* for the Democratic victory in the election. Carmack responded with a lengthy editorial entitled "The American's Effrontery." He declared that "The gall of the Nashville American and its presumption are as great as its influence is small." The newspaper contributed nothing to the victory, he wrote, and in fact sought "to weaken the ticket."[17]

Carmack also claimed that Colyar had committed the most henious of crimes in contributing one hundred dollars to the support of the Republican gubernatorial candidate in 1886. After repeating the allegation almost daily for about two weeks, Carmack summed up his indictment of Colyar in a lengthy editorial. He declared that he had no desire to press the issue "further than the cause of truth demands," but the Democrats of Tennessee had a right to know about "the political masquerade and solemn pharisaism which has cursed the politics of Tennessee for the last few years." Carmack

---

[16]*Nashville Democrat*, 4, 5 August 1888.

[17]Ibid., 5, 7 August, 4 September 1888.

insisted that there had been alleged Democrats who had exercised power and influence "in making the platforms, nominating the candidates and shaping the policy of the party, yet who were all the time secretly voting the republican ticket and spending their money to elect republican candidates." He believed that "THE DEMOCRAT has done some service in showing the true face of some of these masqueraders to the public." Carmack then outlined in detail his charge that Colyar had made the contribution to the Republican candidate. He added the charge that the *Daily American*'s editor had also made a contribution to the Republican legislative ticket from Nashville in hopes of defeating the Democrats. A companion editorial observed that the course taken by the *Daily American* was "full of treachery" and, now that the facts were known, it no longer had any "standing or influence in the party."[18]

Colyar was a superb journalist skilled in the use of pungent language, but, on the defensive, he was unable to match Carmack's abuse. Finally, the maligned editor had had enough and penned a personal letter to his antagonist, which Carmack maliciously printed in the *Democrat*. Colyar wrote that "I am not aware that I have done you any personal wrong. Your paper has teemed with personal references to me which were intended to be offensive, and with pretended facts which you must have known were absolutely untrue. . . . I know of no grounds for the personal assaults and the repeated attempts to insult me, except that I am conducting a rival newspaper." He then denounced as untrue the charge that he had contributed money to the Republican gubernatorial candidate. In reference to the fact that E. B. Stahlman had made a similar charge, he declared that "You know that Stahlman even, who is known to be a malignant liar, in everything he says about me, did not state it as you state it." The charge that the *Daily American* was controlled by Republicans was also false, he said. Colyar concluded with the declaration that "I take the liberty of denouncing you a liar and I brand you as such." Carmack's reply, which followed Colyar's letter, stated that "If I do not retort in kind," the *Daily American*'s editor would doubtlessly think that "I have been awed by the challenge." Carmack insisted that the charges against Colyar were true and that the *Democrat* had a duty to the public to tell the truth "undeterred by abusive epithets, or threats of personal violence." Angry because his personal letter had been

---

[18]Ibid., 23 August 1888.

published by his rival, Colyar's reply was prompt. He explained that he had not published his letter as a matter of taste to keep his paper free of personalities. Carmack published the second letter and accompanied it with a taunting notation: "The above letter is published as a matter of justice, as well as a matter of kindness to Col. Colyar. So long as he is precluded from replying . . . through his own paper, the Democrat will cheerfully yield him as much space as he may require."[19]

How close the two editors came to blows is not known, but the thirty-year age difference made it unlikely that the controversy would lead to any form of physical violence. Despite Carmack's implications to the contrary, Colyar had made no threats of doing bodily harm. Some saw humor in the situation, such as the editor of the West Tennessee newspaper, the *Forked Deer Blade*, who wrote:

> Speaking about thunder and lightning reminds me of a war now on between Ed Carmack of THE DEMOCRAT and Col. Colyar of the American. Ed had been shootin off his lip at A. S. until patience ceased to be a virtue. So he [Colyar] elevated his spine and wrote Ed a letter. In that letter he said that in his opinion Ed Carmack was a dadburned liar, and that he could lick 'im, and that he meant just what he said, and he'd stay in town or perish in the attempt. He insisted that he was sound on the democratic goose, and the man who said that he wasn't was another. The letter went on in this strain at some length, probably a thousand or more m's, and if it had been written in times long since gone, it would have been interpreted as a challenge to mortal combat. It wasn't a cussin' letter, yet it was plain that the colonel's angry passions were up to about 96° in the shade, and that there would probably be a funeral one of these days, and he would take pleasure in providing a bloody corse [sic]. In brief, the colonel intimated that this foolishness had gone just about far enough, and unless it was put to an end he'd be mad at somebody.
>
> Ed Carmack got the letter. Did he get his little gun, hunt Colyar down and murder him in cold, cold blood? Was there a big funeral the next day, among the chief mourners of which were the stockholders of the American? Naw, not much. Did these two belligerents meet and soil each other's collars and muss each other's hair? Did either wipe the earth with the other? Or did both fall at the first round and soil their trowsers and welter in their own gore? Nary welter. Not that anybody knows of.

---

[19]Ibid., 18, 19 August 1888.

Or did they seize their good broad swords, thrust and parry, and thrust again, until the cold steel drank up the claret of the two heroes? Naw, what cher given' us?

What! Was there no blood spilled? No honor satisfied? No sensation for the newspapers? Didn't Carmack say, "Aha villain, I have thee on the hip? My wounded honor cries out for vengeance!" He did nothing of the kind.

When Ed read the letter in which he was called a liar, ha! ha! he smiled, then took down from its accustomed place his little Faber number-two and sassed back at the colonel, and politely informed him that he (Ed) had no objection to his (the colonel) remaining in the city, and, in fact, granting him permission to do so.

"Let not your angry passions rise;
Your little hands were never made
To scratch out each others eyes."[20]

Carmack scored heavily in his assault on Colyar and was applauded by some of his small-town contemporaries. One editor observed that Colyar was in "a very tight box . . . [because] THE DEMOCRAT has clearly established the charge that he contributed money to republican campaign funds two years ago, and also that the Tennessee Coal, Iron and Railroad Company, who virtually own[s] and control[s] the American, has done the same thing on several occasions." Another noted that Carmack had received Colyar's letter with "his impurturbable [sic] good humor apparently unshaken, and again repeated the stinging charges which had aroused the ire of the old man of the American. Carmack seems to be very much on top up to date." A third declared that "THE NASHVILLE DEMOCRAT is making it warm for the American, the greatest fraud that was ever perpetrated upon upon [sic] a people in the shape of a newspaper."[21]

By sheer effrontery, Carmack, using unsubstantiated charges and then repeating them over and over again, placed Colyar in a bad light. The victor in the war of words, he established himself as an aggressive editor. Moreover, by placing himself at the center of controversy and drawing attention to himself, Carmack became something of a celebrity. He was developing a

---

[20]Reprinted in ibid., 28 August 1888.

[21]Ibid.

personal following and was well on his way to becoming a leader in the Democratic party.

A. S. Colyar was not the only journalist to feel the sting of Carmack's caustic pen, for E. B. Stahlman, publisher of the *Banner*, was an occasional target. Rhetorical assaults were sometimes directed against editors in other cities as well. For example, Carmack once singled out the St. Louis *Globe-Democrat*, asserting that that journal was disloyal to the South and an "arrant slanderer of the South" for criticizing Southern social customs.[22] John McLeod Keating and William Armistead Collier, editor and principal owner, respectively, of the *Memphis Appeal*, drew Carmack's attention. Early in 1888, the *Appeal* began a campaign to block the reelection by the General Assembly of Senator Isham G. Harris. The motive may have been personal on Keating's part, but Collier was a "Whiggish" Democrat and probably hoped to rid the state of the old Bourbon leader. The effort to unseat Harris failed as Keating and Collier were unable to prevent the party convention in Memphis from instructing the legislative delegation to vote for Harris. When the embarrassed Keating tried to explain the failure, a gleeful Carmack heaped salt on the *Appeal* editor's wounds. "The Memphis Appeal is sorely troubled in spirit . . . because the Shelby County convention instructed its nominees for the legislature to vote for Senator Harris." The excuse Keating gave for his failure to block the instruction was absurd, but "A man in his semi-crazy condition cannot be held responsible for anything he says and does." The failure also proved, he said, that the editor had very little influence in Memphis. Carmack then turned his fire on Collier whom he charged with treason to the Democratic party. Rather than loyally supporting the regular ticket, the *Appeal*'s proprietor was in reality part of "the little ring [in Memphis] interested in securing the defeat of the democratic party." The issue regarding the reelection of Harris died soon thereafter, but Carmack and Collier engaged in a larger battle a few years later.[23]

Carmack's aggressive editorial style established him as a dynamic editor and his reputation spread across the state. Yet his career in journalism reached a critical point in the fall of 1888 in one of the sudden newspaper

---

[22]Ibid., 14 November 1888.

[23]Ibid., 15, 16, 21 September 1888. See also Thomas Harrison Baker, *The Memphis Commercial Appeal: The History of a Southern Newspaper* (Baton Rouge: Louisiana State University Press, 1971) 151-52.

ownership changes. On 15 October, a syndicate of "Col. D. B. Cooper and other gentlemen closed negotiations by which they became owners of the entire stock in the Nashville American." Cooper's associates were identified as James L. Gaines, John W. Childress, B. Lanier, and George K. Whitworth, most of whom were stockholders in the *Democrat*, resulting in the group's full and at least partial ownership of both papers. Cooper became the president of the *Daily American* and was to direct editorial policy. Simultaneously, Colyar announced that he was severing his editorial connection with the *American* publishing company. However, he retained some $16,000 in second-mortgage bonds in the *American*, and soon after the sale, he brought suit against the company asking for a receiver. It seems likely that he hoped to be able to purchase the newspaper, but after the contest became somewhat acrimonious, Colyar withdrew the suit.[24]

Carmack expressed delight at the merger. He wrote that "THE DEMOCRAT may be permitted to express its profound gratification that the known political convictions of the gentlemen who have now assumed control of the paper [the *American*] gives guarantee that from this time forward it will be conducted as a straight democratic organ in thorough sympathy with and accord with the sentiments of democrats of Tennessee." He noted that he had once declared that he intended to make the *Democrat* the best Democratic newspaper in Nashville and that he "would not be content until we had made the American the next best." That goal, he asserted, had been accomplished.

The profound gratification expressed by the editor was for public consumption only. While he may have known about negotiations, he was not a participant nor did he become a partner in the new company and his future was uncertain. It was questionable how long the owners would maintain two competing newspapers and the decision to suspend publication of one of the papers came soon. On 12 November, the *Daily American* announced the end of the *Democrat* in a terse statement: "As some of the largest owners of the stock of *The Democrat* have become largely interested, by purchase, in the stock of THE AMERICAN, and as the two papers have been covering the same field in politics, it was deemed advisable to discontinue the publication of *The Democrat*, which has been done." Carmack was ap-

---

[24]*Nashville Democrat*, 16 October 1888; Nashville *Daily American*, 16 October 1888. See also Waller, *Nashville in the 1890s*, 79-82.

parently offered a position on the *Daily American* but in a subordinate position, a proposition he rejected. An editorial associate on the *Democrat* observed that Carmack "has refused to go on the American unless he could do so as editor in chief. He has not been given that position as yet, though I would not be surprised to see him as such in a short time." The holdout was rewarded; Carmack was too valuable to lose to a competitor. Before the end of the month, Edward Ward Carmack was editor-in-chief of the Nashville *Daily American*.[25]

---

[25]*Nashville Democrat*, 16 October 1888; Nashville *Daily American*, 12 November 1888; J. D. Anderson to his mother, 13 November 1888, Box 9, Folder 3, James Douglas Anderson Papers, Tennessee Historical Society's Collection, Tennessee State Library and Archives, Nashville.

3

THE DAILY AMERICAN

Edward Ward Carmack had earned his appointment as chief editor of the Nashville *Daily American*. Although only thirty years of age, he had demonstrated a talent for journalism. His writing style varied from classical form to pungent wit as each situation dictated. He was especially skilled in the use of invective and ridicule when challenging a political opponent or another editor. He also had a flair for dramatizing issues, even those of little consequence. These talents had attracted attention well beyond Nashville during Carmack's short stint with the *Democrat*. Like so many dynamic editors of that era, he began to develop a personal following that continued to grow during his years on the *Daily American*.

Soon after Carmack took over the editorship of the *Daily American*, his early benefactor and patron, Duncan Cooper, left the presidency of that journal. Restless, Cooper sold his stock in the newspaper to his associates, and his connection with the journal came to an end. Why he left the *Daily American* is unknown, but it is not without its irony that it wasn't long before it was announced that he was one of the founders and first president of a new paper, the *Evening and Sunday Morning Herald* that began publishing in January 1889. The *Herald* did not challenge the *Daily American* head to head; rather, it became a direct rival to the evening *Nashville Banner*. But Cooper remained with the *Herald* only a year before he once again pulled up stakes and sold his interest.

Carmack thrived on conflict and controversy, but his first year as editor of the *Daily American*, 1889, was relatively quiet. He had no dragons to slay nor an especially challenging issue to debate. Even so, his vitrolic pen was neither silent nor toned down. He regularly damned Republicans, mugwumps, and protectionists while generally praising Democrats. Carmack continued to single out for condemnation those in Nashville and across Tennessee whose political and economic views were contrary to his. Not everyone who was attacked responded in anger, and some readily acknowledged that Carmack was a worthy antagonist. One was William Robert Moore, a wealthy Memphis dry-goods wholeseller and Republican activist whom the Nashville editor vilified unmercifully. At the time of Carmack's wedding in April of 1890, Moore wrote that "Your very frequent editorial notices of myself for several years past, have made me feel like you are an old acquaintance, and for that reason, I take the liberty of offering my sincere congratulations upon your marriage." Moore continued, saying that he had a genuine admiration for Carmack's talent as an editorial writer.[1]

Sectional conflict was a subject frequently addressed by the *Daily American* editor and he was quick to react to Northern criticism of Southern cultural patterns. Northerners, he insisted, were guilty of fomenting persistent sectional antagonism. An editorial entitled "The Persistence of Sectional Hate" provides a good example. It was a response to an editorial in the Chicago *Tribune* critical of Southern politics and treatment of blacks. Carmack declared that "The cool effrontery, the dazzling impudence, the confounded gall of the Chicago Tribune was never so strikingly exhibited as in a recent editorial. . . . No paper has done more to illustrate the persistence of sectional hate or the sleepless activity of a sectional slander than the Tribune." The Chicago newspaper, he said, went even further than the Republican party in "its fierce and vindictive war upon the South."[2]

Carmack was sensitive to the fact that some Confederate veterans had gone over to the Republican party. Thus he responded angrily to an editorial in the St. Louis *Globe-Democrat* that intimated that old Confederates who remained in the Democratic party were responsible for continuing sectional

---

[1]William R. Moore to Carmack, 30 April 1890, Box 1, Folder 1, The Edward Ward Carmack Papers, Southern Historical Collection, University of North Carolina Library, Chapel Hill.

[2]Nashville *Daily American*, 25 April 1890.

conflict. Carmack observed that Republican newspapers argued "that an ex-Confederate is a traitor so long as he is a Democrat, and becomes a patriot as soon as he becomes a Republican." The only thing ex-Confederate Democrats had done to promote sectional animosity was "to vote the Democratic ticket and lawfully resist the efforts of the Republican party to put their State under the domination of ruffian negroes and imported thieves." He pointed out that Republican editors and politicians had often distorted speeches by Democrats in an attempt to create animosity, "but they could as easily find, if so disposed, just as much in the acts and utterances of ex-Confederate Republicans to justify similar tirades."[3]

Carmack insisted that the North, rather than the South, fomented sectional hatred. Nothing, he thought, better illustrated that than the attempt to impose upon the South the proposed "Force Bill," a measure presented to Congress in 1890 by the Republican congressman from Massachusetts, Henry Cabot Lodge. The measure called for federal supervision of elections in the South in order to protect black voting rights. The Force Bill passed the House of Representatives but failed in the Senate. Nevertheless, it remained an issue and Southerners continued to regard the proposal as a threat for several years. According to Carmack, the measure was an unwarranted attempt by Northern Republicans to destroy Southern institutions; it was just another in a long series of attacks on the "Southern way of life." When Tennessee Republicans in convention in 1890 endorsed the Lodge bill, Carmack believed that the Grand Old Party in the Volunteer State had committed treason to the South; that the members of the party had become mere tools of their Northern brothers.

Carmack, as much as anyone, contributed to sectional animosity. Through his editorials, he gained a reputation as an eloquent defender of the Southern ethos. He glorified the romantic myth of the Old South, its traditions and cultural patterns, and, as much as any Tennessee journalist, contributed to creating the "myth of the Lost Cause." He praised Confederate heroes and extolled the virtues of Confederate veterans as illustrated in an editorial occasioned by a reunion in Nashville in 1889. In welcoming the veterans, he wrote:

---

[3]Ibid., 2 September 1889.

> They meet, to-day, in the midst of a peace so secure, so pleasing and so sacred, that the memories of a bitter past are tinged with the halo of forgiveness and the harshness to which Southern people were so long subjected has yielded its place in our hearts to a patriotism that for sincerity defies the world.
>
> There is every cause for these Southern veterans to be happy and proud. Their equal in bravery, in virtue and in forbearance, the world has never yet seen. They came out of the terrible internecine struggle, homeless and without credit. They grappled with the situation and mastered it, and, to-day, without having received, or asked or wanted one dollar of pension money, and without having had the benefit of Federal encouragement, they are the most prosperous, most happy and most respected of people.

They achieved prosperity, he said, despite the fact "that political blackguards" and a "prostituted press" in other sections continued to "slander the South." They had done so much despite "still being called rebels by a party that has always fought them," the inhibitions of hostile legislation, "unjust and inequitable taxes," and the attempt by those in another section to keep aglow the "bitterest of prejudices."[4] As a journalist, Carmack helped reinforce and strengthen established values and beliefs. But while praising the South and its heroes and damning the North and Republicans was satisfying, the exercise was not sufficiently controversial for Carmack's spirit. In 1890, however, there appeared a movement that threatened to further divide an already fractured Democratic party and was ready-made for a man with Carmack's combative nature: the agrarian revolt.

In 1890, as part of a larger mass movement that spread across the South and West, the agrarian revolt burst upon the scene in Tennessee with surprising suddenness. It was the result of pent-up grievances of small farmers across the nation. For nearly a generation, small farmers had been plagued by declining farm prices, high interest rates, high freight rates, and high exactions of middlemen. More important, perhaps, the status of the time-honored mythical yeoman farmer had declined while the political power of industrial and urban America had increased. Generally, farmers placed the blame for their plight on the monopolies of corporate and busi-

---

[4]Ibid., 3 October 1889.

ness interests and their alleged sycophants in political office. Whatever the cause, farmers organized in an effort to obtain relief, and by 1890, with a variety of proposed political and economic reforms, the movement had blossomed into a full-scale revolt against the political establishment.

The revolt originated in Tennessee, as it did elsewhere, within fraternal organizations. During the 1880s, two brotherhoods, the Agricultural Wheel and the Farmers' Alliance, were formed. Understanding their common goal, the two soon joined forces under the name of the latter. Although originally nonpolitical, under the leadership of men of experience and prominence in the small towns across Tennessee, the Alliance turned to political action. Generally, the established politicians did not regard the Alliance as a genuine threat but the agrarian revolt sprang full-blown in Tennessee in 1890 in a way that shocked entrenched factions. The Alliance won control of the Democratic party and an Alliance leader was nominated as the party's gubernatorial candidate.

The established political factions were not unaware of the rumblings of discontent from rural and small-town Tennessee as the gubernatorial campaign of 1890 approached. Carmack, for example, acknowledged that the farmers had legitimate grievances, but cautioned that they would obtain nothing through their own organization. "The Democratic party," he wrote, "is their hope for everything desirable, their protection and guarantee against legislation wicked and in the interests of classes."[5] However, Carmack was less concerned with the problems of the farmers than with maintaining the dominance of the Bourbon regulars in Tennessee. He, with others in the establishment, remained complacent despite the fact that the president of the Tennessee Alliance, John Price Buchanan of Murfreesboro, became a strong contender for the Democratic gubernatorial nomination and gained momentum by winning the endorsement of county conventions across the state. Assuming that the Alliance president had no chance of obtaining the nomination, Carmack made no attempt to block Buchanan by publicly opposing him. Indeed, among the hopefuls—the incumbent Robert L. Taylor, Colonel Josiah Patterson of Memphis, and Bu-

---

[5]Ibid., 2 July 1890.

chanan—"THE AMERICAN has no choice," Carmack said, because all three were men of merit and good Democrats.[6]

He was undoubtedly surprised and shaken when the Alliance won control of the Democratic party in the state convention and proceeded to nominate Buchanan. The platform, however, was not extreme. It did not, for example, include an endorsement of a measure sponsored by the national Alliance: the subtreasury plan proposing that the federal government make low-cost loans to farmers for nonperishable crops. The platform favored free coinage of silver as a desirable monetary policy, something that provoked little opposition from regular Democrats. Somewhat chagrined, Carmack quickly decided that party unity required the support of Buchanan. A few days after the close of the convention, he wrote that the *American* would support Buchanan with good will and enthusiasm. He was a man of "unblemished integrity" and was a sound Democrat. "There is absolutely no reason," he insisted, "why any Democrat should not give his cordial support to the ticket this year."[7] Buchanan encountered some hostility within the party, but the Republican endorsement of the Lodge Force Bill encouraged many dissenters within the Democracy to remain loyal. Buchanan thus won the governorship and a significant number of Alliance men were elected to the General Assembly.[8]

The agrarian revolt in Tennessee was not a radical movement. In fact, Governor Buchanan appointed some conservative non-Alliance men to his official family, and his legislative program was anything but radical. Alliance men in the legislature did not press extreme measures. Yet the entrenched political elements in the Volunteer State viewed with increasing

---

[6]Ibid., 5 July 1890. Normally, as an editor, Carmack did not openly endorse or oppose candidates for nomination, but in 1890 he deviated from custom. He carried on a vicious campaign against one contender, Jere Baxter, a Nashville industrialist and business executive. Carmack noted that "THE AMERICAN has adopted a course which is somewhat unusual, for the reason that the situation" was unusual. A responsible newspaper, he declared, had a duty to warn "the people in general and Democrats in particular of the dangers" of nominating someone with Baxter's background. Ibid. Carmack's real choice in 1890 was probably Josiah Patterson whom he praised several times as a Democratic loyalist who worked for unity and harmony in the party.

[7]Ibid., 18 July 1890.

[8]For the rise of the Alliance to power in Tennessee, see Roger L. Hart, *Redeemers, Bourbons, and Populists: Tennessee 1870-1896* (Baton Rouge: Louisiana State University Press, 1975) 107-54.

alarm the new-found solidarity and power of the small farmers. The fear was less of radicalism than of the threat to the hegemony of the Bourbon regulars. The increasing momentum of the agrarian movement across the nation and the political activity of farmers added to their concerns. A convention of farmers' organizations met in December 1890 at Ocala, Florida, and endorsed a radical program designed to relieve agrarian distress. Another convention of agrarian groups that endorsed the concept of a new political party which would be more responsive to their plight was planned for May of 1891 in Cincinnati, Ohio. This convention was enough to cause near-panic by both Bourbon regulars and Whiggish industrialists.

Carmack had no public complaints about Governor Buchanan or his program in the first months following the inauguration of the new administration in January 1891. Privately, he expressed concern about what he perceived to be a threat to Democratic unity posed by the recent developments. Shortly after the election in November, he wrote to a friend that he was afraid "that the farmers, flushed with their achievements this year, will take the bit in their teeth and put up an independent ticket in 1892."[9] His concern about the Alliance threat was evident in a January 1891 editorial written a few weeks after the legislative session convened. Carmack observed that "the members of this Legislature have, on the whole, shown themselves to be a painstaking, cautious and deliberative body of men; and especially have the 'Alliance members' disappointed the fears of many and the hopes of some by the conservative tendency which has restrained them from all wild and radical legislation." He hoped to see that tendency continue in order to put a "brake on the disposition in some quarters to begin the preparations for a revolutionary reform by beginning at the bottom and reaching to the top of the social, political and economic system."[10] Others shared Carmack's thinly veiled fears and by the time of the Cincinnati convention, it appeared that Bourbon regulars and Whig industrialists had joined forces to discredit the Alliance. The press across the state—the Memphis *Commercial*, the Memphis *Appeal-Avalanche*, the Nashville *Herald*, the *Nashville Banner*, along with other daily and weekly journals—set the agenda: a campaign to crush the political power of the upstart small farmers in Tennessee and to destroy Governor Buchanan.

---

[9]C. H. Jones to Carmack, 27 November 1890, Box 1, Folder 1, Carmack Papers.

[10]Nashville *Daily American*, 30 January 1891.

Although he refused to attack the governor, the *Daily American* quickly joined the campaign and just as quickly, Carmack became a leader in the crusade. Carmack's rhetorical effort was aimed at keeping farmers loyal to the Democratic party. On occasion he stressed the threat contained in the radical proposals of the national Alliance, especially the subtreasury plan which he insisted was unsound. He suggested that it was in the best interests of the farmers to remain conservative and avoid radical schemes. There was no good reason, he wrote, for farmers to interfere with the control of railroads or street car companies, or meddle in the management of gas and electric light companies. It was especially dangerous for farmers to join hands with the forces of organized labor. The two had nothing in common and, in fact, labor's demand for higher wages was contrary to the interests of farmers who paid wages.[11] The crusade against the Alliance resulted in the accusation that the *Daily American*, with other newspapers in Tennessee, ignored the needs of farmers and was in fact engaged in a war on farmers. The charge required an answer. Carmack responded that "The American has no war to make on farmers who happen to be members of the Alliance, nor has it made war against the Alliance as an organization. . . . The farmers have a right to organize for mutual protection and benefits." A little later, he felt it necessary to again defend his position in a long editorial entitled "The American and the Farmer." Thus he wrote:

> We wish to say a few plain words, in a pleasant, friendly way to farmers and to Alliancemen. . . . THE AMERICAN is a genuine—not a pretended—friend to the agriculturalist. It circulates in a purely agricultural section, and it cannot escape any calamity which may befall that interest or fail to share in any prosperity which may come to it. There is no possible way in which it can profit by giving them bad advice. There are others who can, who have and who hope to profit by leading them in false paths.

Carmack concluded that "it is amazing to us that any honest farmer should consider THE AMERICAN his enemy because it gives him truthful information concerning a matter which it vitally concerns him to understand."[12]

---

[11] Ibid., 5 May, 12, 23 June 1891.

[12] Ibid., 27 May, 24 June 1891.

The press was vulnerable to the charge that it was an enemy of the farmers; consequently, consciously or unconsciously, the strategy of the opponents of the Alliance changed. The journals trying to undermine the political power of small farmers ceased attacking the Alliance and concentrated on the organization's leadership. They found a perfect target—John Henry McDowell, president of the state Alliance. Born in Gibson County, Tennessee, about 1845, McDowell served in the Confederate army during the Civil War but moved to Arkansas soon after the conflict where he was for a time a cotton farmer. Returning to Tennessee about 1877, he served three terms in the Tennessee General Assembly as a representative from Obion County. He was active in organizing the Alliance in the state and became editor of the organization's journal, the *Weekly Toiler*. In 1890, he succeeded Buchanan as president of the state Alliance. Governor Buchanan also appointed McDowell as coal-oil inspector at Nashville, one of the most lucrative positions at the disposal of the chief executive and one that allowed McDowell a good deal of free time to continue his Alliance activities. Opponents of the farmer organization soon focused on the vain and arrogant McDowell as the symbol of agrarian radicalism.

Not long after McDowell received his sinecure from Buchanan, a story, reported in a sarcastic manner, circulated that the ambitious Alliance president would seek a seat in the United States Senate. When McDowell reacted to the ridicule with anger, Carmack responded with an editorial dripping with scorn.

> In an interview which appeared in the Herald yesterday our future United States Senator—how far in the future we shall not undertake to say—proceeded to belabor the author of this defamation with some words, the like whereof are not in the hymns of Wesley or eke in those of Watts. Owing to the pointblank refusal of the compositors to set up the hard words which Brother McDowell used with respect to the defamer Halsey we shall not be able to reproduce them in these columns; we can only say, in the language of the shocked hostess to the ancient Pistol, "These be very bitter words, Captain." We entreat Brother McDowell to be easy, under these trying circumstances, and if he cannot be easy to be as easy as he can.

To McDowell's denial that he was seeking a Senate seat, he said:

> Of course our brother in journalism and farming is not a candidate for the Senate—no man ever was. He has only been solicited—'twas ever thus. The office is seeking Brother McDowell and he is simply not trying to hide from it. Brother McDowell's admirers have often said of him that a man always knows where to find him. It is the same way with offices. Whenever Brother McDowell hears that an office is out searching for a man he merely incloses to it his name and address with the information that he is still doing business at the old stand. It may also be said that no office ever came to him for a man and went away empty-handed. He always supplied its wants with the best man he had in his clothes. Sometimes he had been forced to take it himself. For instance, we know it to be a fact that Brother McDowell begged Gov. Buchanan with tears in his eyes not to make him Coal Oil Inspector; and it is a fact that Gov. Buchanan could not accede to his request for fear of the populace.
>
> Of course Brother McDowell will go to the United States Senate. The first time we ever beheld him we were seized with the gift of prophecy and named him a future Senator. We knew that God Almighty never gave him that mass of storm-striken and insurrectionary whiskers and made him look like a weather-beaten tintype of Senator Peffer for nothing.
>
> United States Senator McDowell, noble knight of the horny hand and stone bruised heel, we, the played-out Bourbon, moss-back, upper-case Democrats salute thee—*morituri salutamus*, as it were.[13]

It would be impossible to measure the effectiveness of ridicule in discrediting McDowell, but clearly more was required. Evidence of corruption, fraud, or venality was needed to thoroughly destroy the Alliance president. A small-town newspaper seemed to be on to something when it reported in March 1891 that McDowell had been a Republican when he was residing in Arkansas. The allegation was hotly denied and, after causing a brief stir, seemed to die.[14]

Undoubtedly, the story was ready-made for one with Carmack's journalistic instincts. Sensing the possibilities, he began a quiet investigation by sending a reporter to Arkansas to dig up information about McDowell's

---

[13] Ibid., 9 April 1891. William A. Peffer was a United States senator from Kansas. With a long, flowing beard and rustic manners, he was the caricature of the unorthodox agrarian radical.

[14] Hart, *Redeemers, Bourbons, and Populists*, 169.

activities there. What the reporter actually learned can not be known, but most likely it was neither all good nor all bad. But by selecting bits and pieces of information and embellishing them, Carmack and his staff were able to concoct acts of wickedness by McDowell.

On 25 June, the *Daily American* essayed into the realm of "yellow journalism" by suddenly and dramatically providing its readers with an exposé of McDowell's political activities in Arkansas. The headlines of the story, which covered the entire front page, indicated the thrust of the revelation: "M'DOWELL; His Political Career While A Resident of Arkansas; The Associate of Negroes and a Republican Officeholder." The story declared that McDowell had become a Republican after moving to Arkansas and that he had run for the office of justice of the peace with the support of the radical black Republican organization. Moreover, he had committed what many white Southerners considered to be the ultimate sin—actually dining with blacks. Once elected, McDowell offended whites by collecting excessive fees. Then he served as a deputy under a black county clerk. Within a short time McDowell became so thoroughly disliked by whites that he was forced to move back to Tennessee. The *Daily American* supported its assertions with signed affidavits by several residents of Arkansas who claimed to have known McDowell. The reason for the exposé was explained on the editorial page.

Carmack wrote that "Because this man holds an honorable and lucrative office under a Democratic administration and because he seeks to be the guide and counselor of the people at a time when wise counsel and honest guidance is all important, it is nothing less than a public duty to show him as he is." He also insisted that he had no personal feeling in the matter and no prejudice against McDowell as an individual. "But we should be recreant to our duty to the Democratic party and the public if we did less than expose the pretensions of a man seeking to beguile the people and win their confidence with soft words and fair promises." In an editorial the following day, Carmack declared that "THE AMERICAN is not trying to ruin McDowell; it is simply trying to enlighten the people. We confess that we do not hope to do him any good by telling the truth about him, but we will do other people some good."[15]

---

[15]Nashville *Daily American*, 25, 26 June 1891.

Other newspapers quickly picked up the *Daily American*'s story, and it became the prime ammunition used in the verbal war against the Alliance. In contrast to other journals, the *Daily American* emphasized that it saw no reason to taint Governor Buchanan with McDowell's sins. Carmack made it clear that while "One or two of our contemporaries have made the exposure of McDowell an occasion for criticizing Gov. Buchanan for making the appointment," the *Daily American* "wishes to be understood as not joining in this criticism." The governor, he wrote, could not have known of McDowell's background. There was no good reason to question Buchanan's "honesty and conscientiousness."[16]

McDowell was in Mississippi on a debate tour when the *Daily American* broke the story. He immediately wrote a letter denying the charges and then cancelled the remainder of the tour to return to Tennessee to prepare a rebuttal. Three weeks later, his statement was published. In anticipation of McDowell's reply, Carmack wrote that "It is due Col. McDowell that every man who had read THE AMERICAN'S charges against him should read that which he calls his defense." The reply should be read with careful scrutiny and "If THE AMERICAN has been guilty of slander, it should receive the condemnation and merit the contempt of every right-thinking man." But McDowell would indeed be fortunate if he could "induce Alliancemen to shut their eyes to his record as published . . . and blindly take him and his unsavory record to their bosoms."[17]

McDowell's statement was a thoroughly and carefully documented refutation of the *Daily American*'s charges against him. He denied that he had been a Republican in Arkansas or that he had had any social contact with blacks. He included in his defense a large number of letters containing statements sworn to or notarized that testified to his character and honesty, and that denied the *American*'s allegations.[18] Although McDowell's reply contained some inconsistencies, it had no more than did the *Daily American*'s exposé, and was in fact more believable. Under ordinary circumstances, the Alliance president's defense might have settled the issue, but the editor of the *Daily American* did not drop the charges. In true Machiavellian

---

[16]Ibid., 30 June 1891.

[17]Ibid., 13 July 1891.

[18]*Nashville Banner*, 13 July 1891. See also Hart, *Redeemers, Bourbons, and Populists*, 171-72.

style, Carmack continued to repeat them with even greater emphasis. The day following the appearance of McDowell's statement, Carmack declared that "THE AMERICAN will make a full, complete and explicit reply to this paper as soon as certain facts already within its knowledge have been put in form for publication. This will be very soon." The *Daily American* never did reply to McDowell's rebuttal point by point. Rather, the charges made initially were simply repeated over and over again while taunting the Alliance president to file a libel suit. In the two months following the exposé, Carmack devoted at least nineteen vicious and brutal editorials to damning McDowell. The attacks subsided somewhat in September when the public was distracted by a new issue but not before the Alliance leader had been thoroughly discredited among most Democrats. By the fall of 1891, his influence was limited to a small group of diehard Alliance men.[19]

McDowell's demise contributed to the declining effectiveness of Governor Buchanan. Initially regarded with suspicion and never fully accepted by the established factions, the governor contributed to his own problem by his failure to repudiate or break with McDowell. Problems not of his own making also damaged Buchanan's standing among Democrats. He was censured from all sides for the way he handled an uprising of East Tennessee miners protesting the use of convict labor in the coal mines. He probably handled the situation as well as any one could have under the circumstances, but he was open to criticism any way he turned. By early 1892, the campaign to destroy the political influence of the Alliance had become a juggernaut which now included an additional goal: preventing the renomination and reelection of Governor Buchanan.

Interest in the governor's race had begun to mount when Carmack announced that he was leaving his comfortable position on the *Daily American* to assume a similar position on the Memphis *Daily Commercial*. The notice of his departure, which appeared on 1 February 1892, read in part: "With this issue I cease to have any responsible connection with THE AMERICAN. It has cost me a hard struggle to sever relations which have been so uniformly pleasant, and nothing but the overpowering conviction that my personal interests called me to another field could have parted me from THE AMERICAN and its readers." After expressing appreciation to the staff of the

---

[19]Nashville *Daily American*, 14 July, July-August 1891, passim. See also Hart, *Redeemers, Bourbons, and Populists*, 172.

newspaper for its cooperation and support, he offered special thanks to Duncan Cooper, who had once again become the proprietor of the *Daily American* the previous May. He declared that:

> I desire especially to acknowledge the debt I owe and the regard I feel towards Col. D. B. Cooper, under whose management I first became connected with THE AMERICAN and with journalism. It is a pleasure at this time that I cannot recall one word, act or incident which has marred the harmony of our relations during the whole time of our intimate association. I shall always feel an interest and pride in THE AMERICAN'S success and know that under its present management it cannot fail to deserve and to hold the confidence and esteem of the public, which has made it a power for good in the state of Tennessee.[20]

Carmack's reasons for making the move are not readily apparent. There must have been several considerations, but any attempt to identify them would be based wholly on conjecture. Despite his declaration to the contrary, Carmack's relationship with Duncan Cooper may have been strained, if ever so slightly. It is possible that Carmack chafed at Cooper's lack of total commitment to the principles of Bourbonism.

Legend says that Carmack moved to the *Commercial* solely because he was offered a much better salary. However, the Memphis newspaper was in financial difficulty and may not have been able to improve on Carmack's *Daily American* salary. On the other hand, the owners of the *Commercial* may have realized that the only way to improve the newspaper's profitability was to employ a dynamic editor. It is also quite possible that the politically ambitious editor saw a chance to expand his influence and personal following, looking to the day when he might seek elective office. The Memphis newspaper had a much larger circulation area than the Nashville *Daily American*. Indeed, in 1892, the *Commercial* served several states including all of West Tennessee, southwestern Kentucky, southeastern Missouri, eastern Arkansas, northern Mississippi, and even northwestern Alabama and parts of northern Louisiana. In any case, Carmack was already sufficiently well known and admired to be mentioned as a possibility for the governorship of Tennessee. The day following his departure from the *Daily*

---

[20]Nashville *Daily American*, 12 February 1892.

American, the new editor of that journal noted that Carmack's name had been raised in connection with the governor's race of 1892:

> A number of newspapers of the State have mentioned in terms of highest laudation the name of Editor E. W. Carmack as a proper candidate of the Democracy of the State for Governor.
>
> Mr. Carmack, in his paper, the Memphis Commercial, after publishing a number of extracts from esteemed contemporaries, advises Satan and his temptations to get behind him in the following paragraph:
>
> "For fear that this boom may grow to unmanagable [sic] dimensions unless promptly suppressed, or that it may perish at the most interesting point of its career, the highly complimented subject thereof desires to quietly but firmly decline the unattainable honor and refuse with thanks the unoffered prize. To be the editor of a great newspaper is a bigger thing than being Governor of Tennessee as things go. It takes more than lungs, gall and chin whiskers to make an editor."

Despite the polite rejection, the *Daily American* declared that "If Ned Carmack wants to be Governor we are for him from sorrel top to stone bruises."[21]

Whatever his motives, Carmack's move to the *Commercial* was a challenge, but it involved a considerable risk. The Memphis *Daily Commercial* had been founded in December 1889 by a group of men associated with the "old families"—the traditional ruling class—of that city. This group was allied with the Bourbon regular wing of the Democratic party and Senator Isham G. Harris. The *Commercial* challenged the hegemony of the well-established *Appeal-Avalanche* published by William A. Collier, a Whiggish Democrat and an advocate of the New South creed. In 1887, Collier had obtained a partnership in the *Appeal*, a newspaper founded in 1841, and two years later, he acquired full control. Then in 1890, he purchased the venerable Memphis *Avalanche* and merged the two as the *Appeal-Avalanche*. Collier also moved his newspaper into a new building and purchased new equipment.

In 1892, the *Appeal-Avalanche* seemed to be in good financial condition and in a dominant position in Memphis. Despite the fact that its backers were men of wealth, the *Daily Commercial* operated under some

---

[21]Ibid., 14 February 1892.

difficulties. The initial cost of a physical plant plus day-to-day operating expenses strained the resources of the new journal. Survival of the *Daily Commercial* required dynamic and imaginative leadership. If anyone could keep the newspaper alive and challenging the *Appeal-Avalanche*, it was Carmack.[22]

---

[22]Thomas Harrison Baker, *The Memphis Commercial Appeal: The History of a Southern Newspaper* (Baton Rouge: Louisiana State University Press, 1971) 151-62.

4

THE COMMERCIAL APPEAL

Editor-in-Chief Edward Ward Carmack quickly settled into his position on the Memphis *Daily Commercial* and was soon the dominant personality on the newspaper. As a newcomer to the Bluff City, the speed with which he assumed a position of prominence and influence within the community was remarkable. Although the general readership in the circulation area knew of Carmack only vaguely at best, his reputation preceded him to Memphis and many of the political, economic, and social leaders of that city were either personally acquainted with him or were familiar with his writings and editorial style. Carmack was also knowledgeable regarding conditions in the West Tennessee city and had on occasion revealed an interest in that community. Although he became well established, Carmack did not put down roots; rather, he took up residence in the Hotel Peabody, which remained his abode for many years. Perhaps he did not regard his stay in Memphis as permanent for he apparently made no attempt to obtain a more permanent residence. Moreover, his wife was absent for long periods of time, visiting in Columbia. Even so, he was fully accepted by the conservative establishment in Memphis.

Generally, two political factions vied for control of the Bluff City in the 1890s. One was the "old families" element, which included those whose wealth was based on cotton and related industries. This faction had long controlled Memphis politically, supported Senator Isham G. Harris, and was allied with the Bourbon regulars in the Democratic party. Those belonging to the other faction were "new residents" who were Whiggish in sentiment and endorsed the doctrine of the New South. The conflict between the two factions was reflected in the rivalry between the two morning newspapers—the *Daily Commercial* spoke for the former, while the *Appeal-Avalanche* was the voice of the latter.[1]

Philosophically conservative, Carmack found an easy association with the "old families." Indeed, the owners of the *Daily Commercial* were members of that faction. Because he had been employed to put life into the newspaper and increase its circulation, his appointment portended a lively newspaper war with the rival *Appeal-Avalanche*. Those who expected excitement were not disappointed. Carmack did put life into the *Daily Commercial* and in sensational style—headlines screamed of heinous crimes, horrible disasters, and other dramatic events. There were more illustrations and more circulation stunts. For example, on election night in November 1892, special high-speed trains were employed to deliver the *Daily Commercial* with the last-minute returns to readers throughout the Mid-South. But it was on the editorial page that Carmack created the most excitement, and William A. Collier, owner and publisher of the *Appeal-Avalanche*, became a regular target. Carmack had no sooner arrived in Memphis than he declared rhetorical war on Collier, who quickly entered the fray by returning fire. The conflict soon became so intense and bitter that it appeared that Carmack and Collier were involved in a personal feud and that each was intent on destroying the other.

The editorial warfare between the two journalists focused on local politics and issues, reflecting the contest for control of Memphis by the two political factions. Prior to the city elections in 1889, the "old families" controlled local politics and were headed by D. P. "Pappy" Hadden, president of the Memphis taxing district.[2] However, the opposition, the "new resi-

---

[1] Thomas Harrison Baker, *The Memphis Commercial Appeal: The History of a Southern Newspaper* (Baton Rouge: Louisiana State University Press, 1971) 151-62.

[2] As a result of the devastation caused by yellow fever epidemics, Memphis had gone bankrupt and lost its charter in 1879. The Tennessee General Assembly created a special taxing district for the city. The president of the district was the chief political officer in Memphis.

dent" faction, won control of the Democracy in Memphis in 1889 and nominated W. D. Bethel for president, a nomination supported by Collier's newspaper. However, Hadden did not bow out gracefully and decided to run as an independent, which may have been the impetus behind the founding of the *Daily Commercial*, the organ that became Hadden's press support in the race. Bethel, however, won in a close vote, but the ascendancy of the Whiggish faction in the Bluff City did not end the struggle for political control of the community. If anything, it became more intense. The "old families" charged the new regime with crime and corruption and by 1892, a "Law and Order League," a disingenuous front for the Bourbons, had appeared. The real objective of the league was to discredit Bethel and his supporters and return control of the city to the "old families." Carmack became an active member when he arrived on the scene.[3]

Crime and vice in Memphis was a subject to which the new editor turned often and with good reason, for the city still retained characteristics of a wild river town. Carmack denounced widespread vice and especially the existence of illegal saloons, aiming for those taverns that operated without a license. He conveniently saw a corrupt link between city government and the criminal element in Memphis. It was not, however, the crime-and-vice issue that excited readers—editors and ministers had discussed that issue for years. Rather, it was the feud between Carmack and Collier that provided interesting reading. The two journalists had used intemperate language in reference to each other before Carmack arrived in Memphis and the move only served to increase the frequency of name-calling. The conflict reached a white heat of intensity in the early months of 1893 over the impeachment of a Memphis judge.

In January 1893, Carmack launched a vicious editorial campaign against a member of the ruling faction, Memphis Criminal Court Judge Julius J. DuBose. Denunciation of DuBose became a regular feature on the editorial page of the *Daily Commercial*. The judge was accused of taking bribes from operators of illegal saloons and from the kingpins of vice. He was described as an incompetent and a tyrant with an "insatiate desire for power." DuBose despised "decency and good morals" and had "dragged the ermine of his office in the filth of the gutters." He had "prostituted the power of his office to shield criminals." Finally, the judge, by failing to en-

---

[3]Baker, *The Memphis Commercial Appeal*, 162-63.

force the law, was responsible for the excessive vice and crime in Memphis. Carmack called for the impeachment of DuBose by the Tennessee General Assembly.[4]

Although there may have been substance to the allegations against DuBose, the attack was neither a spontaneous response to exposed villainy nor the result of righteous indignation over the existence of corruption. There was calculation in the campaign against the judge. Carmack could not pass an opportunity to embarrass, and thus weaken, the ruling faction just a few months before city elections were to be held. More important was the attempt to impeach the judge. Although the "old families" had no voice in city government, it still retained control of the Shelby County delegation in the state legislature. The initiative against DuBose coincided with the convening of the General Assembly in January 1893. The advantage of impeachment was obvious. It was a way to bypass the local structure to strike a blow against the ruling faction.

Collier and the *Appeal-Avalanche* quickly came to the defense of Judge DuBose, basing it on the presumed innocence of someone charged with a crime. The *Appeal-Avalanche* observed that the *Daily Commercial* had already convicted the judge before the evidence was in and that the newspaper was creating an atmosphere in which DuBose would not get a fair hearing. Carmack's wit and sarcasm could, when the occasion demanded, destroy an opponent's argument. Generally, he deigned reply to Collier, and in this instance, Carmack followed his Machiavellian principle. He continued his attack, repeating the same charges against the judge.

In the middle of February, however, the object of Carmack's barbs was replaced when significant changes were made on the editorial staff of the *Appeal-Avalanche*. Although he remained president of the company, Collier relinquished his responsibilities for editorial management, and B. M. Stratton was made editor-in-chief with complete control of editorial policy. The reason for the move is not clear, but pressing financial problems may have required that Collier devote more attention to managing business operations. With tongue-in-cheek, Carmack welcomed Stratton to the editor's fraternity "as an active coadjutor and willing assistant to THE COMMERCIAL for we fain believe that his heart is in the right place." He appealed "to Col. Stratton to come over on the Lord's side and bring the Appeal-Avalanche

---

[4]*Daily Commercial*, January-February 1893, passim.

with him" on the DuBose issue. Detecting that Stratton was on the verge of conversion, Carmack concluded:

> We hope we are not mistaken in Brother Stratton; and if through our agency we shall succeed in bringing that tough old reprobate, the Appeal-Avalanche, out of disgrace into grace, we defy any man to dispute our claim to be considered the Sam Jones of American Journalism.
> Let the congregation stand and sing:
> While the lamp holds out to burn
> The vilest sinner may return.[5]

Carmack's forecast of a significant policy change was confirmed a few days later when Stratton editorially conceded the guilt of Judge DuBose. "Judge DuBose has brought this prosecution upon himself by arbitrary acts giving offense to the public and causing thoughtful men to regard his longer presence on the bench as intolerable." A gleeful Carmack commended Stratton for his conversion in an editorial entitled "Bro. Stratton Comes Through." Stratton, he wrote, "has taken his foot out of the mirey clay and set it upon the Rock of Ages. . . . Brother Stratton has done a great work in redeeming what everybody had come to consider a hopelessly tough and redemptionless newspaper." But Carmack did not drop the issue; he regularly reminded Collier of the flip-flop by the *Appeal-Avalanche* in regard to Judge DuBose. For weeks, the *Commercial* published daily brief excerpts from Stratton's editorial. If his intentions were to intimidate Collier, he was probably successful. In the meantime, with the Shelby County delegation in the legislature pressing the case, the General Assembly voted in March to impeach the Memphis judge, and the trial began a few weeks later.[6]

The editorial shift of the *Appeal-Avalanche* displeased Collier, and he objected to Stratton's editorial on DuBose, calling it premature. Undoubtedly under pressure from the president and board of directors, Stratton returned in late April to the original position of the newspaper that DuBose must be presumed innocent until proven guilty. Moreover, the judge was praised as a good jurist and his impeachment must be the result of a campaign by "malignant scoundrels" and character assassins. Carmack was

---

[5]Ibid., 19 February 1893. Sam Jones was a well-known evangelist.

[6]*Appeal-Avalanche*, 23 February 1893; *Daily Commercial*, 24 February 1893.

quick with a response. In a lengthy editorial, he declared that the *Appeal-Avalanche* had completed a circle. It had begun by defending DuBose, grew lukewarm, then assailed him, grew lukewarm, and was now back at the "same old foolish, absurd and preposterous" position. He warned the *Appeal-Avalanche* "that it lays a false and flattering unction to its soul if it really believes that there is any weakening of purpose on the part of Judge DuBose's accusers. Perhaps it was some such notion that emboldened our contemporary to enter the field again." Then, with reference to the financial problems of the *Appeal-Avalanche*, Carmack concluded that "it will live to learn better if it can manage to survive a few days longer."[7]

Collier had had enough. On 3 May, he lashed out at Carmack and the proprietors of the *Daily Commercial* in a bitter, vituperative editorial.

> The Memphis Commercial is so glib to denounce on every occasion gentlemen who do not agree with it as thugs, thieves and social outcasts generally, that its utterances attract no more attention than the billingsgate of the fishwife or the bluster of the bully. . . . Blackguardism is the chief weapon in its armory and the chief pillar in its temple. Without resort to this vulgar practice, existence would be impossible.

Vicious attacks by the *Commercial* were "consistent with its life and history." Moreover, the newspaper was established, owned, and operated by criminals. Collier concluded that because the *Commercial* was "conceived in infamy and nurtured in corruption," it "can not rise higher than its source. The twig was bent, and the tree must always be inclined."[8]

Carmack returned the fire quickly in two editorials, representing one of his most scathing attacks yet. The first was entitled "Remarks To A Slanderer."

> It is not the slander of such evil tongues as that of the person who owns and controls the Appeal-Avalanche or of those who do his dirty work, that can defame THE COMMERCIAL. Every man connected with THE COMMERCIAL in any capacity has lived in vain if he needs any protection except that of his own good name against the splutterings of a thing that has sunk lower than even the lowest in its shameful trade. If

---

[7]*Appeal-Avalanche*, 30 April 1893; *Daily Commercial*, 1, 28 May 1893.

[8]*Appeal-Avalanche*, 3 May 1893.

the person who owns what is left of the Appeal-Avalanche does not know how impotent he is to defame the character of honest men in this community he is the only man who is so ignorant.

Then, referring to Collier's desperate search for funds to keep his financially troubled newspaper from collapse, Carmack declared that "He has indeed succeeded in debauching a once honorable newspaper until it has sunk to the level of a night-strolling trollop, plying its trade in the back alleys of the town, dealing in shame for a morsel of bread and selling its soul to whoever will buy; but in doing so he has made it as impotent as it is infamous."

Responding to the charge that the proprietors of the *Commercial* were criminals, Carmack listed the names of the founders and original stockholders of the newspaper, noting that he needed "only to publish this list" of honorable gentlemen "to hold the author of the article . . . up to public contempt as a corrupt and infamous slanderer." Carmack insisted that the only basis for the charge by Collier was "the fact that one person who was indicted in the courts as a defaulter at one time owned one share of stock in THE COMMERCIAL and was for a few weeks in its employ. Upon such a slender basis as this a body of as honorable, upright and highly respected citizens as live in any community are classed as criminals by the besotted scribblers of this low lampoon. . . . We dismiss this rag with contempt," he said in closing. The accompanying editorial under the title "Editorial Dipsomania" declared that:

> If the Appeal-Avalanche chooses to let its writers have their delirium tremens on the editorial page it is a matter of no particular consequence to THE COMMERCIAL or to any person connected therewith. If the person who does the "dictating" and "surveillance" act has a taste for editorial jim-jams and likes to see the columns of his newspaper full of red snakes and blue lizards he is welcome to indulge his peculiar passion. The bacchanalian orgies that reel and scream through the columns of our esteemed contemporary simply show how reckless it has become of its own reputation as well as the reputation of others. No "dictator" that has not parted company with all considerations of decency and self-respect would permit reckless writers to unload their jags and spew the overflow of their night's debauch on the pages of his newspaper. It is evident that there was no "surveillance," or rather no intelligent "surveillance," exercised over the editorials in yesterday's Appeal-Avalanche. The early morning drunk was given liberty to howl its disgusting impre-

cations without check or hindrance. There was no blue pencil to interfere with the free play of the writer's *mania a potu*. There was nobody to edit his hiccoughs. There was not even a friendly lamp-post to keep him out of the gutter. Driven off the street by the police, he retired to his padded cell in the Appeal building where, like the imbecil Polonius, he could "play the fool in's own house." There in the solitude of his quiet chamber his reeling brain and diseased imagination called up all the grotesque shapes from the nasty deep of his vocabulary and set them to dancing a wierd and hideous can-can. There was never such a dance of brain-born devils since Tam O'Shanter glowered through the windows of Alloway Kirk.

And even thus is the Appeal-Avalanche—the "Old Reliable"—edited! May the good Lord and Dr. Keeley save it!

The rest of the editorial page contained other comments along with a reprint of the *Appeal-Avalanche*'s 23 February editorial in which Stratton had conceded the battle over DuBose to Carmack.[9]

Collier's rebuttal appeared the next day. He was especially incensed at Carmack's comment about the *Appeal-Avalanche* "selling its soul to whoever will buy."

> As one of the owners of the Appeal-Avalanche, I desire to state that the Commercial is so low, mean and contemptible that nothing said of it would be a slander. . . . The Appeal-Avalanche has never received financial aid as a loan or any other way, directly or indirectly, to the extent of one-thousandth part of a cent for its editorial influence or policy, nor has anyone connected with it. There is not enough money in the banks of this city to buy one line of its editorials. It has been conducted in the interest of our city and country and people, and it has prospered and will continue in the same way. In conclusion, I denounce . . . [the defamation in] the Commercial as a wilful and malicious lie, and its author as a wilful and malicious liar. —W. A. Collier

In another column, he suggested that "The Commercial had to order out its last reserve yesterday morning to make one more desperate effort to conceal its vile origin and present phasisaical hypocracy [sic]." He suggested that when the *Commercial* was about to collapse, "a common Blackguard

---

[9]*Daily Commercial*, 4 May 1893.

from the hill country [Carmack] was imported to put a little life in the moribund carcass. And well has he performed his task. Posing as an exemplar of high citizenship, a symposium of all the virtues and the beau ideal of manhood, the Commercial has resorted to every method known to the ingenuity of infamy to blast private characters and defame good names."[10]

The feud between Carmack and Collier had reached the flash point. The insults became so venomous that one of the contestants believed that he had been so pained that his honor required vindication. One of the parties sent word to the other that they should meet face to face on neutral soil to settle their differences. Carmack's loyalists assumed that Collier had issued a challenge to a duel, but who challenged whom is not clear. A duel posed a problem, however, for the Tennessee constitution outlawed prearranged combat of that nature. The fundamental law declared that anyone sending or knowingly bearing a challenge, accepting a challenge, or fighting a duel, or serving as an aide at a duel would be deprived of the right to hold any office of honor or profit in the Volunteer State.

After some negotiations, the contestants, referring to their affair as a matter in dispute which required settlement, agreed to avoid publicity and meet at Holly Springs, Mississippi, a small village about forty-five miles southeast of Memphis. Efforts to keep the affair quiet went for nought. Word leaked out and spread across Memphis, causing quite a stir. Hoping to prevent a tragedy, friends tried to find a way to keep the duel from taking place. An unknown person or persons alerted the authorities and bench warrants were sworn out charging both Carmack and Collier with conspiracy to participate in a duel. The police, therefore, intervened, arresting them on the morning of the duel, preventing possible bloodshed. The events of the appointed day still involved considerable excitement and drama that had all the elements of an old-fashioned melodrama, replete with its characters and exaggerated actions, conflicts, and emotionalism, plus a scene from the "Keystone Kops." One story circulated that the individual who alerted the authorities was an unknown woman dressed in black with a thick veil covering her face.

On the day of the scheduled meeting, as reported in the *Commercial*, Carmack descended from his room and appeared in the lobby of the Hotel Peabody about eight o'clock. "He walked to the counter, got his mail,

---

[10]*Appeal-Avalanche*, 5 May 1893.

walked to the rear of the rotunda and paused a moment as if in deep thought. Then he went into the saloon and took a good stiff drink." He then walked to the *Commercial* office and "went into the editorial-rooms . . . picked up something wrapped in a piece of paper, put the package and his cane under his arm, took up his umbrella and came down stairs." He went into the business office and shook "hands with several men in the office" before returning to his hotel. A few moments later, he boarded a hack that took him to the station. Carmack had already seated himself in the smoking car of the train when a deputy sheriff found him and "placed him under arrest and conveyed him to the courthouse."

About 9:45, Collier left his office at the *Appeal-Avalanche* and got in a hack. After he had seated himself, a deputy appeared and announced that Collier was under arrest. Associates with Collier quickly grabbed the deputy, who was "jerked within the carriage and the door was slammed." The hack raced through the streets of Memphis to the station with the officer under restraint. Collier quickly boarded the train and locked himself in a compartment. The train pulled out of the station with the deputy still under restraint. The proprietor of the *Appeal-Avalanche* arrived in Holly Springs on schedule.

Carmack's appearance at the Memphis courthouse drew a large crowd and after a brief conference with the judge, he was allowed to go, presumably on his own recognizance, but the delay caused him to miss the train for Holly Springs. West J. Crawford, president of the *Commercial*, arranged for a special train to take Carmack and his party to the Mississippi community and then began a series of telegrams attempting to make alternate arrangements. The special arrived after the designated hour of 2:30 P.M. and Collier, accepting this as vindication, refused to consider alternate arrangements. Both the *Commercial* and the *Appeal-Avalanche* reported the events in lead stories the following day, but giving biased accounts; the former implied that Collier was a coward for not agreeing to a later meeting, and the latter suggested that Collier's honor had been vindicated.[11]

Both men were embarrassed by the affair and perhaps sobered by narrowly escaping an event that might well have resulted in a tragedy. Personal attacks were toned down, but the newspaper war and the factional struggle continued. When Stratton resigned as editor because of his newspaper's de-

---

[11] Ibid., 7 May 1893; *Daily Commercial*, 7 May 1893.

fense of DuBose, Carmack gloated. He observed that it was a "stinging blow to the Defense when a man who is one of the principal directors and stockholders of the paper which supports DuBose feels himself called upon as a patriotic citizen to express himself as opposed to the present policy of his own paper." He had even more to crow about when DuBose was convicted of impeachment on 2 June. He declared that it was "The Triumph of Right."[12] The factional struggle warmed up again in late fall of 1893 during the city election campaign. In the mayor's race, the *Appeal-Avalanche* supported Lucas Clapp while Carmack's *Commercial* endorsed John Joseph Williams, a politician who would subsequently become something of a legend in Memphis. Carmack lampooned Clapp and described Williams as a thoroughbred whose "record is stainless, his personal character clean." Clapp won, however, and the *Commercial* editor rationalized that Republicans had been the cause of the defeat of the "regular" Democrat.[13]

If Carmack was embarrassed by the events of the aborted duel with Collier, he gained a measure of satisfaction at the financial misfortunes of the owner of the *Appeal-Avalanche*. Using the easy credit of the boom years of the late 1880s and early 1890s, Collier had built a seemingly prosperous and successful business from the *Appeal* and the *Avalanche*. He spent lavishly on the physical plant, equipment, and promotional schemes. So when the nationwide panic of the spring of 1893 hit, Collier was caught overextended. The newspaper's revenue declined, but expenses and debts remained fixed. By September, the financial condition of the journal was serious; the newspaper's creditors went to court, and were granted a receivership. Collier fought the court action, the legal battles occupying several months, but in June 1894, the court ordered the sale of the *Appeal-Avalanche*. The high bidder was West J. Crawford, president of the *Commercial* Publishing Company; the purchase price was a bargain at $65,200. The acquisition led to the formation of a new newspaper, *The Commercial Appeal*, whose first edition hit the streets 1 July 1894 with Edward Ward Carmack as editor. The merger left Memphis with only one morning daily and one evening daily, the *Evening Scimitar*.[14]

---

[12]*Daily Commercial*, 28 May, 3 June 1893.

[13]Ibid., December 1893-5 January 1894.

[14]Ibid., 17 June 1894; see also Baker, *The Memphis Commercial Appeal*, 156-57.

The exciting newspaper war diverted reader-attention from some very witty and eloquent editorial debates between the editor of the *Commercial* and his counterparts in other cities. At times Carmack took on more experienced and more famous journalists and often did well enough. Henry Watterson, editor of the Louisville *Courier-Journal* and exponent of the New South creed, was a favorite target for editorial barbs. An exchange in the summer of 1893 provides a good illustration of both editors' skill with words.

In June, Watterson became involved in a controversy with the editor of the Charleston, South Carolina, *News and Courier* over the wisdom of secession. Although a strong Unionist, Watterson had committed himself to the Confederacy during the Civil War. In the debate with the South Carolina journalist, Watterson asserted that secession had been wrong. Carmack then entered the fray and wrote: "Mr. Watterson may admit that he fought for a cause which he believed was wrong, and that he sinned. . . . He must confess for himself alone. . . . We enter our most emphatic protest when he undertakes to make it appear that the people of the South entered a wicked and causeless rebellion knowing that they were wrong."

Watterson took note of the Memphis editor's comment and replied: "Our young friend, the editor of the Memphis Commercial, should beware of tackling anything more exciting than an ice-box during the heat of the dog-days. In particular, as a not unpromising cadet of that journalism, which, although precocious, is all too quick-of-the trigger, he should steer clear of conclusions about matters" he knows little about. "With the characteristic bravery of youth and ignorance . . . seeking to while away the tedium of a summer afternoon, our juvenile oracle delivers . . . broadsides of blank cartridges and pop-gun rhetoric."

Carmack could not let that pass without a response. "We suppose we have written as much and as fulsomely of Hon. Henry Watterson, of his genius, his character, and his service" as anyone. "It may be that 'youth and ignorance' are partly responsible for the admiration we have always felt and avowed for this Kentucky oracle, and that with years and ripening wisdom we may learn that Our Hero is nothing more than a gifted penstagger and lip artist. . . . From what Mr. Watterson says of us we are convinced that we are doomed to live always in ignorance." Watterson replied, observing that "Such is the towering vanity of this word swollen egotist that he cannot endure a temperate and dispassionate criticism." Who won the exchange is open to debate, but the young Memphis editor proved he could hold his own with those of more experience and with a larger reputation.[15]

The local conflict with Collier and debates with other editors in no way distracted Carmack from his other concerns. Not the least of his interests were national issues, and he often commented on them. He continued to call for the end of the protective tariff, and he got on the bandwagon for a national progressive income tax. Not surprisingly he supported the leader of the Democratic party, President Grover Cleveland, even on the occasions when the president pressed policies contrary to Carmack's views. His chief concern, however, remained the influence of the Farmers' Alliance in Tennessee. This was one issue upon which he and Collier agreed.

The press campaign to destroy the Alliance politically in the Volunteer State and to prevent the renomination of Governor Buchanan was well underway when Carmack left the Nashville *Daily American* for the *Commercial* in February of 1892. Buchanan faced an uphill struggle with virtually every major daily newspaper opposing him. He became especially vulnerable when the national Alliance played a leading role in the formation of the new People's party, or Populist party, in St. Louis, Missouri, in February 1892. The threat of the third party became more ominous when it met at Omaha, Nebraska, in July, wrote a platform, and nominated a candidate for the presidency. Many Tennessee Alliance men were opposed to the third party, and Buchanan tried to disassociate himself from the movement. His efforts were futile, and he was abused without letup in the press. He was literally read out of the Democratic party.

Although Carmack attacked the Alliance, he did not vilify Buchanan; but neither did he endorse the governor's renomination. Without significant press support or the backing of one of the established factions of the party, Buchanan became one of the few governors of Tennessee to be denied renomination for a second term by his party. The Democrats selected for that honor a Bourbon Democrat, Chief Justice of the State Supreme Court, Peter Turney, a choice Carmack applauded. Buchanan, however, entered the race as an independent and garnered the support of several groups, including one known as "Buchanan Democrats" and the Populist party in Tennessee. The governor now became fair game and Editor Carmack had reason to attack him.

---

[15]*Daily Commercial*, 5, 9 July 1893; Louisville *Courier-Journal*, 3 July 1893.

Late in the gubernatorial campaign, it was reported that the past-president of the Farmer's Alliance, John Henry McDowell, now one of the Populist leaders, had entered into a deal with some Republicans. Both parties in the agreement pledged to avoid certain legislative and congressional districts to ensure victory for the other; McDowell was to keep Buchanan in the race to draw votes from Turney so that the Republican candidate for governor, G. W. Winstead, would win; and the Republicans would support McDowell in his race for the Senate against Democrat William B. Bate. McDowell also received $15,000 from the Republicans, presumably to be used in the campaign. Although there was nothing illegal or immoral about the deal, the Democratic press jumped on the issue.

Carmack gave the story front-page coverage with a headline and subheadlines that read: "Judas and His Silver; The Corrupt Deal Between John H. McDowell and the Republican Committee Laid Bare; A Cold-Blooded Cash Transaction, In Which John Henry Agrees to Sell Buchanan and All of His Followers; Populites to Support Harrison; In Return, Republicans Have Agreed to Support McDowell for the Senate Besides Paying Him the Sum of $15,000." The story included copies of the correspondence to prove the charges. An editorial in the same issue under the title "Bought and Paid For" referred to Buchanan as "Our poor, weak, wretched Governor—God pity him—is included in the trade." From that point until election day, Buchanan was the subject of several brutal editorials. What effect the McDowell deal had on the outcome of the gubernatorial election is difficult to measure, but there is reason to believe that a number of "Buchanan Democrats" returned to the fold. When the election was over, Carmack happily wrote that "We have seen the last of McDowellism and the proud old State of Tennessee has been delivered of its captivity" from McDowell and Buchanan.[16]

The election of 1892 involved a presidential contest as well as contests for most state and county offices across the Mid-South. Carmack endorsed the Democratic presidential candidate, Grover Cleveland, without qualification and, reflecting his usual party regularity, supported all other candidates of the party. He sought to influence the voting public all across the

---

[16]*Daily Commercial*, 23 October, 9 November 1892; see also Roger L. Hart, *Redeemers, Bourbons, and Populists: Tennessee 1870-1896* (Baton Rouge: Louisiana State University Press, 1975) 179-98.

Mid-South and especially did he warn his readers about the menace of populism. He cautioned that "A vote in the South for the third party means a vote for the Republican party."

The year 1892 was a Democratic year as the party swept many offices across the nation. The *Commercial* cheered. One headline read: "Hell and Vermont; Are All That Is Left Of the Grand Old Party; The Democrats Have Grabbed the Rest of Creation." The election was also the background for one of Carmack's promotional stunts. The *Commercial* chartered special fast trains to carry news of election results to its Mid-South readers. The editor claimed that the efforts to get the news to its patrons quickly was an overwhelming success. He also noted smugly that one train was sent on its way "after dumping off a lot of Appeal-Avalanches that were trying to steal a ride." The Democratic sweep was also an occasion for blatant self-praise by the *Commercial*. In an editorial entitled "THE COMMERCIAL'S Part," Carmack claimed that the newspaper had played a vital role in defeating both Populists and Republicans. "No false modesty need prevent our recognition of the fact that the people believe that THE COMMERCIAL has done valiant and effective service for the cause of straight Democracy."[17]

The election of 1892 signaled the end of the influence of the Farmers' Alliance and Populism in Tennessee's Democratic party. Although a legacy of unresolved problems remained, the agrarian revolt in the Volunteer State peaked during the administration of Governor Buchanan and began to fade with his defeat. Scholars have attempted to identify the reasons for the failure of the farmers' revolt in Tennessee. These include ineptness and incompetence of the leaders of the Alliance, the threat of increasing the black vote, loyalty to the Democratic party, and fear that the movement might weaken the party and allow the Republicans to rise to power.

Overlooked was the influence of the press. Except for a few small-town newspapers and the organ of the Alliance, the *Weekly Toiler*, the movement had virtually no press support; to the contrary, the major daily newspapers were outspoken in opposition to the agrarian reformers. If social scientists are correct in the assertion that the press can have a significant influence in shaping public opinion in the establishment of new cultural patterns, the farmers' revolt, as a legitimate social movement, might have been far more

---

[17]*Daily Commercial*, 4, 10, 14 November 1892.

successful in the state, and elsewhere, if it had had significant newspaper endorsement. Instead, the press, both Bourbon and New South, regarded the movement as a threat to established norms, values, and beliefs, and rallied public opinion in opposition, even among those who stood to gain from proposed reforms. The press set the agenda—destroy the political influence of the Alliance—and then contributed to the achievement of that goal.

Although the political influence of the Alliance was minimal after 1892, its opponents still found the organization useful as a whipping-boy. The agrarian movement remained a threat because the complaints of the farmers had not been resolved and because of the continued activity of the Populist party across the nation. Carmack was among those who regarded the new party as a threat, and he regularly called attention to "The Menace of Populism." He declared, for example, that the party included "all the turbulent, incendiary and vicious elements of society" and was in sympathy with criminals and anarchists. "The party indeed is an organized menace to the peace of society. Its rule means social and industrial chaos."[18]

Conforming to tradition in 1894, the Democrats renominated for governor the incumbent Peter Turney, a choice that pleased Carmack. The Republicans placed in the field a Chattanooga businessman, Henry Clay Evans. Throughout the campaign, the Memphis editor reminded his readers of the sins and errors of the Republican party at both the national and state levels. According to Carmack, the national party continued to follow policies that hurt the South, and the state party was guilty of associating with the national party. Although unable to win alone, the Republicans could endanger Democratic hegemony in Tennessee if allied with the Populists. This was a very real threat, a fact which Carmack acknowledged. He warned that a "fusion" of Republicans and Populists could threaten Democratic control of the governorship and General Assembly; therefore, as he so often did, he urged Democrats to stay loyal and remain united.[19]

Despite continuing internal discord and the threat of a Republican-Populist fusion, Carmack and other Democrats were supremely confident, perhaps overconfident about the prospects of victory in the general election in November. The results in Tennessee and elsewhere were, therefore, stunning. Even in Democratic Tennessee, a Republican won the governorship,

[18] Ibid., 17 July 1894.

[19] Ibid., July-October 1894, passim.

albeit narrowly. At first, Carmack ascribed the debacle to the failure of Democrats at the national level to solve problems in the economy. The people, he wrote, "put the Democratic party in power [in 1892] to restore prosperity. It has failed to accomplish the result as promptly as expected." Indeed, it was saddled with the blame for the panic of 1893 and the depression that followed. He concluded "that it is not a time to perpetuate antagonisms within the party, but rather a time for Democrats to counsel soberly together with a view to meeting the enemy in the next campaign with closed ranks." Conceding the Tennessee gubernatorial election to Evans, Carmack accurately put his finger on one of the reasons for the Republican triumph in the state—too many Democrats had stayed away from the polls through "over confidence."[20]

Although Evans won a narrow but clear victory, the Democrats challenged the vote. A Democratic-controlled legislative committee that investigated the election invalidated numerous Republican votes. In the end, the Democratic General Assembly overturned Evans's victory and returned Turney to the governor's office. Carmack had always espoused honesty, fairness, and majority rule, but he did not condemn the way the Democrats deprived a properly elected official of his office.

To Carmack, the rejection of the Democracy by so many voters in 1894 was simply a rejection of the policies and programs offered by the party. It was convincing proof of the need for the party to pursue new directions. Especially important, it seemed, was the need for the party to adopt a monetary policy that would be attractive to the electorate. The proposal to expand the money supply by increasing the use of silver in the currency was available. Thus free silver became Carmack's next crusade.

---

[20]Ibid., 7, 8, 11 November 1894; Hart, *Redeemers, Bourbons, and Populists*, 213-14.

5

SILVER AND POLITICS

A vital national issue in the generation following the Civil War was money supply. Generally, the question involved a conflict between those who favored hard money, or gold, and those who advocated easy money—inflating the currency by issuing greenbacks or silver. In 1878, Congress adopted a bimetalist policy by authorizing the purchase of a nominal amount of silver by the treasury department to circulate as currency. Although the Sherman Silver Purchase Act of 1890 increased the amount of silver circulating as currency, the per capita amount of money in circulation declined relative to population. A number of groups believed that this was the cause of many of the nation's economic problems. Farmers especially thought that the decline in the money supply was a cause of their plight. By 1890, advocates of easy money had come to believe that the free and unlimited coinage of silver would solve the problem of the money supply and improve the nation's economy. Free silver was one of the demands of the Populist party.

Carmack was initially ambivalent on monetary policy. In 1891, for example, he declared that although the "silver question should not be ignored," the most important issue was the tariff. "It would . . . be a dangerous tactical mistake" for the Democratic party to abandon its traditional economic issue, the tariff.[1] Carmack's conversion to free silver began

---

[1] *Daily American*, 15 March 1891.

after the Wall Street crash and the onset of a severe depression in 1893. He suggested that the depression was caused by the East's control of the money supply—Easterners were lenders and holders of mortgages; Southerners and Westerners were borrowers and debtors. When a financial collapse occurred, he wrote, "money disappears like magic in the South and West and goes to the Eastern or manufacturing states where it is locked up in bank vaults, safety deposits, and strong boxes."[2]

When President Cleveland called Congress into special session in August 1893 to repeal the Sherman Silver Purchase Act, Carmack expressed a willingness to support him, but he declared that "There can be no such thing as stability with a single standard." He would accept repeal of the Sherman Act only with assurances that it would not be a step backward and "provision is to be made for the continued use of silver in adding to the volume of our currency."[3] Congress, under prodding from Cleveland, repealed the silver act and the Democracy became a bitterly divided party. The economic distress intensified and, as suffering increased, planters and small farmers alike became convinced that the only solution to the depression was a return to silver. Carmack found it easy to go with the trend, and, in the company of Senator Isham G. Harris, boarded the bandwagon for silver.

In the state Democratic convention in August 1894, Carmack was one of the leaders instrumental in persuading the delegates to adopt a pro-silver platform. Carmack's acceptance of the cause of silver was complete after the Democratic party's setback in November 1894. Pragmatic politics, rather than adherence to economic principles, dictated his transition. The continued threat of populism and the need to restore unity in the Democracy were the overriding concerns. Accordingly, he became totally committed to the cause of free coinage of silver.[4]

The silver crusade gained momentum in Tennessee and the Mid-South in 1895, but the split in the Democratic party over monetary policy became more pronounced. In May, supporters of the gold standard held a "Southern Sound Money Convention" in Memphis. The meeting had no official sanc-

---

[2]*Daily Commercial*, 29 May 1893.

[3]Ibid., 17, 29 September 1893.

[4]*The Commercial Appeal*, 21 August 1894; see also Thomas Harrison Baker, *The Memphis Commercial Appeal: The History of a Southern Newspaper* (Baton Rouge: Louisiana State University Press, 1971) 168-69.

tion; rather, it was a call for interested parties to convene to show support for gold and a "Sound money policy." Not surprisingly, those in attendance, amid sustained applause, voted endorsement of the gold standard. Not to be outdone, the silverites held a rally that moved into Memphis the day following the gold convention. Carmack was chairman of the meeting and, judging from reports in his newspaper, the enthusiasm far exceeded that of the gold meeting.

In contrast to the 695 at the hard-money convention, more than 2,000 attended the silver caucus. The keynote speaker was a young Nebraska lawyer named William Jennings Bryan, "an orator of such marked ability that he has attracted attention from ocean to ocean." Bryan displayed "forensic abilities of the highest caliber" and was given an ovation at the close of his address. The convention, amid cheers, called for the restoration of silver. Less than three weeks later, the silverites held a second convention that had been expanded to include delegates from other sections of the country. Bryan was also present at the second silver meeting. However, when all was said and done, neither the gold nor the silver meetings accomplished anything except to dramatize the issue and publicize the split in the Democratic party.[5]

Carmack's editorials and activities in the silver crusade brought him into conflict with some of the members of the board of directors of the *Commercial Appeal*. The board was divided on the monetary issue with two in support of free silver and three advocating the gold standard, one of whom, West J. Crawford, was one of the organizers of the gold rally. By early 1896, the differences within the newspaper's organization were common knowledge across the city. Finally, in a confrontation with the board in April, Carmack dramatically resigned as editor. According to his version, one of the gold-bug directors declared that the only thing preventing his discharge as editor was the five-year contract that assured Carmack control over editorial policy. The editor reached into his pocket, took out the contract, tore it up, and said "I have resigned, and the contract is at an end." Shortly, Carmack announced his resignation in the *Commercial Appeal*: "My connection with The Commercial Appeal as its editor has ceased with this date. Reasons that seem to me imperative, but of which I need make no

---

[5] *The Commercial Appeal*, 24-26 May, 12-14 June 1895; Baker, *The Memphis Commercial Appeal*, 170-73.

statement to the public, impel me to take this step." The implication in the statement could hardly have escaped his readers.[6]

The difficulty within the newspaper's organization appears to have been a personality conflict rather than differences over monetary policy. The historian of the *Commercial Appeal* suggests that the principal owner and chairman of the board, West Crawford, resented Carmack's popularity and the fact that in the public's mind, the editor's name and the newspaper were synonymous. Moreover, the journal did not suddenly shift to support of the gold standard after Carmack left. Many of the readers in the circulation area were silverites and a change to advocacy of gold might have alienated subscribers. The *Commercial Appeal*, therefore, continued to be as enthusiastic for the white metal as it had been under Carmack.[7]

Carmack's resignation was contrived. He had a flair for dramatizing public issues and staging events to his own benefit. He could also make it appear that he had been personally aggrieved in his efforts to lead in a just cause. He made it seem that he parted company with the *Commercial Appeal* to avoid compromising his principles. However, it is quite probable that Carmack had already decided to enter politics as an active candidate for office and had discussed his availability with friends long before his resignation as editor. He certainly had opportunities to remain in journalism, for he received a number of offers of financial backing to establish newspapers both in Memphis and elsewhere, as well as offers of editorships on established journals.

There were those who liked to believe that they were responsible for persuading Carmack to seek public office. Kenneth Douglas McKellar, a young attorney associated with a prominant law firm in Memphis and later a United States Senator, described how Carmack visited his firm's office shortly after his resignation. The editor related what had happened and, in the course of the discussion, McKellar had a sudden thought—he suggested that Carmack run for Congress. But the editor's decision to run for political office was not the result of a sudden inspiration. Carmack was the manipulator and very much in control of the situation. He hoped to arouse pop-

---

[6]*The Commercial Appeal*, 28 April 1896; see also Kenneth D. McKellar, *Tennessee Senators as Seen By One of Their Successors* (Kingsport: Southern Publishers, Inc., 1942) 465; Baker, *The Memphis Commercial Appeal*, 170-71.

[7]Baker, *The Memphis Commercial Appeal*, 171-72.

ular sympathy by his dramatic resignation, and he must have been gratified by the response. He received a large volume of mail expressing regret that he had been forced to leave the newspaper, applauding his stand on free silver, and condemning the "gold bug" directors of the *Commercial Appeal.* Some of his correspondents urged that he run for Congress, and a mass meeting of interested citizens at Brunswick, a village near Memphis, endorsed a resolution that declared "that therefore we decidedly prefer E. W. Carmack to any man we know to represent us in the next Congress, and we pledge ourselves to use every honorable effort to secure his nomination and election." When Carmack eventually announced his candidacy for the tenth district seat in Congress, it appeared that he was simply responding to popular demand.[8]

Tennessee's tenth congressional district was composed of Memphis, Shelby County, and the adjacent counties of Fayette, Hardeman, and Tipton. The latter three were cotton-growing counties with large populations of blacks. The incumbent congressman was Colonel Josiah Patterson, a native of Alabama and a veteran of the Civil War. Long a respected leader in the Democratic party, Patterson was of the Bourbon persuasion, an ally of Isham G. Harris, and a bitter foe of both the New South creed and populism. In 1890 he had been a serious contender for the Democratic gubernatorial nomination. A loyalist, he had occasionally gone on the campaign trail in support of others, a practice that once drew editorial praise from Carmack.

Like most of his conservative contemporaries, Patterson had advocated an inflationary monetary policy. However, some time in the early 1890s, for unknown reasons, Patterson converted his support to the gold standard. The first evidence of his shift came in 1893 when he became one of the leaders in guiding Cleveland's proposed repeal of the Sherman Act through the House of Representatives. The following year he chaired a House elections subcommittee that investigated a contested election case from a Missouri district. The subcommittee eventually denied the seat to the certified winner, incumbent silverite Republican Charles Joy, and awarded it to a supporter of the president's monetary policy. Concerned

---

[8]Correspondence, Box 1, Folder 2, The Edward Ward Carmack Papers, Southern Historical Collection, University of North Carolina Library, Chapel Hill; McKellar, *Tennessee Senators,* 465.

with Patterson's apparent defection, party leaders, most of whom were silverites, decided to try to force his hand. The state chairman of the Tennessee Democratic party went to Washington to secure a pledge from the entire delegation to support free silver. An angry Patterson refused. The congressman then wrote an open letter to his constituents in which he defended his position in favor of "sound money." The letter accomplished little as silverites in Tennessee now regarded him as a turncoat, a view confirmed when Patterson spoke at the gold rally in Memphis.[9]

Party leaders determined to eliminate this traitor in their midst. The first move was an attempt to arouse popular indignation against Patterson in his own district. The popular maverick congressman from Mississippi, "Private" John Allen, was invited to stump the renegade's district. As a speaker, Allen was a master in the use of wit and ridicule and invariably kept his audiences in an uproar of laughter. Heaping scorn upon Patterson, he likened the Memphis congressman to the owner of a Mississippi woodworking shop who had posted a sign that read: "All Kinds of Twisting and Turning Done Here." Patterson, he said, was doing a lot of twisting and turning on monetary policy. Stung by the sharp attack, Patterson retaliated by stumping the Mississippi congressman's district, but he had little success in wreaking vengeance, for Allen was popular among his own constituents.[10]

The next move against Patterson was to find an available candidate to challenge the congressman in the 1896 election. Carmack had all the prerequisites: he was popular with a strong personal following, a superb speaker, an advocate of free silver, and he had a record of consistent loyalty to the party. Reasoning that because Patterson still controlled party machinery in the district, Carmack's forces, with the blessing of the State Democratic Executive Committee, decided to bypass regular channels. Therefore, a convention of silverites was called and, to give it greater legitimacy, Senator Harris was persuaded to preside. The convention enthusiastically nominated Carmack as a candidate for Congress. Likewise, the Patterson forces held a convention that called a primary, and because the canvass was uncontested, the incumbent was nominated. Patterson was

---

[9]Clyde J. Faries, "Carmack vs Patterson: The Genesis of a Political Feud," *Tennessee Historical Quarterly* 38 (Fall 1979): 332-33.

[10]Ibid., 334-36.

then endorsed by the Republican organization in Shelby County, whose "Black and Tan" faction worked to secure the black vote for the incumbent. The congressman also received the endorsement of Carmack's old employer, the *Commercial Appeal*. Ironically, the journal also supported the Democratic presidential nominee, silverite William Jennings Bryan.

Carmack won an important victory when the State Democratic Committee certified him as the rightful nominee. The committee declared that Patterson's primary was held without sanction and that his gold platform displeased a majority of Democrats. Patterson responded that Carmack was a bolter, that the committee lacked jurisdiction in the matter, and that he had been nominated in the proper manner. The circumstances of the nominations and the cleavage in the party resulted in a bitter campaign.[11]

The tenth district race eclipsed all other contests in Tennessee for excitement. Early in the campaign, Carmack challenged Patterson to a debate, but the incumbent declined, declaring that to do so would give tacit recognition to a bolter. Although he entered the race highly optimistic, Carmack had periods of depression. He wrote to his wife that he was "making a desperate and doubtful fight against heavy odds." He was especially dejected over rumors of the black vote "being solidified against me." He did not care if he lost so he could "get out of this dirty business."[12] Yet he could not help but be elated when presidential candidate Bryan came to Memphis and gave his blessing, an endorsement which was a boost to his cause. Carmack must have also been encouraged by the large and enthusiastic crowds that greeted him at every stop on the campaign trail. The charges of irregularities, voter intimidation, bribery and vote buying, and other chicanery in the tenth district on election day in 1896 are legendary. Evidence produced afterwards demonstrated that there was substance to the charges, but neither side had a monopoly on unethical or illegal practices.

Carmack won the election by a little more than four hundred votes. Patterson carried Shelby and Tipton Counties by narrow margins, but the challenger's larger majorities in Fayette and Hardeman gave him the victory. In other races in 1896, Robert L. Taylor, recruited once again to unify the Democratic party, won the governorship, and Bryan carried Tennessee de-

---

[11]*The Commercial Appeal*, 25 August-2 October 1896, passim.

[12]Carmack to Cobey Carmack, August 1896; Carmack to Cobey Carmack, no date; Carmack to Cobey Carmack, no date: Box 1, Folder 2, Carmack Papers.

spite a strong effort by the Republicans for their candidate, William McKinley, and a ticket presented by bolting Democrats.[13]

Carmack's victory was certified by Governor Peter Turney in late November and he took his seat in March 1897. But he could not rest easy for the narrowness of the election almost dictated a challenge. As one of Carmack's friend's wrote, "Josiah would prefer death to retirement," and he "will not hesitate to resort to any means to hold his seat, and can confidently invoke monied influences." Moreover, Patterson would contest the election because the gold Republican contingent controlled Congress, and thus would be sympathetic to his petition against a silver Democrat.[14] Patterson did as expected. Three days after Carmack's election was certified, he filed a legal notice of contest with the House of Representatives, charging that his opponent's forces had committed fraud in the election and denied him an honest count. Carmack then filed an answer in which he charged Patterson with outright purchase of black Republican votes, bribery of election officials, and other illegal activities. He turned to the law firm of William H. Carroll for counsel; junior partner Kenneth McKellar was assigned to the case.

With the prospect of facing a Republican-controlled Congress, few of Carmack's friends were optimistic about his chances of defeating the challenge. Nevertheless, Carmack took his seat in Congress in March 1897 while the attorneys for both sides began to take evidence. Although circumstantial, Patterson's lawyers were able to produce some evidence of fraud, voter manipulation, and an illegal appointment of election officials. McKellar also offered evidence of wrongdoing by the incumbent and his supporters. Some months later, a house elections subcommittee held hearings. Carmack did not attend the hearings; he was occupied in Nashville as a manager of Thomas Battle Turley's campaign in the General Assembly to win a seat in the United States Senate. McKellar traveled to Washington to argue the case before the subcommittee and, according to his own account, gave a good performance. Still, the Republican majority report recommended that Patterson be awarded the post; the Democrats filed a minority report favorable to Carmack. The full elections committee subsequently ratified the majority report. Resigned to defeat, Carmack wrote to his wife

---

[13]*The Commercial Appeal*, 8 November 1896.

[14]J. L. Bullock to Carmack, 7 November 1896, Carmack Papers.

SILVER AND POLITICS

predicting "that the House will follow the committee and turn me out. As you know I have never been too hopeful of the situation."[15] He did not foresee the dramatic way in which his case would be resolved.

On 21 April 1898, the day following the adoption of a joint congressional resolution initiating war with Spain, the full House of Representatives took up the issue of the contested election. The debate that followed revealed that the contest was more a partisan political issue than a simple case of a fraudulent election. The first speaker for the majority report was Representative Charles Henry Grosvenor of Ohio. Rather than addressing the issue of vote frauds, Grosvenor sought merely to prove that Carmack "has been guilty of unprecedented acrobatic performances in politics." Quoting from Carmack's editorials, he demonstrated how the former journalist had once been an opponent of free silver but had gradually become an outspoken advocate. He also observed that Carmack had once declared that blacks were savages and undeserving of the franchise, and now he was willing to accept black votes. Grosvenor concluded that he would like for Carmack to explain "how much improvement there has been in the various elements of the politics he denounced so bitterly a short time ago." The minority was then awarded a turn and Congressman Stephen Brundidge spoke for Carmack. The only speaker to deal with the evidence, Brundidge went through the charges item by item and refuted Patterson's claims, noting that the witnesses for the challenger included sworn bribers and ballot-box stuffers. The House then turned to other matters before adjourning for the day.[16]

The following morning, the House again took up the contested election. In an unusual move, the managers of the majority report requested and received permission from the House for Patterson to speak in his own behalf. Patterson had few peers for eloquence and he was at his best on this occasion. Although he briefly restated his charges of irregularities in the election, he devoted most of his time to the monetary issue and directed his remarks to the Republican side of the House. He admitted that at one time he had favored free silver but had concluded that he was wrong, and now

---

[15]Carmack to Cobey Carmack, 3 March 1898, Box 1, Folder 4, Carmack Papers; McKellar, *Tennessee Senators*, 467-68; Robert Dean Pope, "Senatorial Baron: The Long Political Career of Kenneth D. McKellar" (Ph.D. dissertation, Yale University, 1976) 24.

[16]*Congressional Record*, 55th Cong., 2d Ses. (1898) 4171-77.

he advocated a sound money policy. Many Democrats in his district, he said, agreed with him and they, along with Republicans, nominated him in 1896 because of his position on gold. Patterson insisted that Bryan's intervention had created dissension in the district. He concluded with an appeal to the Republicans in the House to seat him in the name of sound money.[17]

The next speaker for Carmack was "Private" John Allen. The real question in the case, Allen declared, was whether Patterson was the rightful representative from Tennessee's district, not the monetary issue. The simplest thing to do was to let the Democrats in the state settle their own problems. Allen then reminded the Republicans of Patterson's rigid partisanship, of his bitter denunciation of Republicans, and that he had once been especially vindictive toward former Confederates who had joined the Grand Old Party. Moreover, the man who was now appealing to Republicans for support had admitted to voting for Bryan. Allen noted that while Patterson had frequently declared that blacks were unfit to exercise the franchise, he was now complaining that they were defrauded of the ballot. Allen made the telling point that Patterson was inconsistent and a hypocrite and could not be relied upon to remain a gold-bug. Throughout his speech, he kept the House and the galleries in an uproar of laughter by making Patterson the butt of humor.[18]

Carmack then rose to speak in his own defense. The effort proved to be one of his finest performances and, following Allen, he had a large audience. Using most of the tricks of the orator's trade, he skillfully wove rational argument and documentary evidence with sarcasm, satire, and humor with emotion. He was frequently interrupted by applause and laughter. He opened with an apology for taking the valuable time of the House. He declared that "it is only as a matter of justice to my constituents and against my own inclination that I consume the time of this House. I should rather prefer that the House would proceed with all possible swiftness to the final act of this little drama." He was, he said, truly indifferent to the issue because he knew in his own heart that he had earned "the esteem and confidence" of his people at home. Carmack then took time to respond to some of the earlier speeches, particularly the one made by Grosvenor. He declared that he trembled "at the thought of confronting so valiant a tongue

---

[17]Ibid., 4183-86.

[18]Ibid., appendix, 453-56; Faries, "Carmack vs Patterson," 339.

slugger and so accomplished a lip artist as the gentleman from Ohio. His prowess in this arena entitled him to be regarded as the veritable 'blue-gum nigger' of debate, an oratorical scorpion whose tongue is his tail." Yet it was necessary to remind the House that Grosvenor was also guilty of acrobatic performances in politics. "It seems but yesterday," he said, "that the gentleman from Ohio was denouncing the contestant [Patterson] upon this floor as a 'political guerrilla' and a 'political tramp.'" Moreover, Grosvenor had once been an advocate of the white metal.

Carmack then turned to Patterson. The challenger, he asserted, "has made his appeal, not to the law, not to the evidence, not to a sense of right and justice upon the part of this House, but to the very personification of party spirit and of party power." Patterson was also a political acrobat, he countered. "Among Democrats he was a Democrat; among Republicans he was a Republican." The challenger, he said, reminded him "of the Mississippi flatboat man who declared that he was 'half horse and half alligator, with a heavy cross of snapping turtle.' [Laughter.] He seems to have been one of those hybrids sometimes begotten in the hot lust for office, a political mule, having neither pride of ancestry nor hope of posterity. [Laughter on the Democrat's side.]" Carmack suggested that if the Republicans wanted Patterson, they were welcome to him. "If you want him, take him. If you can make him useful in your business, you are welcome to him. [Laughter.]" Then after reviewing in some detail the evidence concerning Patterson's charges, he concluded with a melodramatic defense of his constituents and of the South:

> Mr. Speaker, I now close this case and submit it to the judgment and conscience of this great jury. My duty has been done and I am ready to receive with patience the verdict of this House. . . . I would that the words I have uttered were more worthy of the noble constituency whose cause I plead.
>
> In their name I appeal from whatever there may be of sectional prejudice and passion in this House, to whatever there may be of a broader, higher and nobler sentiment. These people, sir, are of high and noble lineage. The blood of the heroes who fought at Kings Mountain and at New Orleans is in their veins. They are the sons of the sires who blazed the pathway of civilization through the primeval forest of America and builded [sic] a temple of liberty in the wilderness of this western world. [Applause.] In whatever sphere of action it has pleased God to place them, whether in the quiet walks of peaceful citizenship, or in the high-

est stations of civic power and duty, or amid the storm of death on the red field of battle, they have everywhere illustrated those high qualities of American manhood that have made glorious the history of this Republic. [Applause.]

I am proud to be the champion of such a people. I speak, sir, for my native State, for my native South. It is a land that has known sorrows; a land that has broken the ashen crust and moistened it with her tears; a land scarred and riven by the plowshare of war and billowed with the graves of her dead, but a land of legend, a land of song, a land of hallowed and heroic memories. To that land every drop of my blood, every fiber of my being, every pulsation of my heart, is consecrated forever. [Applause.] I was born of her womb, I was nurtured at her breast, and when my last hour shall come, I pray God that I may be pillowed upon her bosom and rocked to sleep within her tender and encircling arms. [Loud applause.][19]

The House thundered with applause as Carmack took his seat. One member was said to have expressed his appreciation by pounding his desk with a large book. The debate continued with two speakers for the majority report. Representative George White of North Carolina, the only black in the House, denounced the use of "darky" plantation language by both sides and William Bourke Cockran of New York summarized the evidence favoring Patterson. Debate closed, and after briefly considering other matters, the speaker called for a vote. Most observers agreed that the vote would be close, but all indications were that Carmack would be denied his seat, for the Republican leadership exerted intense pressure on the membership to award the post to Patterson. It was, therefore, a surprise when the House voted to seat Carmack by a slender margin of eighteen votes. An elated Carmack was swamped by his supporters on the floor of the House. He later received a large volume of telegrams and letters from pleased friends and constituents, many of whom requested a copy of his speech.[20]

Observers immediately began to search for the reason for Carmack's victory. Barely mentioning Carmack's speech, the *Washington Post* awarded credit to John Allen, asserting that "he probably saved the seat of a Dem-

---

[19]*Congressional Record*, 55th Cong., 2d Ses. (1898) 4185-93.

[20]Ibid., 4194-98; Faries, "Carmack vs Patterson," 344; and Box 1, Folders 5, 6, Carmack Papers.

ocratic member of Congress" by keeping "the House in a roar of laughter with several Darky stories." In Tennessee, a legend quickly developed that Carmack, by his eloquence, swayed the House in his favor and plucked victory from certain defeat. A more likely reason for the House action may be found in the vote. Carmack received 136 votes to Patterson's 118. Although a large number were paired, 100 members of the House, many of whom were present in the chamber when the roll call was taken, did not vote on the contested-election case. The vote reveals that the Democratic lines held, and the Republican lines broke. In all probability, friends of Charles Joy, the congressman Patterson had ousted a few years earlier, abstained, thus leaving the Democrats with a majority. Revenge, therefore, played a part, and very likely Allen and Carmack together convinced some Republicans that Patterson was not dependable and could not be trusted to remain firm on gold.[21]

The excitement of victory in the House was tempered by the fact that another campaign was imminent; the immediate concern became winning renomination and reelection. Patterson publicly stated that he would retire, but Carmack was warned not to believe him.[22] The victory in the contested-election case had put Carmack in a commanding position in his district and if Patterson tried to mount a challenge, the effort never got off the ground. The incumbent won renomination and reelection to another term without opposition. Thus in 1898 he was safe in his own district and secure in his seat in Congress. Yet like so many congressmen, he aspired to move up to the United States Senate. Although few ever have the opportunity, one was soon presented to Carmack.

Back in July 1897, Senator Isham G. Harris had died with three and a half years remaining in his term. Governor Robert L. Taylor was required to make an interim appointment to serve until the General Assembly could elect a successor. Because he had been involved in the challenge to his congressional seat at the time, Carmack was not given serious consideration. Besides, Taylor and Carmack were not allies. The governor had senatorial aspirations himself, and he must have been sorely tempted to resign

---

[21]*Washington Post*, 23 April 1898, 10 November 1908; *Congressional Record*, 55th Cong., 2d Ses. (1898) 4199; Faries, "Carmack vs Patterson," 345.

[22]D. P. Hadden to Carmack, 23 April 1898, Box 1, Folder 4, Carmack Papers.

with the agreement that his successor appoint him to the Senate.[23] Such a move, however, would not have been politically wise and in August, the governor appointed Thomas Battle Turley of Memphis as interim senator. A member of the Memphis aristocracy and a veteran of the Civil War, Turley had never held political office before this appointment. He was, however, associated with the Harris "regular" faction of the Democratic party. The General Assembly met in extraordinary session in early 1898 and took up the task of electing a senator to complete the Harris term. Turley was nominated by the Democrats in caucus, but Congressman Benton McMillin's name was placed before the legislature and he became a strong contender. A native of Celina, McMillin had served eight terms in the House of Representatives and was a member of two important committees—Rules, and Ways and Means. Although Taylor disclaimed candidacy, friends placed his name in nomination. The popular McMillin led in the early balloting, but Turley's managers, one of whom was Carmack, gradually obtained the necessary votes and Turley was elected to a Senate term that expired 3 March 1901. Turley, however, simply did not like political life and as early as December 1898 there were rumors that he would retire at the expiration of his term.[24]

No sooner had Turley been elected to the short term than attention turned to the other Senate seat occupied by former Governor William Brimage Bate. His term expired in March 1899, and the General Assembly would fill that post in the next regular session to meet in January 1899. Although stiff challenges were occasionally mounted, Tennessee normally returned incumbent senators to Washington. However, Bate appeared to be vulnerable, as many Democrats did not have high regard for the abilities of the seventy-two-year-old senator.

A challenge, however, was complicated by Tennessee's nominating process. The usual method was by legislative caucus, a method more easily controlled by an incumbent. It was also possible for the State Executive Committee to call a nominating convention. There was strong sentiment

---

[23]Some of Taylor's supporters encouraged him to resign and accept the senatorial appointment. One wrote that "this would be the crowning glory of your life." Arthur Traynor to Robert L. Taylor, 12 July 1897, Governor Robert L. Taylor Papers, Tennessee State Library and Archives, Nashville.

[24]*Shelbyville Gazette*, 8 December 1898; see also McKellar, *Tennessee Senators*, 450, 453, 456, 467.

in the state for a direct primary, but that method was not made available until the General Assembly enacted enabling legislation in 1901. Whatever the method used, an aspirant had to campaign intensely in order to secure the endorsement of local factional leaders, county conventions, or otherwise demonstrate strong public support. Believing that Bate could be beaten, Governor Taylor announced for the Senate, but soon withdrew his candidacy, possibly because there was no rush of support. With the governor's seat open, McMillin entered that race and soon built up such a commanding lead that all opposition collapsed. He won both the Democratic nomination and the general election in November 1898 with ease. Then in January 1899, the General Assembly reelected Bate to the Senate without opposition.[25]

Attention once again turned to Turley. In the summer of 1899, the senator announced that he would retire at the end of his term. Thus without an incumbent seeking reelection, the senatorial contest in Tennessee became a wide open race and potentially a free-for-all. All aspirants began to jockey for position. Clearly the strongest possible candidate and favorite was former Governor Taylor; he had long coveted a Senate seat and was one of the most popular politicos in the state. For months following Turley's retirement announcement, the state awaited word from Taylor that he would be a candidate. It never came. Why he did not enter the contest is something of a mystery. Possibly his financial condition prevented him from embarking on a costly campaign. Governor McMillin, also anxious to go to the Senate, took Taylor's place as the leading contender. Another candidate was the popular and respected chief justice of the state Supreme Court, D. L. Snodgrass. Carmack was also regarded as a possibility, for he had a loyal following in both the western and middle sections of the state.[26]

Soon after Turley announced his retirement, Carmack began quietly to feel out sentiment across the state. He wrote to intimate friends to determine his strength; their responses were positive. One correspondent, a close friend and an astute political observer, wrote that if former Governor Taylor entered the race, it would be very close. But, he emphasized, he did not believe Taylor would be a candidate. McMillin would then be the strongest rival and would have the advantage of being the state's chief ex-

---

[25]*Shelbyville Gazette*, 7 July, 1 October 1898.

[26]Box 1, Folder 7, Carmack Papers.

ecutive. It would be a hard fought race but Carmack, he insisted, could defeat McMillin.[27] Others were even more optimistic. A Nashville friend declared that Carmack would carry Davidson County; a resident of Dresden in West Tennessee reported that "I have felt, in a quiet way, the pulse of a number of prominent Democrats . . . [and] I do not think you would have any trouble in this part of the state."[28] A Memphis attorney wrote, "I think you would make a great mistake if you should not become a candidate for United States Senator. No more auspicious time is ever likely to come." Kenneth McKellar suggested that Carmack might regret it if he did not try now.[29] Despite the positive response, Carmack was a little hesitant about the commitment. He probably wanted to be certain he could win. However, in July 1899, he became seriously ill with typhoid fever and his recuperation was slow. Finally, in October, Carmack made public his intention to seek the United States Senate seat to be vacated by Turley. Thus the senatorial contest settled down to a race between Carmack and McMillin with Snodgrass as a long shot.

As Carmack's bandwagon began to gather speed, McMillin's forces tried in subtle ways to sidetrack it. Even before Turley's rumored retirement was confirmed, McMillin's managers began to circulate the story that Carmack wanted to run for governor, a report that was kept alive for some months. Appealing to tradition, McMillin's supporters also argued that Carmack was "young enough to wait." Tennesseans had long regarded a Senate seat as a reward bestowed upon elder statesmen. Therefore, McMillin, with eighteen years in the House of Representatives and one term as governor, was more deserving than Carmack. They reasoned that the congressman from Memphis was young and should follow precedent, gaining experience in one or two terms as governor. Too, Senator Bate was getting old and because it would not be long before his seat was vacant, Carmack should wait. The appeal to tradition, however, did not elicit much enthusiasm from the electorate. McMillin, despite his years of service and popularity, was not held in sufficiently high esteem for such a reward. Many

---

[27]F. M. Thompson to Carmack, 25 June, 8 July 1899, Box 1, Folder 7, Carmack Papers.

[28]R. W. Cantrell to Carmack, June 1899; T. K. Reynolds to Carmack, 26 June 1899, Box 1, Folder 7, Carmack Papers.

[29]G. T. Fitzhugh to Carmack, 20 September 1899; K. D. McKellar to Carmack, 23 August 1899, Box 1, Folder 7, Carmack Papers.

no doubt agreed with a small-town editor who wrote that there was no reason for Carmack to wait, because the important things were knowledge of issues and political wisdom, not long experience.[30]

Unable to produce enough excitement for his cause, McMillin announced in March 1900, that although his ambition was for the Senate, he would stand for reelection as governor. He subsequently won a second term in that office without serious opposition. When Snodgrass withdrew in August, Carmack was the only senatorial candidate. An excited McKellar, having just returned from a trip to Europe, wrote that "it gave me great pleasure to learn . . . that both your competitors had quit the field, thereby giving the Senatorship to you without a contest. . . . You were certainly born lucky."[31] Indeed, few who have sought to win a United States Senate seat have been so fortunate as to obtain it so easily. The Democratic caucus in January 1901 nominated him without dissension and the General Assembly elected him without a serious challenge. Accordingly, on 4 March 1901, Edward Ward Carmack became a United States senator. Ironically, he was succeeded in the House by Malcolm Rice "Ham" Patterson, the son of his former antagonist, Josiah Patterson.

---

[30]*Shelbyville Gazette*, 9, 16 November 1899.

[31]K. D. McKellar to Carmack, 31 August 1900, Box 1, Folder 8, Carmack Papers.

6

CONGRESS

In March 1901, Edward Ward Carmack reached the summit of his political career and there was no reason to believe that he would have anything but a long tenure in the United States Senate. Standing six feet tall, his slender frame topped by a thick shock of red hair and a blunt mustache, Carmack was a handsome man with a look of dignity. He was "full-chested as becomes an orator" noted *Harper's Weekly* in 1907. But "he lacks the common-artifices of the politician, for it is very difficult for him to remember the face of one he has met but a few times and utterly impossible to recall unfamiliar names. He never won success by practice of the gentle art of handshaking. Nevertheless," observed *Harper's*, "his is a personality toward which one warms intuitively, for it makes an impression of rugged sincerity quite in keeping with the man's reputation."[1]

Carmack lived in an age in which oratory was important and on the platform he had a charismatic quality that attracted supporters. Although some in Tennessee merely attached themselves to a rising star, he had an intensely loyal following that would have gone with him on almost any issue. The years after 1901 were not propitious years for Democrats in Congress; nevertheless, Carmack was in his element there and his forensic

---

[1]William Inglis, "A Democratic Presidential Possibility: Edward Ward Carmack, Ex-Senator From Tennessee," *Harper's Weekly* (29 June 1907) 942.

talents won for him the admiration of both friends and foes. His oratory earned for him a national reputation; the *Washington Post* suggested that he "would have been an ornament to British Parliaments that knew Burke and Fox and Pitt. He would have been distinguished in American Senates that contained Clay and Calhoun and Webster."[2] Philosophically, Carmack was inclined toward the old Bourbon conservatism and he was the spiritual descendant of the likes of Isham G. Harris whose Senate seat he now occupied. He was, therefore, not a maverick nor the leader of a mass reform movement.

The views expressed in Congress by Carmack, and his votes, reflected those of the old aristocracy and thus constituted no break with the past. Ironically, the issue upon which he based his first campaign ceased to be a vital national concern soon after he arrived in Washington. Rapid recovery from the depression of the 1890s aided by an increase in the amount of money in circulation quickly silenced the demand for the free and unlimited coinage of silver. As a result, Carmack had little reason to speak out on monetary policy. But there was another economic issue upon which he was able to voice a concern: tariff protection. In his maiden speech before the House in 1897, for example, he declared that the proposed increases in the Dingley Tariff would "pile higher and heavier the burden of taxes on the shoulders of the people." High tariff rates, he said, "breeds trusts and combines, which enthrones monopoly, which strangles competition, which arbitrarily restricts production," and denies the American workingman "the full employment of his energy and his faculties."

Carmack also expressed concern for the concentration of wealth into the hands of a few individuals and their alleged malignant influence on government. He, therefore, found it easy to advocate a progressive income tax as an equitable source of revenue. When Congress began debating an emergency revenue bill after war with Spain was declared, Carmack expressed preference for an income tax, rather than the proposed increase in the excise tax on beer and tobacco. He was also in favor of regulation of big business. Carmack endorsed the Hepburn Rate Bill of 1906 which provided for more stringent controls over railroad freight rates. Indeed, he was the author of an amendment to the act that made interstate carriers of merchandise liable for damage of goods in transit. Although interested in matters of

---

[2]*Washington Post*, 2 February 1907.

tariff, taxation, and regulation, it was not economic issues that occupied Carmack's attention. His chief concern was foreign affairs, and his involvement in that area brought him to the attention of the nation.[3]

Carmack had been in Congress for only a little more than a year when conflict with Spain over the latter's rule in Cuba led to war in April 1898. The Memphis congressman supported the war resolution, as well as endorsed the principle of the Teller Amendment to the war resolution that disclaimed any intention on the part of the United States to annex Cuba. To Carmack, the purpose of the war was to expell Spain from Cuba and nothing more, but he began to suspect that the administration's policy was directed toward territorial acquisition.

During the debate over the war appropriations measure, he made an impassioned plea for the Congress to arrest the apparent trend toward imperialism. He declared that "we are about to enter upon a policy of aggression, of foreign conquest, of territorial acquisition. Instead of a vast but compact territory, every acre of which can summon to its instant aid the utmost power and protection of this Government, we are to scatter our broken frontiers all over the globe." The United States, he said, was following "a policy which finds its parallel in the jungle or the slums, which delights to compare itself to a drunken ruffian who pummels a cripple for the mere 'joy of fighting' or to a tiger mad with the taste of blood." The nation, he exclaimed, was entering "a destiny that was never in the hearts or minds of those vain dreamers who established this Republic, believing that it was to lead the world to purer and serener heights and teach it by example that there may be grandeur without bloodshed and glory without crime. [Applause.]" Carmack then quoted a few lines from George Washington's farewell address that warned against involvement in European affairs and observed that "only in this mad hour have they [Washington's words] been forgotten." Waxing eloquent, he concluded:

> Sir, if at last we are to turn from the path of safety and of honor and from our lofty ideal as a nation, then let us cover with oblivion all the precious wisdom of our ancestors. Let us never again invoke the names of the fathers, whose dust we have dishonored, lest they curse us from the grave. . . . Let us never again raise our eyes to the figure of Liberty, where

---

[3]*Congressional Record*, 55th Cong., 1st Ses. (1897) 147-48; ibid., 55th Cong., 2d Ses. (1898) 4376-77; ibid., 59th Cong., 1st Ses. (1906) 4444, 5895.

she stands symbolizing the spirit of this great Republic and lifting her torch on high to light the nations of the earth. Let us cast her down from her proud pedestal and quench her torch in the sea; and let us erect in her place a statue of warlike Ambition, with fiendish face and bloody hands, and death and crime and famine treading upon his heels. [Loud applause.][4]

Carmack's principal reservation with the drift toward territorial acquisition, a concern voiced by many others, was the prospect of acquiring noncontiguous lands peopled by nonwhite stock, who he believed could not be assimilated. After it became apparent that the Republican administration was indeed following a course of territorial expansion, Carmack became one of the most severe critics of President William McKinley and his successor, Theodore Roosevelt.

The war with Spain was brought to a speedy and successful conclusion, with peace protocol signed on 12 August 1898 and a treaty formalized the following December. The United States received Puerto Rico, Guam, and the Philippine Islands as the spoils of war. Carmack bitterly assailed the portion of the treaty ceding the Philippines to the United States. He also objected to the annexation of the Hawaiian Islands in 1898, a prospect he had long opposed. When it was first proposed in 1893, Carmack had protested, claiming that Hawaii contained nothing more than "a lot of untamed barbarians, for the most part." The nation, he said, already had enough of that type.[5] In 1898, Carmack argued that because the United States already monopolized trade with the islands and had a lease on the naval base at Pearl Harbor, there was no reason to take on the responsibility of ruling the natives.

Carmack was sharply critical of the administration's post-war policy toward Cuba as well. McKinley adhered to the Teller resolution in principle, but Cuba remained occupied for some time by American forces while health, sanitation, and financial problems were solved and government organized. Then in 1901, the administration sponsored a resolution known as the Platt Amendment that would make Cuba a quasi-protectorate of the United States. During House debates on the resolution, Carmack declared:

---

[4]Ibid., 55th Cong., 2d Ses. (1898) 571-75.

[5]*Daily Commercial*, 10 July 1893.

"This is no time, Mr. Speaker, to mince words. The passage of the" amendment "will be an act of infamy" and a wilful, deliberate, and premeditated violation of the pledge to set Cuba free from foreign domination. The attempt to force the Platt resolution through Congress "is but one more chapter in this Administration's monotonous and unbroken record of perfidy, falsehood, and dishonor." It would "be the deliberate judgment of history that no Administration in this country . . . had ever shown such brazen and cynical contempt for the nation's honor or for its own."[6]

Carmack was even more outspoken in protesting the administration's policy toward the Philippines. When it became clear that the United States had no intentions of giving up the islands, a native force under the leadership of Emilio Aguinaldo revolted against the new owner. Whereupon the McKinley administration launched a military operation to suppress the insurrection. In a lengthy speech denouncing the American use of force against the Filipinos, Carmack exclaimed that the nation had lately conducted "a successful war for a declared and definite purpose." But "the President of the United States is now waging another war upon his own responsibility and for purposes of his own." The nation "fought to destroy military despotism . . . and to confer the blessings of liberty upon" the Filipinos. McKinley's "war is to establish despotism . . . and to destroy the liberties of its people. . . . The first war was blessed of Heaven and approved by the enlightened conscience of mankind; the second war is a crime against liberty, and the curse of God is upon it," he declared. "For the sake of my own country and for the welfare of my own countrymen," Carmack concluded, "I make my humble protest against launching this nation upon a career of conquest and 'criminal aggression.' I protest against the policy . . . because it is an abrupt and violent departure from those established principles and rules of conduct which have conducted this nation to glory and power."[7]

The administration persisted in its Philippine policy and in putting down the insurrection. The final tally showed that the United States used more manpower and had more casualties than in the Spanish-American War. Although fighting continued until 1902, the revolt was effectively suppressed by the end of 1899, but not before guerrilla warfare was prose-

---

[6]*Congressional Record*, 56th Cong., 2d Ses. (1901) 3348.

[7]Ibid., 55th Cong., 3d Ses. (1899) 612.

cuted with ruthless measures by both sides. Reflecting on the problems attendant to its new role as an imperial power, the United States had to decide what to do with its new Asiatic possession. President McKinley appointed a commission to study conditions in the Philippines and to make recommendations concerning civil government in the islands. In June 1899, the commission made its report recommending ultimate independence but that the United States should maintain its rule until the Filipinos were ready for self-government.

Widespread opposition to this policy led to the founding in February 1899 of the Anti-Imperialist League, an organization that sought to alert the American people to the dangers of overseas expansion. The league's membership was diverse and included conservatives, business tycoons, labor leaders, intellectuals, and reformers. Names such as Grover Cleveland, Andrew Carnegie, Samuel Gompers, Charles Francis Adams, William James, and Mark Twain appeared on the rolls. Launching a propaganda campaign in the press, through pamphlets, and speeches at public gatherings, the league hoped to arrest the trend toward imperialism. Carmack was called upon for assistance, and he became one of their leading congressional spokesmen. After McKinley's reelection to a second term in 1900 and imperialism ceased to be an issue, the league began to fall apart. Nevertheless, the Tennessee congressman remained an outspoken opponent of overseas expansion. Because of rules limiting debate, Carmack did not have many opportunities during his service in the House to voice his concerns about imperialism. But the Senate, to which he moved in March 1901, had unlimited debate and was a better national forum from which he could assail the foreign policies of the Republican administration. He also was appointed to the Senate's Philippines Committee which provided him with better access to information about problems in the islands. In his freshman year in the Senate, he had an opportunity not only to attack the policies of the administration and carry the flag for anti-imperialism, but to also make a name for himself.

Early in 1902, Theodore Roosevelt's administration presented Congress a package of measures ranging from a proposal for a tariff concession for the islands to provisions for civil government. The issues were made-to-order for Carmack. On 3 February 1902, he made his maiden speech before the Senate, a performance characterized by the Memphis *Commercial Appeal* as "a rhetorical gem."[8] The subject under consideration was the tariff concession, but Carmack devoted little attention to the merits of the proposal. Rather, he directed his remarks to the "whole question of our policy in the Philippine Islands." He insisted that the Congress was not familiar with the facts concerning the Philippines and was, therefore, unprepared to deal with the bill. The measure had been fashioned not for the benefit of Americans or Filipinos, but for the benefit of a few carpetbaggers. The Republican administration, he declared, disguised a war of criminal aggression in the Philippines and censored or suppressed information concerning atrocities there. Republicans, he exclaimed, "are outraged and indignant when you hear of an occasional lynching of a negro criminal in the Southern states. But you are engaged in lynching 10,000,000 people, who were but lately your allies and your brothers in arms, and who have committed no crime but the crime upon which this Republic was founded." The natives of the islands, he asserted, though they were savages, only wanted their freedom. It should be given them. Carmack concluded that the American flag should be hauled down when it supported despotism and the killing of people for the salvation of their souls.[9]

Carmack's speech received a good deal of attention in the nation's press. The *New York Times* noted that

> The tradition that new Senators should be seen and not heard for a year or two after they begin their service was practically annihilated today, and the oldest Senators in the body took a hand in wrecking it.
>
> Heretofore, when new Senators have violated the custom, there has been little debate or comment on their speeches, and they have been made to feel that they have done something rash and uncalled for. But Mr. Carmack's set speech of two hours was followed by a debate in which the new Senator himself was the storm centre.

A Florida newspaper described Carmack as "one of the brainest [sic] young men in the Senate. . . . It needs no prophet to foresee that Senator Carmack will be recognized available Presidential timber long before the next National Convention assembles." Carmack also struck a responsive cord among many of his constituents, receiving a large volume of mail applaud-

---

[8]*The Commercial Appeal*, 5 February 1902.

[9]*Congressional Record*, 57th Cong., 1st Ses. (1902) 1236-42.

ing his speech, and editorial comments in the Tennessee press were favorable. The special tariff consideration failed to pass; how much influence Carmack had on the defeat can not be measured. It is evident, however, that he attracted considerable attention to himself and from that point was recognized as one of the sharpest critics of the administration's foreign policy.[10]

In April, the Senate took up the proposal to establish civil government in the Philippines and once again Carmack spoke in opposition. When word spread that he was addressing the Senate, the galleries filled with spectators. His message was a scathing attack upon the bill, the Republicans in the Senate who supported it, and the president and his policies. He declared that it required "a great deal of effrontery for any man to openly champion a measure so utterly bad, so utterly destitute of any virtue or of a single redeeming quality." Supporters of the bill revealed "indifference to the story of all the horrors and barbarities being perpetrated in the Philippines" by the administration. The measure before the Senate, he said, was "a confessed departure from the principles and traditions of our own country." Yet "a majority of the Senators upon the other side of the Chamber are ready to vote for it without debate . . . [or] without knowing or caring to know the meaning of a single provision that it contains." The important question was whether the nation had a right "to frame laws and devise a system of government for an alien and unwilling peoples."

He observed that one of the arguments favoring the bill was the need to educate the Filipinos in the art of self-government before freeing them. He then asked: "But how much time do you propose to consume in your ridiculous experiment? How many ages of spelling and parsing, how many centuries of wrestling with the parts of speech, before your pedagogue statesmanship will have done its perfect work?" It would be more appropriate, he argued, to allow the Filipinos to "develop along their own racial lines, not ours. We cannot recreate them in our own image."

Carmack then turned his attention to Roosevelt, assailing the president with ridicule. Referring to public statements made by Roosevelt in which he criticized Democrats for not supporting his policies, Carmack said

---

[10]*New York Times*, 4 February 1902; see also *Chicago Tribune*, 4 February 1902; *Washington Post*, 4 February 1902; scrapbook newspaper clipping, Box 6, Volume 7, Box 1, Folder 10, and Box 6, Volume 6, The Edward Ward Carmack Papers, Southern Historical Collection, University of North Carolina, Chapel Hill.

that he did not believe the president was vindictive. "I do not believe that he hates Democrats any more than he hates grizzly bears or mountain lions. He just loves to shoot them. He is an always loaded gun, and can only go off with the full force of the powder that is in him." The military leadership in the Philippines was condemned for sanctioning atrocities. Carmack observed that although Major General Frederick Funston, leader of the American forces that suppressed the Filipino rebellion, was regarded as a hero, he was guilty of provoking insurrection and ordering the hanging of natives without judge or jury. He concluded his harangue with the prediction that "if the government we are about to establish in the Philippines is not ten thousand times better than the carpet bag government you established and maintained with the bayonet here in your own country, over your own people, may the Lord God have mercy upon the people of the Philippine Islands." Once again Tennessee's senator drew nationwide attention and a large volume of approving mail. A New Jersey farmer encouraged Carmack to continue his attack on the administration's Philippine policy. "Lay on McDuff, and damned be he Who first says, hold enough," he wrote.[11]

Two weeks later, discussion of the Philippines bill resumed and Carmack returned to the attack. In a bitter debate in which tempers sometimes flared along with occasional good natured banter, he scored heavily in denouncing atrocities committed by the American army in the Philippines. In spite of the opposition of Senator Carmack and many of his Democratic colleagues, the Philippines civil government act passed. However, he was not inclined to immediately abandon an issue that had served him well. Several months later, he discoursed at length on atrocities committed by the army and condemned the military authorities for failure to court-martial those involved in burning villages and in torturing unarmed and helpless noncombatants. Carmack's protests did not change the course of the administration's policies, but he clearly gained a reputation in opposition.[12]

Carmack crossed swords with President Roosevelt on another issue: the Panama Canal. Although opposed to territorial expansion, he acknowl-

---

[11]*Congressional Record*, 57th Cong., 1st Ses. (1902) 4667-720; James M. Frazier to Carmack, 28 April 1902, Box 1, Folder 10, Carmack Papers.

[12]*Congressional Record*, 57th Cong., 1st Ses. (1902) 516ff; ibid., 57th Cong., 2d Ses. (1903) 1931-35. Carmack's files contain a number of letters and affidavits attesting to cruelties perpetrated by the army, Box 1, Folder 13, Carmack Papers.

edged the desirability of having a canal in Central America, connecting the Atlantic and Pacific Oceans, under United States' control. Carmack favored a route across Nicargua and supported a congressional resolution to that effect. President Roosevelt took other action. When the province of Panama revolted against its parent state, Columbia, the president quickly recognized Panama as independent, and within a short time, a treaty had been negotiated granting the United States the right to build a canal. Carmack took to the Senate floor on two occasions to protest the president's hasty action. Among other things, he charged that Roosevelt's conduct violated "a fundamental principle of international law, . . . the obligations of a solemn treaty," and "the Constitution of the United States." Like the Philippines government act, the treaty with Panama was ratified and construction of the canal begun despite Carmack's opposition, but the Tennessee senator was able to maintain his reputation as one of the administration's most strident critics.[13]

Reasons for Carmack's opposition to territorial acquisition, like most of his contemporaries, were mixed. In part, it stemmed from traditional isolationism and a fear of conflict that might result from increasing contacts with European and Asiatic powers. He also feared that the nation was on the road to militarism. Like others, he also believed that territorial acquisition violated the Constitution and the Declaration of Independence relative to the principle of government by the consent of the governed. The most important objection, however, was his belief that it would be impossible to assimilate into the American culture those of different races and traditions. This latter related directly to Carmack's racial views.

In many ways Carmack was a pragmatic politician with the prerequisites for successful public life—flexibility and a willingness to compromise. But he was also a crusader and inflexible on issues that he regarded as important, and on no subject was he more rigid than race relations. He was emphatic in his insistence that the United States was a white man's nation. He once told a political gathering that "I went to the Senate as a white man and a Democrat. I have never practiced the African dialect, and I can only speak a white man's language in a white man's cause. I believe this is a

---

[13]*Congressional Record*, 58th Cong., 2d Ses. (1904) 703-707, 1765-71.

white man's country, a white man's civilization and a white man's government. . . . This land is ours," he exclaimed.[14]

Carmack was convinced that the white race was mentally and emotionally superior; blacks were innately inferior. Early in his editorial career, he wrote that "in a struggle for supremacy the negro cannot compete with the Anglo-Saxon and it will be well for him if he does not try."[15] Still later, he wrote in response to the proposition that the blacks had made progress since redemption that "it is a patent, notorious fact that the younger generation of negroes is far, very far, from being an improvement on the older. They have a smattering of book learning, but they are none the better off on account of it. They are shiftless, lazy, idle, insolent, vicious, turbulent, and born thieves." Moreover, blacks are still slaves "to the superior race. In so far as he is free he is still a savage. As a whole, the people of this country must sooner or later awake to the fact that the negro is impervious to the influences of civilization and so incapable as to make him have no place in shaping the destinies of a great people."[16]

Carmack did have a sense of justice toward blacks. Brutality and mistreatment was unacceptable. On the occasion of a lynching of a black accused of rape, he angrily charged that "the authorities in charge . . . betrayed their trust" for allowing it to happen. It was "the duty of his captors to have guarded him if possible. It was possible, and was not done." But Carmack qualified his sense of justice with the assertion that "we consider the fate he received as being no more than his deserts."[17] In short, "the negro should have full justice and right . . . so long as he remembers common sense and the relation of things."[18] Blacks must stay in their place.

Senator Carmack acknowledged that the South had a "race problem." Part of the problem, he believed, was the fact that blacks were involved in politics and had the franchise. He reduced this to the most simplistic terms. Because they were inferior and ignorant, blacks constituted "a great mass of corrupt and venal voters, with no enlightened conception of the duties

---

[14]Scrapbook newspaper clipping, no date, Box 6, Volume 6, Carmack Papers.

[15]*Nashville Democrat*, 7 August 1888.

[16]*Daily Commercial*, 23 April 1893.

[17]Ibid., 26 July 1893.

[18]Ibid., 9 December 1892.

and responsibilities of citizenship" and were easily manipulated by corrupt political bosses. The black vote thus debauched politics, and Carmack made no attempt to hide his concern that the Republican party controlled those votes. Yet he revealed a cynical self-interest and a blatent paternalism when he was the recipient of their votes in 1896. Aside from the franchise, the race problem was simply a matter of the insolence, arrogance, and aggressiveness of many blacks who would not remain in their subordinate position in society. The cause, he believed, was the activities of blind or corrupt agitators beyond the South, especially Northern Republicans.

This view was illustrated in an editorial written in 1892 under the title "Our Colored Brother." He wrote that "it has always been plain that the relations between the whites and the blacks in the South would have been principally peaceful and pleasant if they had been left alone to work out their destiny according to the logic of necessity and the evolution of events." Unfortunately, it was "the constant policy of the Republican party to foment hostile sentiments and feeling among the negroes, and to keep them inspired with prejudices and hatred against the whites." Carmack went on to say that Republicans had "taught him [blacks] that he was abused and down trodden, that he was defrauded of his political privileges and cheated out of the fruits of his labors." But now, he believed, there was a better day at hand, for the Republicans had "no longer any hope of breaking the solid South." When the Grand Old Party left the South alone, "we may look forward to a far better state of things for the negro" as well as for the whites.[19]

Carmack's prediction that a better day in race relations was at hand was more hopeful than accurate. He remained obsessed by the continued black involvement in politics and the continued harassment of the South by Northerners. He revealed frustration and exasperation at the continuation of the race problem in a rambling article published in 1903 in a short-lived, Nashville-based magazine, *The Olympian*. He declared that the race problem was serious and imperiled the nation. If it were not solved, the United States would decline as had ancient Rome. The solution, he suggested, was to separate the black from the franchise by repealing the Fifteenth Amendment to the Constitution which guaranteed black suffrage.[20]

---

[19]Ibid. See also E. W. Carmack, "The Race Problem," *The Olympian* 2 (October 1902): 308-16.

[20]Carmack, "The Race Problem," 308-16.

Carmack was tilting at windmills in advocating repeal of that amendment. Moreover, there was no widespread demand in Tennessee to follow the lead of the Deep South in disfranchising the black by statute. A nationally circulated journal, the *Independent*, observed in 1910 that "there has never been a movement [in Tennessee] to deprive the negro of his franchise. The races have lived together in comparative peace. The election laws have not been tainted with unfair educational qualifications or grandfather clauses. The negro has exercised his voting rights without interference."[21] There were two factors that inhibited the demand to deprive blacks of the vote. Statewide, the black vote was not large enough to threaten white supremacy. Indeed, in some communities the black vote was useful to white political leaders. Second, the black vote was controlled by intimidation, economic pressure, and the institution of the white-only primary. In short, white Tennesseans saw no need to deprive their black brothers of the vote by statute.[22]

Although unable to achieve his goal of black disfranchisement, Carmack nevertheless found the race issue politically useful. Many of his constituents applauded when he called for white supremacy and damned Northerners and Republicans for fomenting trouble in the South. He reflected the incredulity of many of his white contemporaries when he publicly accused President Roosevelt of turning the White House into a "nigger restaurant" by inviting Booker T. Washington to lunch. An incident involving a black postmistress at Indianola, Mississippi, was an opportunity to express his views regarding the race problem on the Senate floor. A group of whites had signed a petition requesting her resignation and she had complied. A government investigation and report declared that she had been forced to resign under intimidation by white rowdies; President Roosevelt, therefore, authorized the closing of the post office. Carmack defended the white citizens of Indianola and scorned the president for closing the post office in a speech before the Senate. He used the occasion to discuss at length the race problem in the South and his concern with black voting.

Carmack drew national attention again when, in 1907, he addressed the Senate regarding an affair involving black soldiers in Brownsville,

---

[21]"Political Hysteria in Tennessee," *Independent* (22 September 1910) 553.

[22]Lester C. Lamon, *Black Tennesseans, 1900-1930* (Knoxville: University of Tennessee Press, 1977) 37-58.

Texas. One night in August 1906, a group of black soldiers stationed at Brownsville, possibly bored and irritated at slights by some whites in that city, marched into town and fired into houses. When investigators were unable to identify the culprits, Roosevelt ordered dishonorable discharges for 159 men from three companies. The president's action came under fire from some members of his party, and Senator Joseph Benson Foraker of Ohio introduced a resolution that called for an investigation. Despite his lack of admiration for the Republican chief executive, Carmack defended the president for discharging the soldiers. He took malicious delight in condemning the Republican senators who criticized their own president. He declared that the real purpose of the investigation was "to break the power of the only leader of the Republican party who ever arrayed it against the enemies of the people." Carmack's speech on the Brownsville affair was one of his last in the Senate; it received national press coverage.[23]

As an editor and public servant, Carmack helped to reinforce and perpetuate the racist dogma of a great many of his white Southern contemporaries. But in espousing white supremacy, Carmack was not supporting a view entirely Southern. There were those beyond the South who were sympathetic, for Carmack lived in an age in which the implications of natural selection as expressed in social Darwinism had made the idea of racial superiority intellectually and academically respectable. He was, therefore, no prophet shouting in the wilderness; his views found acceptance among a receptive white population in the North. Racist dogma thus did not prevent Carmack from establishing a following outside of the South.

Carmack's reputation as an orator had caught the attention of the nation soon after he entered Congress. He was much in demand for commencements and after-dinner speeches. The Anti-Imperialist League called upon him and he made a number of appearances in places such as New York City, Philadelphia, and Boston. With his reputation for devotion to Southern traditions, Carmack was continually solicited to speak at the dedications of Confederate monuments across the South. One request for his services was a distinct honor—the unveiling of the Jefferson Davis monument in Richmond, Virginia, in 1907. In his remarks dedicating the Jefferson Davis monument, he insisted that the cause of the South was not wrong but just:

---

[23]*Congressional Record*, 57th Cong., 2d Ses. (1903) 2565-67.

Whether for chieftain or private, we make no confession of wrong, we plead for no forgiveness of error, we ask no tenderness of the future historian, no charity from the enlightened judgment of mankind. If there are those who are shocked by such sentiment, let me add that this reunited country will not be best defended by conscious criminals begging for mercy at the victor's feet. Thoughtless people have sometimes reproached us for such scenes as this, and have demanded as a pledge of our loyalty to a reunited country that we give the memory of our heroes to oblivion and their graves to the wilderness. They know not what they ask. They would have us prove our loyalty to the Union by proving ourselves recreant to the noblest sentiments that could swell the bosom of an American patriot.

I say that the valor of our Southern soldiers, the fortitude of our Southern women, the fidelity with which we cherish the memory of their deeds and their sufferings are but the measure of our loyalty to a reunited country and to the flag that floats over it from the lakes to the gulf and from sea to sea.

Talented in the use of words, he invariably rose to the occasion, mesmerizing his audiences. He extolled the virtues of Southern soldiers, using such terms as valor, fortitude, unselfish devotion, patient self-sacrifice, and heroic suffering. He also had appropriate words for Southern traditions and the lost cause of the Confederacy. In his address dedicating the Confederate monument at Gallatin, Tennessee, in 1903, he declared that the purpose of the monument "is to proclaim that you, my countrymen, are proud to honor their deeds and to claim them as the noblest heritage of yourself and your children forever." In his dedicatory addresses, other speeches, and editorial writings, Carmack tried to justify Southern secession and was, therefore, a contributor to the myth of the "Lost Cause." Moreover, he helped bring about sectional reconciliation by making the Southern cause a symbol of nationalism and patriotism.[24]

---

[24]Paul Franklin Bumpus, *Carmack: The Edward Ward Carmack Story* (Franklin: Paul Franklin Bumpus, 1977), contains Carmack's dedicatory addresses. For treatment of the Lost Cause rationale and reconciliation, see C. Vann Woodward, *Origins of the New South, 1877-1913* in vol. 9 of *A History of the South*, ed. Wendell Holmes Stephenson and E. Merton Coulter (Baton Rouge: Louisiana State University Press, 1951) 154-58, 456-81; Thomas L. Connelly, *The Marble Man: Robert E. Lee and His Image in American Society* (New York: Alfred Knopf, 1977) 91-122; Charles R. Wilson, *Baptised in Blood: Religion of the Lost Cause, 1865-1920* (Athens: University of Georgia Press, 1980) 139-82.

One of Carmack's most famous speeches was a commencement address entitled "Lecture on Character" delivered at the University of South Carolina, 11 June 1907. A Columbia, South Carolina, newspaper reported the following day that Carmack "spoke for near an hour and held attention riveted. . . . His address was beautiful in sentiment, lofty in spirit, and refined in tone, and it was such an effort as to hold the admiration of young men who long for a high ideal. There was none of the ranting or affection of so many public men of the day, but a dignified, undramatic, and yet brilliant, powerful and true talk to young men."[25] It was, however, a rambling, sententious effort. Nevertheless, it was presented on other occasions under the title "Character, or the Making of the Man." Printed in booklet form, it was widely distributed and quoted. Carmack's forensic talent was also used to produce an income. The Lyceum Bureau of Chicago, Illinois, discovered that he was in demand and used him on the Chautauqua tour as a paid lecturer.

Despite the provincialism of much of Carmack's philosophy, he earned respect and a goodly following outside the South. An editor of the *Washington Post* expressed the admiration of many when he asked rhetorically: "Where is the man who does not respect him? Where is the man who does not admire him? All the wealth of either Ind would not buy for the base his lofty character, his unblemished honor."[26] An article in *Harper's* identified Carmack as a possible Democratic candidate for the presidency in 1908.[27] It is unlikely that the Democrats would have seriously considered someone so parochial in his views and certainly Carmack did not regard himself as presidential timber. Nevertheless he was one of the most respected members of the United States Senate.

Carmack closed out his senatorial career in the winter of 1906-1907 in a blaze of glory. His speech regarding the Brownsville affair on 16 January drew widespread attention and a few days later he addressed the Senate eloquently, eulogizing the late Senator William B. Bate. On 3 March, he tied up the Senate just prior to adjournment with a filibuster. The issue was a proposed ship subsidy, a measure backed by President Roosevelt, designed

---

[25] Bumpus, *Carmack*, 13.

[26] *Washington Post*, 2 February 1907.

[27] Inglis, "A Democratic Presidential Possibility," 942-43.

to improve the merchant fleet of the United States. Opposed to subsidizing private enterprise, Carmack joined with a handful of senators to talk the bill to death. The *New York Times* commented that "what Carmack is talking about no Senator can say. He just rambles cheerfully on, gossiping pleasantly about anything that comes into his head."[28] The publicity attendant to his speeches in the winter of 1906-1907 gave Carmack a measure of satisfaction in light of the fact that he had failed to win reelection to the Senate. It was an anomaly that a man so respected and popular in both his native state and beyond was not returned to office. Stranger still was the fact that Tennessee traditionally returned incumbents to the Senate. His failure to retain his seat was an aberration. Politics in the Volunteer State was in turmoil.

---

[28]*New York Times,* 4 March 1907.

7

A CAT FIGHT

Fierce factional conflict was long a characteristic of Democratic party politics in Tennessee and that tradition was maintained during Edward Ward Carmack's tenure in Congress. After the collapse of the agrarian movement in 1892, the party was rent by the silver issue and turned once again to Robert L. Taylor as a harmony candidate in the gubernatorial election of 1896. Taylor stepped down after one term and was succeeded by Benton McMillin, who served two consecutive two-year terms. In 1902, James Beriah Frazier, a Chattanooga attorney, won the Democratic nomination for governor and was successful in the general election in November. Although his ancestors on his mother's side were in the planter class, Frazier's father was a unionist and allied with Andrew Johnson. Nevertheless, a record of party loyalty made Frazier acceptable to the Democratic "regular" wing and he was soon allied with both United States senators—William B. Bate, the last of the old Confederates, and Carmack, the spokesman for latter-day conservatives.

Politics is not a profession for either the timid or the complacent. By its very nature, it is an insecure business, and successful politicians are wary and constantly alert for the shifting moods of constituents and plots by opponents. Carmack was no exception, and as any senator in the nation's capital, he had a corps of some very astute watchdogs in Tennessee to keep him informed. A few of these watchdogs exhibited neurotic fears.

For example, one wrote in 1902 expressing concern about the activities of "certain elements" that threatened party harmony. "My fears may be entirely groundless," he admitted, "we may not have a word said to disturb the harmony of party action; yet I am in constant dread of certain elements here."[1]

Fears of certain elements were not entirely groundless. The very existence of Benton McMillin and Robert L. Taylor, two popular and strong leaders, was sufficient cause for concern. Both were out of office and both were ambitious to go to the Senate. Clearly, if both went after the same post, the chances of unseating an incumbent would have been significantly weakened. It is entirely possible that as early as 1903 McMillin and Taylor had entered into an informal agreement: McMillin would try for Senator Bate's seat which expired in early 1905, and Taylor would challenge Carmack, whose term ended in 1907. There were persistent rumors throughout 1904 of such an alliance and the subsequent actions of both McMillin and Taylor seemed to give substance to the gossip. In 1903, Taylor announced that he would not run against Bate and that he, in fact, favored the incumbent's reelection. But, as the *Shelbyville Gazette* observed, "Bob means what he says. But he does not mean that if he sees a chance to get there himself that he wouldn't do it."[2] For whatever reason, Taylor remained out of the race, but he did not work for Bate. McMillin declared against the aged incumbent.

Senator Bate seemed vulnerable. He had done little to excite the enthusiasm of his constituents, and the seventy-seven-year-old senator appeared to be getting feeble and unable to carry out his normal duties. Indeed, political leaders across the state privately agreed that Bate would probably not live out another term. Thus to factional leaders, the occupant of the governor's office was an important consideration, for the chief executive would make an interim appointment if the old senator died in office. Nevertheless, McMillin began a concerted campaign to wrest the Democratic nomination from Bate and, by the spring of 1904, appeared to have captured a commanding lead in commitments from local leaders.

---

[1]N. W. Baptist to Carmack, 30 April 1902, Box 1, Folder 10, The Edward Ward Carmack Papers, Southern Historical Collection, University of North Carolina Library, Chapel Hill.

[2]*Shelbyville Gazette*, 30 July 1903.

However, Carmack and his friends, along with Governor Frazier's organization, were in a fever of activity behind the scenes for Bate.³ Carmack was kept busy putting out fires. Stories that probably originated in McMillin's camp circulated to create doubt concerning Bate's health along with questions regarding his sobriety. Carmack was forced to respond to inquiries about the gossip. One rumor which quoted Carmack as saying "in substance that Senator Bate spent the greater part of his time drunk and staggering aroung [sic] the capitol and unfit for Senatorial duties" required an answer. Carmack replied that he was "outraged that such a bare faced lie should have been given circulation on my authority. . . . There never was a more more [sic] baseless or unfounded statement circulated against any living man. I never saw Senator Bate in the least degree under the influence of intoxicants in my life." He admitted that Bate "takes a toddy in the evening on his return from the Senate and no more—one drink a day."⁴

Bate's situation reached a crisis when Democrats in Carmack's home county, Shelby, appeared on the verge of rebellion and about to endorse McMillin. Carmack found it necessary to make a hurried trip to Memphis to straighten out "the mess."⁵ He apparently succeeded, for the Shelby Democrats soon swung to Bate and the incumbent's fortunes then began to improve across the state. Bate's bandwagon gradually gathered speed and McMillin, seeing the inevitable, withdrew from the race. The senator was then reelected by the General Assembly in January 1905. Governor Frazier, winning renomination in the state convention, was reelected to a second term in November 1904. The alliance of Carmack, Bate, and Frazier remained intact and in power.

McMillin's withdrawal from the senatorial contest brought little comfort to Carmack. There were rumors that Taylor would challenge him and stories of an alliance between McMillin and Taylor persisted. The editor of the *Shelbyville Gazette* observed that "perhaps there is nothing in the talk and perhaps there is. As a fact we do know that Bob Taylor is just now feeling mighty kindly toward Governor Benton McMillin and that McMillin is

---

³Correspondence, Box 1, Folder 13, Carmack Papers; Box 9, Folders 4, 5, The Governor James B. Frazier Papers, Tennessee State Library and Archives, Nashville.

⁴Unknown correspondent to Carmack, 18 April 1904; Carmack to W. C. Whitthorne, 18 April 1904, Box 1, Folder 13, Carmack Papers.

⁵Carmack to John I. Cox, 17 April 1904, Box 1, Folder 13, Carmack Papers.

nursing no wrath towards Bob Taylor. These things being true it strikes us that it would not be difficult for them to become friends. But whether or not that would lead to a combination against Senator Carmack we are unable to say." The editor concluded that "if it does we are frank to say that it would be a very strong one and Carmack would have a job bursting it. Bob Taylor is perhaps the most popular democrat in the State and McMillin is no great distance behind him."[6] Taylor would be a formidable opponent under normal circumstances, but a series of events in March 1905 gave Taylor a significant issue and perhaps the edge for a contest with Carmack.

On 9 March 1905, Senator Bate died suddenly in Washington less than two months after his reelection and only five days after he had begun his new term. The senator's death came as no surprise, but the timing was propitious for the alliance in power and an inopportune time for aspirants to mount a campaign for the Senate. Bate had scarcely been interred when the Frazier-dominated Democratic State Executive Committee met and issued a call for a nominating caucus of members of the General Assembly which was then in regular session. The caucus met a few days later, nominated Frazier for the Senate, and a week later the legislature elected the governor to fill the remainder of the regular Senate term. John Isaac Cox of Bristol, Tennessee, a Frazier ally and speaker of the state senate, and constitutionally next in line, became governor.

The motives for the precipitous filling of the Senate post are clear. Aside from the governor's own ambitions, the alliance in power sought to retain its hold on both Senate seats. It was not, however, a wise political move. There were rumblings of anger from both friends and foes across the state over the "snap caucus." The loudest outcry came from Taylor who, if indeed he had an agreement with McMillin, was next in line for the Senate. Taylor was out of the state on an extended speaking tour when Bate died and he protested that the snap caucus prevented him from organizing a campaign and denied the people the right to express their preference as well. Carmack's part in the chain of events is not clear. He later denied having anything to do with the hasty selection of Bate's successor. Yet he had a vested interest in who would become his junior colleague. He had an opportunity to discuss the matter with his friends as well as those of Frazier, for he had accompanied Bate's body to Nashville for the funeral, and it is

---

[6]*Shelbyville Gazette*, 1 September 1904.

reasonable to assume that the subject of the Senate post was brought up in conversation. In any case, because of his alliance with Frazier, he had to share the guilt by association for the snap caucus. Taylor had an issue to exploit.

In an attempt to capitalize on the snap caucus issue, Taylor wasted no time in organizing a campaign against Carmack. Significantly, McMillin remained on the sidelines. In what was one of the earliest formal announcements of candidacy, Taylor declared in June of 1905 that he would challenge Carmack for the Senate, more than a year and a half before the election would take place. As one newspaper observed, it forecast an early primary. In his statement, Taylor declared that it had long been his ambition "to represent my native State in the United States Senate. . . . I therefore announce myself a candidate for the United States Senate before the next Legislature." He challenged Carmack to a joint debate, which he said, would be like a cat fight. When cats meet, there is a "rain of hair—cat hair." If he and Carmack met, he said, "there'd be a rain of hair—red hair." Carmack responded quickly with his formal announcement and exclaimed that he was "ready for the fray" but would let Taylor "do all the boasting in this matter." He also agreed to a joint debate. Taylor's proposed debate was made in haste and, a bit embarrassed, he quickly backed away from it. In a letter to Carmack, he declared that "it is contrary to all precedents in Tennessee for candidates for the United States Senate belonging to the same political party, to enter into joint discussions for that high office." Senator Harris, he said, once declined to debate an opponent and Bate once rejected a similar confrontation with McMillin. "You, yourself, refused to meet Judge D. L. Snodgrass . . . presumably for the same reasons." Reflecting widespread disappointment, the *Commercial Appeal* observed that "Gov. Bob may be right in principle, but principle is always knocking folks out of a lot of fun." Implying that Taylor was guilty of cowardice, Carmack dubbed him "Knight of the White Feather," an allusion to the title of "Knight of the White Rose" in the War of the Roses of 1886. The red feather was adopted as a symbol by Carmack's friends. The symbols remained although the issue of the debate soon died.[7]

Taylor based his appeal to the electorate on tradition. His friends insisted that a senatorship was a reward to party statesmen, and Taylor de-

---

[7]Scrapbook newspaper clippings, Box 6, Volumes 6, 8, Carmack Papers.

served it for his long and loyal service to the Democratic party. One newspaper, however, asked the poignant question: "Does the Democratic Party or the State owe any man a Senatorship?" The paper concluded that distributing offices as a reward was a dangerous policy. Carmack countered with an appeal to tradition. "It has been," he wrote, "the uniform Democratic practice whenever a public official in his first term has rendered honorable and faithful service to give him the endorsement of reelection." Tradition, however, was less important than the snap caucus.[8]

Hoping to take advantage of the issue of the snap caucus while it was still fresh in the minds of the electorate, Taylor began pressing for an early primary. He proposed that a senatorial primary be held in December 1905 to "separate the Senatorial from the Gubernatorial and other races . . . [to] save the party from possible dissension and discord." Carmack replied that Taylor's scheme was a "snap primary." In an open letter, he charged that Taylor was trying to force the issue in order to deny him renomination. "You must know," he wrote, "that the effort now proceeding to force hurried and ill-considered action from twelve to fifteen months in advance of the election is inspired by a purpose to deny me the opportunity to meet the false accusation and reports which my opponents have spread broadcase throughout the State." He proposed instead that the primary be held concurrently with the general election in November 1906. The issue of the primary was compromised when the Democratic State Executive Committee met in September 1905 and set a direct primary for 12 May 1906. The primary would be for whites only, supervised by county committees, and held without regard to registration or poll tax. The committee also issued a call for a convention to meet 29 May to nominate a candidate for governor. Both Taylor and Carmack agreed to the provisions for the primary, for "Not a ripple [of protest] marred" the meeting of the executive committee.[9]

The chief issue in the senatorial campaign was the snap caucus. Taylor made it the issue from the outset when he charged that Carmack was part of a conspiracy to put Frazier in the Senate in order to keep him out. Taylor kept repeating the charge throughout the hard-hitting campaign. Carmack, he explained, hurriedly left Washington for Nashville after Bate's

---

[8]*Clarksville Leaf-Chronicle*, 8 May 1906; form letter, Box 6, Volume 8, Carmack Papers.

[9]Scrapbook newspaper clippings, Carmack to the general public, copy, 25 August 1905, Box 6, Volume 8, Carmack Papers.

death to "fix up the election" for Frazier. Carmack, working with Frazier and Cox, thus prevented Taylor and others from having a fair chance to present themselves to the electorate. Carmack countered with the accusation that Taylor conducted "a telegraphic campaign for General Bate's seat before his remains were shrouded for the coffin," dishonoring the senator's memory.

Taylor's accusation brought Frazier into the race. Although there was often some behind-the-scenes participation, senators and governors avoided open commitment to candidates for other offices. Frazier issued a statement expressing regret that the manner of his promotion to the Senate had become an issue in the Carmack-Taylor race. He explained that he had no desire to injure any candidate, but he was forced, "in the interest of truth and to vindicate myself," to deny the charges that his election was the result of a conspiracy. Frazier insisted that Taylor had told him privately that he had given up his political ambition, "that he never expected to run for the Senate . . . [and that] he would be for me to succeed" Bate if the senator should die. Taylor had, therefore, broken his word. By going into the open and attacking Taylor, Frazier publicly allied himself with Carmack and quite likely added substance to the snap caucus conspiracy charge.[10]

Because Taylor's allegations seemed to carry weight among the electorate, Carmack was on the defensive from the beginning, remaining in that undesirable position throughout the campaign. He had achieved success in politics by being aggressive, but now he found himself forced to continually deny charges. In both public statements and private correspondence, he sought to counter the accusations with what he declared was the truth. To one constituent he wrote that "I know I am being charged with having taken a hand in the late Senatorial fight when as a matter of fact I never lifted a hand or voice in it. I did not ask a single member of the Legislature to vote for or against any proposition before the caucus and did not ask anyone to take a hand one way or the other." He complained that in Rutherford, Bedford, Moore and other counties that "Taylor's confidential lieutenants are openly supporting Cox [in the governor's race]. He seems to be willing enough for one of the authors of the alleged 'outrage' to be rewarded if he can punish a man who never lifted hand against him."

---

[10]Ibid.

Carmack tried to counter Taylor's assault with charges that the challenger had a record of broken promises and ingratitude. He insisted that Taylor had promised to be active in support of Bate in 1904, but gave only lukewarm support in the beginning and later abandoned the old Confederate for McMillin. He also went to great lengths to prove a contention that Taylor had mistreated old General George Gibbs Dibrell of Sparta. Taylor, he declared, sought Dibrell's assistance in getting a job in the Knoxville office of the pension agency and promised in return that he would support Dibrell for governor in 1886. He broke that promise and ran himself, Carmack asserted. Carmack's claim may have appealed to old Confederates, but he was unable to divert the the electorate's attention from the snap caucus conspiracy charge.[11]

Both contenders for the Senate were excellent speakers, so it was not surprising that the campaign was characterized by superb oratory. Their different styles only enhanced the debates. Taylor was gifted in storytelling and humor and drew large, excited crowds. More serious, Carmack had the edge in eloquence and his audiences were equally attentive. Contemporary Carmack watchers and devoted followers were of the opinion that his opening address of the campaign at the Vendome Theater in Nashville that November was one of his best efforts. It was a lengthy recital of his record, emphasizing his position on such issues as imperialism and the tariff. He attacked Taylor for his failure to agree to a debate and for a lack of sincerity and true loyalty to the Democratic party.

Oratory, however, important as it was in campaigning, was not the decisive factor. The senatorial primary was an unusual contest. The incumbent possessed a satisfactory, if not a commendable, record and according to precedent, clearly deserved renomination and reelection. A West Tennessee farmer wrote that "Carmack is an extreme man it is true, but a man of much more ability and as this is his first term ought to have been returned especially as his record is clean." Yet, as the farmer observed, his opponent was one of the most popular political figures in Tennessee. The editor of the *Marshall Gazette* expressed the dilemma of many Tennesseans

---

[11]Carmack to C. W. Crockett, 11 July 1905, Edward Ward Carmack Correspondence, Tennessee State Library and Archives, Nashville; campaign pamphlet, Box 6, Volume 8, Carmack Papers.

when he wrote: "we regret that we shall have to oppose one whom we greatly esteem and one who is a deserving and splendid Democrat."[12]

Carmack could expect support from his loyalists as well as most of the votes of the old Confederates. But that alone was not enough to win. He was tagged with the onus of conspiracy, and Taylor was riding the crest of personal popularity. Recognizing his handicap, Carmack noted that he "entered the fight with hardly a hope of success." There was one consolation. He wrote to his wife that "the evidence that the best people of all classes are with me is so strong that I feel that it amounts to a substantial victory. . . . Taylor's majority over me will be small."[13] It was, therefore, no real surprise when Taylor won in a close vote, approximately 65,000 to 58,000. The challenger won all the urban areas except Memphis; Carmack's strength was primarily rural. The incumbent had been able to narrow the gap and make a much closer race than it might have been had the primary been held in December as the challenger had urged. Outsiders found it difficult to believe that Tennessee's senior senator had gone down to defeat. The *Washington Post* was mystified:

> Verily it is the "new" South, especially the Tennessee part of it. In abilities, in character, in brilliancy, Edward W. Carmack is to his State what John C. Breckinridge was to the Kentucky of the "old" South, what Alexander H. Stephens was to the Georgia of the "old" South, and now he has been retired by the State which he had made so conspicuous in the greatest parliamentary body on earth.
>
> There was no fault alleged against his course in the Senate, no objection to a vote he cast, no criticism of a word he said, no question of the splendid service he rendered as a leader there, one of the ablest—and concededly the most dashing—men in public life. And this we say without a thought of Gov. Taylor. It may be that Gov. Taylor is an abler and a fitter man than Senator Carmack. If he shall so approve himself, it will be a grand day for Tennessee when the fact becomes apparent.
>
> We do not recall a single instance in the entire history of the country that parallels the defeat of Senator Carmack.

---

[12]May 12, 1906, Box 4, F 1, Cartmell Diaries, Tennessee State Library and Archives, Nashville; scrapbook newspaper clipping, Box 6, Volume 8, Carmack Papers.

[13]Carmack to Albert T. McNeal, 21 May 1906, Box 2, Folder 19; Carmack to Cobey Carmack, no date, Box 4, Folder 50-B, Carmack Papers.

After citing several similar but different situations, the *Post* concluded that:

> It is not conceivable that the defeat of Senator Carmack is a personal or political reproof. It is rather a manifestation of a discontent with present political conditions and present prevailing economic policies. We can account for it on no other ground. Senator Carmack happened to be in office and the public of Tennessee happened to be possessed of a whim.[14]

Although Carmack was not surprised at the outcome of the primary, defeat came as a stunning blow to his devoted followers, and reactions ranged from disbelief and dismay to anger and bitterness. One associate wrote that campaign workers did not want to quit; they wanted to keep the headquarters open and keep working. In a long letter to Carmack, state campaign manager George Harrison Armistead described the depth of the devotion of the senator's loyalists. Carmack's friends, Armistead wrote, believed "that a political tragedy has been enacted in your defeat." Yet, "you are a stronger man today in the affection, esteem and confidence of the people of Tennessee than you would have been in the hour of victory. Your friends are staggering under a sense of personal bereavement." Carmack's loyalists "meet and greet each other as if they were comrades, wearing common scars of a struggle which had enlisted all the affections of their hearts. Not only do your friends come from every direction to manifest this sense of keen personal bereavement, but they display indignation and a feeling that Tennessee has been humiliated in the eyes of our sister states." Armistead concluded that:

> There will be no wavering in the Carmack column in Tennessee; these men will cling to you as long as you live, and your very defeat has bound you to them with ties of tenderness which will be more enduring than the mere glow of enthusiasm which would have followed your victory. They are proud that they stood by your colors; they hold themselves as men who have the right to stand proudly in the hour of defeat and look the world squarely in the face. They know you emerged from this conflict without the shadow of stain upon your record, and though the spoils of

---

[14]*Washington Post*, 15 May 1906.

the office may go to another, that the honors of the field are yours and theirs.[15]

Others reported a wave of regret, even from Taylor-supporters, that such a man as Carmack had been denied reelection. There were also charges of fraud and claims that Taylor had been nominated by unqualified voters. One correspondent, reflecting on Taylor's speaking style, observed that he expected that after Carmack's "retirement next March, that the Senate Chamber will be turned into a Vaudeville Theater, and that Bob Taylor, with his Uncle Rastus, and Aunt Dina, will be the leading actor therein." A West Tennessee farmer wrote in his diary in disgust that "Taylor in U.S. Senate will be Small, a mere clown." Another writer reflected the bitterness of some by pointing a finger of blame toward Frazier who "precipitated all this trouble upon the State." Carmack's defeat caused deep wounds in Tennessee's Democracy that did not heal quickly. Interestingly, his name was immediately injected into a hot gubernatorial race.[16]

The Democratic party was concurrently involved in a bitterly fought race for the gubernatorial nomination. The convention to select the nominee was scheduled to meet on 29 May, only seventeen days after the senatorial primary. Frazier's successor, Governor Cox, sought the nomination to a full term. He was challenged by Malcolm Rice "Ham" Patterson. Born in 1861, educated at Christian Brothers College in Memphis and at Vanderbilt University Law School, Patterson had entered politics and was elected attorney general of Shelby County in 1894. He managed his father's race for Congress in 1896 and was himself elected to that body in 1900, replacing Carmack. He was reelected in 1902 and again in 1904.

The snap caucus was also an issue in the gubernatorial race. Patterson emphasized that episode and charged that it was the result of the maneuverings of a state machine. The Memphian's campaign gathered momentum as he won commitments of delegations, but the outcome was still in doubt at the time of the senatorial primary. The fear that the bitter gubernatorial race would disrupt the party and lead to a Republican victory in

---

[15]G. H. Armistead to Carmack, 17 May 1906, Box 2, Folder 15, Carmack Papers.

[16]Sam P. Irvins, Jr. to Carmack, 13 May 1906; George W. Gorrell to Carmack, 14 May 1906, Box 2, Folder 14, Carmack Papers; 10 May 1906, Box 4, F 1, Cartmell Diaries.

November led some to urge the nomination of Carmack as a compromise—a unity candidate.

The introduction of Carmack's name in the governor's race was neither spontaneous nor of sudden inspiration. The scheme apparently originated as early as February and made the rounds in East Tennessee. It was likely that talk of Carmack for governor came from Taylor's camp in an effort to blunt the incumbent's momentum and, if a boom developed, it would make it easier for the uncommitted to vote for Taylor. After the senatorial primary, the scheme was revived as some urged that Carmack be drafted as a compromise between Cox and Patterson. Again, some of the talk came from within Taylor's organization. The motive is not clear, but one of Carmack's friends warned him not to allow his name to be put in the governor's race. He wrote that "the game of the Taylor crowd [is] to put you entirely out of the way & put Gov McMillin in when Senator Fraziers time expires. Taylors friends would revel in your slaughter next November. They would like to put you out for all time. And if you run for Gov that would be their chance."

Carmack's state campaign manager struck another cord and suggested that "a small but respectable element of citizens well intentioned but misinformed, who, moved by prejudice aroused out of wrong information as to your attitude in the Frazier election, and swayed by the sentimental belief that they owed Governor Taylor a debt for 'saving the Party in 1896' cast their ballots for him in the Primary last Saturday." Because of the result, the "wide spread manifestations of regret, and indignation" over Carmack's defeat had "aroused this class of voters to a realization of the wrong they had done the State and themselves. Feeling that they should make the earliest reparation possible, this class have [sic] called upon you to accept the Governorship. They are acting in good faith toward you in generous sympathy."[17]

Some of Carmack's friends favored the governor's race. Senator Frazier was one. His alliance in Tennessee had collapsed, and Carmack wrote that

---

[17]Scrapbook newspaper clippings, Box 6, Volume 9; Wiley Harbison to Carmack, 15 May 1906; G. H. Armistead to Carmack, 17 May 1906, Box 2, Folder 15, Carmack Papers. Armistead suggested that another element urged Carmack for governor in order to protect Taylor. "They reason that if you could be provided for . . . with the office of Governor, that the keen edge of indignation and injustice would be dulled, to the benefit of Governor Taylor."

"he is deeply troubled over the political situation and I think has it very much in his mind that I ought to take the nomination for Governor if it comes to me and indeed I think he would be glad to have my friends encourage such a movement." Others at the grass roots, anxious to keep fighting for their hero, urged that he make a commitment to the governorship. They believed that he would take the convention by storm and sweep to victory if only he gave the word.

The more astute of Carmack's followers advised against getting involved in the governor's race. Armistead wrote that "as to the Governorship; it is evident that if you want it you can have it." Moreover, if a deadlock ensued at the convention, he would undoubtedly be drafted, but most of his true friends "are opposed to your taking the nomination for Governorship. They want you to maintain the position of a dignified, manly withdrawal from the arena of politics for a season, and then return to the Senate under conditions that will be an absolute vindication of yourself in every sense of the word. Nothing but death can prevent you from returning to the Senate upon the first opportunity." Accepting the wisdom of his closest advisors, if indeed they had to sway him, Carmack was emphatic in his veto of any movement to put his name before the state convention. To seek the gubernatorial nomination so soon after his senatorial defeat, he wrote, would give the impression that he was merely an office-seeker. Also, if he got involved in the fray, he would perpetuate the devisiveness that already plagued the party. Carmack quoted Patterson to the effect that he (Patterson) would see to it that Cox won before allowing Carmack to get the gubernatorial nomination. A divided party would also open the door for a Republican victory in November. Finally, Carmack insisted that he did not want to be governor.[18]

In an effort to avoid involvement or to encourage those who urged his commitment to the governor's race, Carmack did not appear at the convention, and likewise those adherents of his who were present carefully avoided disruptive action. Yet they were still keenly interested in who would be the next governor, for the victor at the convention would dominate the party for at least the next two years. It must be noted that their inaction

---

[18]Carmack to F. M. Thompson, 19 May 1906, Box 2, Folder 18; G. H. Armistead to Carmack, 17 May 1906, Box 2, Folder 15; correspondence, Box 2, Folders 14-19, Carmack Papers.

stemmed in part from the fact that Carmack and his allies had lost control of the party, and there was nothing they could do about it. The senator's organization clearly abandoned Cox. One of Carmack's confidants wrote that Cox could not be trusted, and even if he received the nomination, he could not be elected. Carmack agreed. He wrote that "under the circumstances [we should] keep hands off and let the situation work itself out as it will. Cox is a man no one can safely co-operate with because you never know what he is doing behind your back."[19]

Quite likely there was substance to Carmack's allegation that Patterson meddled in the senatorial primary, but how much influence he had would be hard to measure. The very nature of political factionalism in Tennessee made it difficult, if not impossible, for a statewide leader to establish rigid discipline in his own organization. Local and regional factions exercised a good deal of independence. No one since the Civil War had been able to establish a cohesive state machine. Some of Cox's supporters worked for Taylor while others pulled for Carmack in the senatorial primary; and some of Patterson's partisans were for Taylor and undoubtedly there were a few Carmack sympathizers in his camp. Statewide political control could only be achieved by coalitions or alliances such as the Frazier-Cox-Carmack combine, but alliance systems did not last long. By May 1906 this one had fallen apart. Led by the youthful and flamboyant Nashville attorney, Luke Lea, the Patterson forces wrested control of the convention from Governor Cox and the challenger received the nomination for governor by acclamation. Significantly, no Carmack partisan was placed in any responsible position or on any committee at the convention.[20]

Thus after 12 May 1906, Carmack was a "lame duck" senator whose term would not expire until the following March. Moreover, he was no longer in a strong influential position in the Democratic party in Tennessee. Yet, being a consummate politician, when the Democratic State Executive Committee requested that he help the party ticket in the general election campaign, Carmack readily agreed to do so. One assignment was to speak

---

[19] F. M. Thompson to Carmack, 21 May 1906, Box 2, Folder 19; Carmack to Thompson, 23 May 1906, Box 2, Folder 20, Carmack Papers.

[20] Correspondence, Box 2, Folders 14, 17, 20, Carmack Papers. See also J. M. Shahan, "The Rhetoric of Reform: The 1906 Gubernatorial Race in Tennessee," *Tennessee Historical Quarterly* 35 (Spring 1976): 65-82.

in reply to an address given in Nashville that October by President Roosevelt's Secretary of the Treasury, Leslie Mortier Shaw. Carmack devoted most of his speech to an attack on the Roosevelt administration's economic policies. Some of Carmack's loyalists agreed that his willingness to help the ticket was wise for "you and your future." A few, however, were upset. One wrote to Cobey Carmack, perhaps facetiously, that she had "sufficient and just grounds" for a divorce. Carmack admitted privately that "I shall be helping my most vindictive personal and political enemies who had conspired to destroy and disgrace me. But I have always spoken for the party in the days of my political prosperity and I can not afford to be a sulker now." It was a sacrifice, he said, but he would promote the party and "not sultify myself" by praising his enemies. In spite of inner turmoil, a measure of outward unity remained in the Democratic party and Patterson was elected governor in November 1906.[21]

Carmack was deeply hurt by his defeat, but in public statements and in numerous letters he declared that he would leave the Senate on good terms. He would, he said, be able to bear his misfortune with dignity and patience, insisting that he had no further ambition and would retire to private life, taking up the practice of law once again. David Lipscomb, an old family friend, believed that Carmack's defeat was providential. Lipscomb had tried many years earlier to lead a youthful Carmack into the ministry, but the two had had little contact since. He thought that the time was right to once again try to persuade Carmack to devote himself to "the cause of Christ among men." He wrote, urging that Carmack "give his zeal and life to the preaching of the gospel." The reply was polite but firm. Carmack thanked Lipscomb for his interest, but declared that "I am too old, perhaps, to radically change my life work." Politics was in his blood; he could not give it up.[22]

Although Carmack announced that he would retire to the practice of law when his Senate term expired, he quietly investigated the possibility of a return to journalism. He found at least one opportunity. A group of Chat-

---

[21]Cleander Cleon Mooney to Carmack, 29 August 1906; W. W. Ogilvie to Cobey Carmack, 30 August 1906, Box 2, Folder 21; Carmack to Gilbert _____, no date, Box 4, Folder 47, Carmack Papers.

[22]Correspondence, Box 2, Folders 14-20, Carmack Papers; *Gospel Advocate* 52 (8 December 1910): 1364.

tanooga businessmen, for example, offered to establish a newspaper in that city and give Carmack editorial control. He declined the offer because at that moment he was enthusiastic over a proposal to return to the *Nashville American*. Some time in December 1906, a syndicate that included T. R. Preston, president of the Hamilton National Bank of Nashville, E. B. Craig, vice-president of the Volunteer State Life Insurance Company of Chattanooga, both Carmack loyalists, and possibly Senator Frazier and others, was organized for the purpose of purchasing the *American*. Carmack was to be the editor if the purchase were consummated.

The principal owners of the newspaper were executives of the Louisville and Nashville Railroad. Although willing to sell, the owners seemed to be reluctant to transfer title of the *American* to a group that intended to employ Carmack as editor. Negotiations continued for several weeks. The syndicate would not agree to purchase the newspaper without Carmack so in February 1907 talks ceased and the attempted purchase fell through. Two of Carmack's friends wrote that it appeared that the Patterson crowd got wind of the deal, put pressure on the *American*'s owners to back off under threat that the administration would press legislation then pending in the General Assembly that the railroad executives opposed. A return to journalism was blocked and it seemed that Patterson had become Carmack's nemesis.[23]

Talk of Carmack as a candidate for governor did not cease after Patterson's nomination, but the emphasis shifted to the race of 1908, two years hence. Pressure on Carmack to make that race increased in intensity after the first of 1907. Some of his friends discouraged his running for governor, noting that it would be against an incumbent and be a hard, bitter contest. Carmack, they believed, had nothing to gain and everything to lose by becoming involved in a factional struggle. They advised him to stay aloof and wait for the next Senate race.

Carmack also received an increasing volume of correspondence urging him to challenge Patterson in 1908. The tone of his mail was optimistic and positive. A recurring theme was that Carmack was stronger and more popular than before his defeat by Taylor and that he could win. Another theme was that he was needed and that it was his duty to run and destroy the Pat-

[23] E. B. Craig to Carmack, 4 February 1907; F. M. Thompson to Carmack, 9 February 1907, Box 2, Folder 25, Carmack Papers.

terson machine. In imploring Carmack to make the race, one writer declared that "I believe now that circumstances over which you have no controll [sic] will force you to run. . . . The office now seeks the man, they, the people, are going to press this matter on you in such a way that I fear it will do you a great injury not to accept this nomination." Another writer who had originally opposed the governor's race explained that "at first some of his best friends . . . including myself, were opposed to his entering the race," but his friends now "are so anxious for him to run and have brought such pressure to bear on him, that it will be difficult, and might be dangerous, for him to decline to make the race." By the summer of 1907, the demand that Carmack try for the governorship reached significant proportions. He was clearly interested and was beginning to sound out friends and political leaders across the state.[24]

Why was Carmack so easily influenced to undertake a formidable, if not impossible, task? Patterson was entrenched; he had been elected on a progressive platform and had achieved at least modest success in his programs and no serious problems had upset his administration; and Tennesseans normally rewarded successful governors with second terms. Patterson would, therefore, be hard to beat. Some of Carmack's more politically astute friends urged that he remain out of politics for a time and quietly mend his fences. As the *Nashville Banner* later observed, "a few years of absolute retirement from the public view after leaving the Senate would, no doubt, have been to his advantage."

Retirement was neither his nature nor his style. He was also bitter and vindictive toward those who had contributed to his defeat in 1906, and he may have been deceived by the enthusiasm of his loyal following. By the summer of 1907, he was convinced that he could win and thus yielded to the pressure and made his commitment. He could also rationalize this move. To a friend, he wrote that "I feel that it is my duty to make this race. I do not do so because I want the office, and indeed, I would give much if

---

[24]Sid R. Clark to G. H. Armistead, 31 August 1907, Box 2, Folder 26, Carmack Papers. One of those encouraging the race for governor was Kenneth D. McKellar; see K. D. McKellar to Carmack, 23 August 1907, Carmack Papers. McKellar wrote later that Carmack "came to me for advice. I urged him not to run . . . but those having different views . . . induced him to make the race." Kenneth D. McKellar, *Tennessee Senators As Seen By One of Their Successors* (Kingsport: Southern Publishers, Inc., 1942) 474-75. See also correspondence, Box 2, Folder 26, Carmack Papers.

I could feel at liberty to decline the unpleasant task before me—but I cannot." Therefore, in late September 1907, Carmack announced that he would be a candidate for the Democratic gubernatorial nomination in 1908. He needed an issue and he chose the most readily available one—prohibition.[25]

---

[25]*Nashville Banner*, 9 November 1908; Carmack to James Wood Jones, 23 September 1907, Box 12, Folder 3; The Jones Family Papers, Tennessee State Library and Archives, Nashville.

8

PROHIBITION AND POLITICS

Efforts to control the manufacture, sale, and consumption of intoxicating beverages have had a long history in the Volunteer State. There were attempts long before the Civil War to regulate the liquor traffic and in the years after the war, a minor but highly vocal political party, the Prohibition party, was established. Their goal was absolute prohibition in the state. A partial victory was won in 1877 with the passage by the legislature of the "Four Mile Law," a measure that forbade the retail sale of liquor within four miles of any chartered school outside incorporated towns. The law was extended from time to time so that by the first decade of the twentieth century, the sale and consumption of intoxicating beverages was prohibited in virtually all of rural and small-town Tennessee; only the metropolitan areas remained legally wet. Efforts to achieve mandatory statewide prohibition continued under the leadership of groups such as the Women's Christian Temperance Union, the Anti-Saloon League, and some of the Protestant evangelical religious denominations, chiefly the Baptists and Methodists.[1]

---

[1] For the history of the prohibition movement in Tennessee, see Paul E. Isaac, *Prohibition and Politics: Turbulent Decades in Tennessee, 1885-1920* (Knoxville: University of Tennessee Press, 1965). For a shorter treatment, see Eric Russell Lacy, "Tennessee Teetotalism: Social Forces and the Politics of Progressivism," *Tennessee Historical Quarterly* 24 (Fall 1965): 219-40.

The proponents of statewide prohibition were loud and vociferous in espousing their cause. Indeed, their enthusiasm gave the impression of a much larger movement than was warranted by their numbers. Prohibition was never a major issue in any statewide political campaign, for there was simply no widespread demand for prohibition in Tennessee. It appears that political leaders responded to the prohibitionists by passing the Four Mile Law and its subsequent amendments merely to get rid of an annoying issue. Like most groups with one goal, the forces seeking the end of the liquor traffic in Tennessee were single-minded in purpose, judging other issues as they thought those issues affected their goal.

This mentality is illustrated by a letter Carmack received in February 1907 from Edgar E. Folk, editor of the *Baptist and Reflector*. The missive referred to the Tollett "Good Roads Bill," a measure designed to stimulate road building that would be paid for in part by revenue from the tax on saloons. Folk wrote that "while we believe in good roads and are anxious to have them, we do not believe in building them out of blood money." The bill, he declared, would be "an entering wedge on the part of the liquor people to secure after a while the abolition of all our temperance laws. The argument will probably be made: The more saloons, the more revenue; the more revenue, the better roads; therefore, we favor more saloons. At least, it means the retention of saloons in our larger cities in order to secure good roads." Folk concluded that "a crisis in our temperance work" had been reached and urged Carmack to use his influence with members of the General Assembly to defeat the Tollett bill.[2] Because prohibitionists demanded total commitment, professional politicians found the issue irritating at the very least. Most tried to sidestep or straddle the issue. No one was more adept at this than Carmack; he was able to avoid commitment to prohibition while maintaining a good relationship with most of their leaders. Actually his record on the liquor issue should have alienated the most diehard prohibitionists.

Implying a moderate stance in his attitude toward efforts to regulate the liquor traffic, Carmack wrote in 1906 that he "had never been among the extreme or fanatical advocates of temperance" although he had "always opposed the political domination of the whisky power." Although a reason-

---

[2]Edgar E. Folk to Carmack, 9 February 1907, Box 2, Folder 25, The Edward Ward Carmack Papers, Southern Historical Collection, University of North Carolina, Chapel Hill.

ably accurate self-assessment, Carmack was not always consistent in moderation. He was no teetotaler, but how much and how often he imbibed can not be known. There were occasional rumors that he consumed alcohol to excess. In 1908, for example, a story circulated that Carmack was so intoxicated one night during a campaign swing of West Tennessee that he had to be put to bed; another tale suggested that he had remained drunk for some time after the close of that campaign.

Early in his career, Carmack had opposed temperance legislation. In 1885, in the one term he served in the General Assembly, he voted against a resolution that proposed an amendment to the constitution of Tennessee that would ban the manufacture of intoxicating beverages in the state. As an editor, he was sharply critical of the temperance movement. Once, in a long editorial, he ridiculed the Prohibitionist party. "Prohibition might or might not be a wise and proper policy," he wrote, "and men might honestly believe in it, but a party to successfully administer the government should have well-defined opinions and policies on other questions besides the mere question of prohibiting the sale or use of certain beverages." The Prohibition party was a mistake, for it was a single-issue party. Those elected to office had to deal with many issues. Suppose, he said, the prohibitionists were able to win control of government and impose prohibition, then what? How would they deal with other issues? "The Lord only knows—the prohibitionists themselves have no idea." They would leave "wreck and ruin behind. . . . A wild bull in a china shop would be gentle and harmless compared with the wild work" of the prohibitionists. Finally, he warned, the prohibitionists were dangerous because they favored granting women the right to vote. On another occasion he lashed out at the temperance crusaders for destroying the the property of whisky sellers. He exclaimed that "a temperance crusader is as much bound to obey the law as anyone, and no sentiment can sanctify a crusade against another's legal right. This is a country of law," he declared.[3]

When he was an editor in Memphis, Carmack frequently railed against the existence of unlicensed saloons and gambling houses in that

---

[3]Carmack to James C. Beck, 16 May 1906, Box 2, Folder 16; Carmack to J. C. Bradford, 21 October 1908; J. C. Bradford to Carmack, 23 October 1908; and other correspondence, Box 3, Folders 29-32, Carmack Papers; Tennessee General Assembly, *House Journal*, 44th General Assembly of the State of Tennessee (Nashville, 1885) 688-89; *Nashville Democrat*, 28 October 1888; Nashville *Daily American*, 20 February 1890.

city. He declared that Memphis was in a desperate struggle to end the domination of the city by the illegal "grog shops." He once exclaimed that "we are growing weary of the rule of men that carry on their business in open and notorious violation of the law." Party machinery, he declared, was "managed in the interest of whisky shops. There is no reason why saloon men should not take an active and honorable part in politics, but there is every reason why politics should not be under the influences of the saloons."

Attacking the existence of unlicensed saloons and their alleged political influence was, however, a safe proposition. It was common for editors and ministers to fulminate against the saloons of Memphis, which allegedly had influence in high places and paid no taxes. Moreover, the Memphis government was in the hands of Carmack's political enemies and charges of a corrupt relationship between the whisky power and the city fathers was part of his continuing attack on the faction controlling the community.

Carmack's voting record in Congress had pleased temperance leaders. He had supported measures to end interstate shipment of whisky into dry areas, to prohibit liquor sales in Alaska, and to require new states to forbid sales of liquor to Indians. More important, he had endorsed the proposed Hepburn-Dolliver bill, a measure that would have placed intoxicating beverages in interstate commerce under the police power of the states through which they passed. Thus Carmack was able to please the temperance forces without committing himself to absolute prohibition in Tennessee. Yet his voice in Congress alienated a strong interest in the state—the liquor industry.[4]

Although prohibition was not an issue in the senatorial contest of 1906 between Carmack and Taylor, the liquor industry, presumably upset over Carmack's votes in the Senate, endorsed Taylor and contributed heavily to the challenger's campaign chest. A vested interest thus threw down the gauntlet and lit the fuse of Carmack's crusading nature. He reacted in anger, and in his opening campaign speech at the Vendome Theater in Nashville in March 1906, he lashed out at the liquor industry. Whereas once he had condemned only illegal saloons, consciously or unconsciously, he now made no distinction between the illicit whisky business and legitimate manufacturers and distributors. He declared that:

---

[4]*Memphis Commercial*, 10 January 1893; *Commercial Appeal*, 22 August 1894; *Congressional Record*, 59th Cong., 1st Ses. (1906) 7517. See also Isaac, *Prohibition and Politics*, 108.

It is not my purpose tonight to deal with the liquor question except as it comes within the sphere of my duties as a Senator.

But I cannot help saying that the activity of the saloon in politics is a question of interest to every man who holds or seeks a public office. So far as I am concerned, I am weary of a condition of things where the man whose business it is to make the laws must hold his office by consent of the man whose business it is to break the laws. I am weary of the insolent and dictatorial spirit which so largely pervades the saloon business of this State; of its open alliance with vice; its open contempt of law; its assumption that the right to sell whisky in accordance with law carries with it the right to sell whisky in violation of the law; that the license to run a saloon carries with it the license to run a gambling house and flaunt its black banner in the very face of innocence, purity and public decency. It seems that I have given mortal offense to some of these gentlemen because I have publicly said that the man who runs a saloon has no more right to violate the law than the man who runs a barber shop.

One of my competitor's chief lieutenants not long since said to a friend of mine that I would surely be defeated because the saloons of the State were solidly arrayed against me. I only wish to remark that if they accomplish that result, they will at the same time give me plenty to do to keep me from brooding over my defeat. If they defeat me for the Senate, it shall be my next ambition to be handed down in history as the last man who was ever defeated for office by the saloon power of Tennessee.

Carmack did not emphasize the temperance issue in his campaign with Taylor, but he repeated his threat on a number of occasions throughout the canvass.[5]

Carmack emerged from his loss to Taylor convinced that the liquor manufacturers and distributors had organized against him and contributed to his defeat. Shortly after the senatorial primary, he expressed his anger "with regard to the insolent and intolerant attitude of the whisky element in Tennessee." He declared that "they are not content with pursuing a lawful business in a lawful way but insist on pronouncing sentence of death

---

[5]For a copy of Carmack's Vendome Theater speech, see Paul Franklin Bumpus, *Carmack: The Edward Ward Carmack Story* (Franklin: Paul Franklin Bumpus, 1977) 174. See also pamphlet "Contest for United States Senator," Box 6, Folder 17, Governor Malcolm R. Patterson Papers, Tennessee State Library and Archives, Nashville.

upon every man who demands that they obey the law. This condition of things is intollerable [sic] and self respecting people will not long submit to it." It was clear, he said, that "the saloon has sinned away its day of grace and must be dealt with as an incorrigible offender against society."[6]

Thus the liquor industry, by assisting Taylor, pushed Carmack toward the temperance side, who welcomed him with open arms. Undoubtedly, the advocates of prohibition recognized that what the movement needed in Tennessee was a charismatic leader. Carmack was their man. Yet in spite of his condemnation of liquor interests in the state, he was strangely reluctant to commit himself to immediate prohibition, favoring instead strict regulation of the industry through high fees. He argued that the public was not in favor of statewide prohibition and, therefore, it could not be enforced. The time was not right. The public had to be educated to accept prohibition, and it should be enacted only when "sentiment is strong enough to carry it through."[7] Carmack did not declare for statewide prohibition when he announced his candidacy for the Democratic gubernatorial nomination in September 1907. Not until March of 1908, well after the governor's race had gotten under way and it was necessary to give life to a faltering campaign against Governor Patterson, did he commit himself to ending the liquor traffic by statute.

Tennessee has experienced many hard-fought political campaigns but few have exceeded in bitterness the Carmack-Patterson race for governor in 1908. Personal animosity was a factor in the intensity of the contest, but there were other issues. Well before the campaign got under way in March, conflict developed over the method of selecting the nominee. In January, Carmack sent an open letter to the Democratic State Executive Committee urging that the committee order a direct popular primary. The *Nashville Tennessean*, a newspaper founded in April 1907 by Luke Lea and the major daily that supported Carmack, quickly took the lead in pressing for a direct primary.[8] Although Patterson had campaigned in 1906 in favor of a mandatory direct primary, he remained silent on the issue. However, because he was an incumbent and controlled party machinery, the committee was ex-

---

[6]Carmack to James C. Beck, 16 May 1906, Box 2, Folder 16, Carmack Papers; *Nashville American*, 19 September 1906. See also ibid., 6 October 1906.

[7]Interview, *Baptist and Reflector* 16 (2 August 1906): 2.

[8]*Nashville Tennessean*, 4, 6 January, 5 February 1908.

pected to select a method that would be to the governor's advantage. When the committee met on 20 February, Carmack spoke to the group for about an hour making an impassioned plea for what he called the only right, just, and democratic way to select a nominee: a direct primary. It did little good for the committee set a delegated primary for 27 June.

The scheme was a county unit system whereby voters in each county would express preference at the ballot box, but delegates apportioned according to population would attend a convention and select the nominee. The candidate receiving a majority of votes in each county would receive all of the delegates from that county. Under this method it was possible for one receiving less than a majority statewide to win the nomination. The delegated primary clearly favored Patterson who had strong support in the more heavily populated counties. The delegated primary was an issue that Carmack sought to exploit. Senator Taylor also spoke out in criticism of the scheme. He declared that "the State Committee overlooked the fact that a great majority of the Democrats of Tennessee demand a direct primary. . . . I am sure they have not reflected the will of the majority of the people."[9]

The most exciting feature of the campaign was a series of debates between Carmack and Patterson. The possibility of a series of debates between the two was raised early in the year and when Carmack issued a formal challenge in March, surprisingly, the governor quickly accepted. Why Patterson agreed so readily is not clear. He was the incumbent and the party leader, therefore having more to loose and apparently nothing to gain. Joint encounters were not common to political races in Tennessee, for most political professionals regarded them as more perilous than rewarding. Presumably Carmack, starting from behind, had more to gain.

It was also surprising that the campaign managers, G. H. Armistead for Carmack and Austin Peay for Patterson, were able to reach agreement on a format. They initially arranged a series of forty-two engagements, later adding eight for a total of fifty debates. Reaction to the debate agreement

---

[9]Ibid., 27 February 1908. That was Taylor's only public involvement in the governor's race. Conforming to tradition, the senator remained quiet, but privately he may have given some support to Carmack. The challenger apparently sought Taylor's support and one correspondent wrote that "my own belief is that he will be a strong supporter in your behalf." Another writer also believed that Taylor was committed to Carmack. See Jerome Templeton to Carmack, 26 September 1907; W. A. Owens to Carmack, 28 September 1907, Box 2, Folder 27, Carmack Papers.

was mixed. The small-town press and the rural constituency applauded; those in the countryside welcomed the prospect of an exciting diversion as well as an opportunity to hear the candidates discuss the various issues. The urban press, on the other hand, concluded that joint debates would serve no useful purpose and would, in fact, cause increased animosity and weaken and divide the Democratic party. One, noting that both candidates were temperamental redheads, predicted clashes that would lead to bitterness and party strife.[10]

The first scheduled debate at Chattanooga on 16 April was a festive occasion with a parade, bands, banners, and flowers, and a large, excited crowd. Carmack was handicapped, for he was suffering with a painful eye infection, a problem that had required several days of bed rest. He was not fully recovered at the time of the Chattanooga debate, and he wore a protective patch. Whether the problem affected his ability to perform can not be known. Subsequent debates had similar pageantry, and while the degree of enthusiasm was not repeated everywhere, all of the joint discussions drew excited crowds. Because both candidates were temperamental and because the issues in the campaign were highly emotional, the prediction of clashes proved accurate.

At Fayetteville, Carmack lost his composure and tried to attack Patterson when the incumbent asserted that the challenger was unfit to be governor. Carmack was restrained, but fights broke out in the audience. Patterson lost his temper on one occasion and, at Paris, Carmack was forced by an unruly crowd to leave the platform. There was fighting in the audience at other stops before the series of debates closed at Tullahoma in June.

Although the debates seemed to have clarified some issues and policy differences, it is questionable whether the confrontations served the interests of the Democratic party. It seems likely that the end result was more anger and bitterness, widening the rift in the Democracy. Carmack may well have erred in agreeing to appear on the same platform with Patterson. The challenger was a good debater and an eloquent speaker, but the governor was at least his equal in oratory and perhaps superior in debate. As the *Morning Jacksonian* observed, "Malcolm R. Patterson can always get an audience. . . . The gift of language and the art of delivery have been given

---

[10]Will Dunn Smith, "The Carmack-Patterson Campaign and its Aftermath in Tennessee Politics" (M.A. thesis, Vanderbilt University, 1939) 32-33.

him in wonderful degree." Thus Carmack's ability to score points was cancelled by Patterson's forensic talent.[11]

Except on prohibition, the debates proved that the contenders had similar platforms. Patterson had campaigned in 1906 on a reform program and, as governor, he had tried to follow through on his promises. Because the governor had an image as a progressive, Carmack was forced to present a platform more reform-oriented than was his inclination. His programs included a call for a statewide mandatory popular primary, strict regulation of public-service franchise corporations to improve services, an end to free passes and freight rate discrimination by railroads, strengthening of antitrust laws by making individual corporate officials responsible for violations of laws, better education, better highways, and state-guaranteed bank deposits. The platform was almost identical to the one offered by Patterson; the only difference of significance was the incumbent's call for a commission to regulate banks rather than guaranteed deposits. The governor also advocated a statewide popular primary despite his acceptance of the delegated primary in 1908. He rationalized that he had merely accepted the dictates of the party.[12]

Without substantial policy differences, Carmack was forced to rely upon charging Patterson with a variety of illegal, immoral, and unethical practices. He asserted that the governor was the head of an evil and corrupt state political machine, a charge that was neither ingenious nor rare. Patterson, he said, built a state machine by flagrant abuse of his patronage power. The governor retorted, in truth, that every administration since the Civil War had been accused of being a machine. The only factor that gave substance to the charge of machine politics was the governor's quiet willingness to accept the delegated primary.

During one of the debates, Carmack asked Patterson if he would accept the nomination if he received less than a majority of the popular votes. When the governor said yes, the challenger declared that the answer proved his contention that a machine controlled state government. Patterson re-

---

[11] Ibid., 36-67; newspaper clipping, Box 2, Folder 10, Patterson Papers.

[12] Scrapbook newspaper clippings, Box 7, Volume 10, Carmack Papers. Carmack was emphatic in damning the practice of giving railroad passes to public figures, but as an editor he was happy to receive free transportation. See Carmack to Cobey Carmack, Box 4, Folder 47, Carmack Papers.

sponded that the delegated primary was the method of nomination established by the party and he merely acquiesced to the will of Democrats. Carmack's accusation and Patterson's reply may have influenced some voters.

Carmack also charged Patterson with pardoning an excessive number of felons. He observed that the governor had pardoned 380 criminals, far more than previous governors for the same period of time, and he insisted that the pardons were political payoffs. Patterson, however, was able to effectively answer the allegation. He declared that many in prison were boys between the ages of twelve and fifteen who had committed minor crimes. When the General Assembly failed to appropriate enough money to build a reformatory, he released those boys from prison, declaring that he had removed children from the evil influences of hardened criminals.

Carmack also claimed that the governor had offered a bribe to a member of the legislature to vote in favor of a measure in which Patterson had a vested interest, a bill to amend the charter of the city of Memphis. However, Carmack also had an interest in the act and had traveled to Nashville when the General Assembly was in session to lobby against it. In effect, the charter revision as passed was a "ripper bill" that called for evacuation of all municipal office-holders, some of whom were Carmack's allies. Under the act, Governor Patterson was authorized to appoint the new city council and, as expected, placed his friends in office. The courts, however, struck down the charter revision as a violation of due process. Interestingly, Carmack did not mention the Memphis charter issue in the debate held in the Bluff City. Ironically, both candidates charged the other with having participated in fraudulent elections in Shelby County.

On another issue, Carmack claimed that Patterson conspired to reduce Confederate veterans and veterans' widows pensions, an allegation that the governor branded a lie and an attempt to turn the veterans against him. Finally, Carmack insisted that the Louisville and Nashville Railroad was a shadowy, evil influence in the Patterson administration. But all of the charges and countercharges paled compared to the issue of prohibition.[13]

The liquor question was the dominant issue in the campaign and the one most frequently discussed during the debates. Carmack, after months

---

[13]Smith, "The Carmack-Patterson Campaign," 23-68. For a discussion of the Memphis charter battle, see William D. Miller, *Memphis During the Progressive Era, 1900-1917* (Memphis: Memphis State University Press, 1957) 153-55.

of hesitation, declared for statewide prohibition in a speech before a group of prohibition leaders at a luncheon in Nashville on 12 March. Subsequently, the Women's Christian Temperance Union and the Anti-Saloon League endorsed him. Governor Patterson declared that he would accept the principle of local self-government. Thus Carmack called for mandatory prohibition, and Patterson advocated local option. Ironically, the stance of both candidates reflected changed positions by both prohibitionists and antiprohibitionists. For years the opponents of the liquor traffic had sought local option because it suited their purpose; in 1908, they abandoned local option for absolute abolition of the traffic. Antiprohibitionists had earlier opposed local option as the foot-in-the-door approach of their opponents; in 1908, they saw local option as a means to block prohibition in the cities. Both sides charged the other with breaking faith; the prohibitionists admitted that they had used local option to indeed get their foot in the door. They had always advocated absolute prohibition and their goal now seemed attainable.[14]

In the first of the debates at Chattanooga, Carmack barely mentioned the liquor issue, possibly because the sentiment in that city was generally opposed to prohibition. At other stops, however, he unmercifully assailed Patterson's record on temperance, insisting that the governor was not only inconsistent but a hypocrite on the issue. He claimed that Patterson had opposed the Pendleton Act, a measure enacted by the General Assembly in 1907 that extended the Four Mile Law to large cities provided they surrender their charters and reincorporate. Carmack declared that the governor had tried to block the measure during the legislative session and had put his signature to it only because he was afraid to veto it. Moreover, despite a promise to sign all prohibition measures, Patterson had vetoed two important pieces of temperance legislation.

Carmack asserted, correctly, that Patterson had the enthusiastic support of the liquor industry, particularly the Model License League. The Model License League had been organized in Kentucky in 1907 by responsible members of the liquor industry who belatedly came to realize the need for reform and to end the abuses of the illegal saloons. The league became active in Tennessee early in 1908 as a lobby against prohibition. The group had endorsed Patterson for governor, possibly contributing heavily to his

---

[14]Isaac, *Prohibition and Politics*, 146-47.

campaign fund. As additional evidence of the industry's support for Patterson, Carmack quoted an article in a leading liquor trade journal, *Bonfort's Wine and Spirit Circular*, that declared that in Tennessee, "The nomination of Carmack would mean the destruction not only of the wholesaler and retailer in Tennessee, but the brewer and distiller as well." The article stated that the trade was making a determined fight against heavy odds and concluded with a request for "assistance from the outside in the way of writers and speakers, and also contributions to aid the creation of a strong organization." Carmack also produced a letter allegedly broadcast by a Nashville distillery executive asserting that "we think it would be to your interest to vote for Patterson as Carmack is more out on the whisky question. . . . We thank you to vote for Patterson and tell your friends to do the same." The evidence, Carmack concluded, proved the close tie between the governor and the saloon power.[15]

Although Carmack was the aggressor on prohibition, Patterson was able to score heavily on the issue. He did not hesitate to damn the prohibitionist leaders as faultfinders and troublemakers, and the movement as a threat to harmony in the Democratic party. He exclaimed that the Democracy would not be led around by such purveyors of discontent as Edgar E. Folk. Patterson asserted that his opponent was in good company with the prohibitionists, for "no man in Tennessee is better fitted to lead the forces of discontent, criticism, cavil and fault finding than ex-United States Senator Carmack." The governor called attention to the challenger's record on the temperance movement, citing Carmack's public positions and quoting from editorials that ridiculed the Prohibition party. Patterson also quoted from remarks made in 1906 in which Carmack declared that he was opposed to a general law requiring mandatory statewide prohibition. In the first debate, Patterson concluded his recitation of Carmack's temperance record by asking "now gentlemen, what do you think of a man who, in order to lead the Democratic party, goes to the very front of the prohibition column and waves the prohibition flag? What is he doing it for?"[16]

In order to reinforce his assertion that Carmack was unreliable and inconsistent on prohibition, Patterson quoted from a letter written by a min-

---

[15]Scrapbook newspaper clipping, Box 7, Volume 10, Carmack Papers. See also Lacy, "Tennessee Teetotalism," 224; *Nashville Tennessean*, 12 May 1908.

[16]*Nashville Tennessean*, 26 April 1908; *Chattanooga Times*, 17 April 1908.

ister who was a leader of the Anti-Saloon League in Jackson. The minister wrote that Carmack had "shunned his duty" by remaining in Nashville while "the temperance people of Jackson were begging him to come help them out" at an especially trying time. Caught by surprise, Carmack hurriedly tried to repair the damage. He declared later that the minister confessed doing him an injustice; that the minister admitted to making the statement without knowing that Carmack was detained by important business in Nashville. Even so, Carmack was hurt by the letter.[17]

Patterson's attempt to portray Carmack as a political opportunist undoubtedly succeeded in influencing the attitude of some thoughtful Tennesseans. He was also successful in raising doubts of the challenger's loyalty to the Democratic party, an interesting twist because Carmack had an image as a party regular. The governor presented himself as a loyalist when he declared that although he opposed mandatory prohibition, he would follow the dictates of the party on the issue. If the platform advocated prohibition, he would sign such an act if it passed the legislature; if the platform opposed prohibition, he would veto an enactment to that end. Carmack observed that the governor was safe in this position because any convention that nominated him would never put a prohibition plank in the platform. Still, Patterson's point was telling, for Carmack had made a commitment to prohibition regardless of the party platform.

The governor also charged that the Anti-Saloon League was a tool of the Republican party, an allegation some Democrats found easy to believe. In 1906 the Republican party came under the domination of the Henry Clay Evans/Newell Sanders wing, a faction committed to statewide prohibition. Many Democrats believed that Evans and Sanders hoped to win control of state government by splitting the Democracy over the temperance issue. Moreover, Patterson claimed that Sanders was helping finance Carmack's campaign. In one of the debates, the governor asked his challenger if he would enter into an alliance with the Republicans if he lost the primary. Carmack responded with an emphatic no, but Patterson had made his point—Carmack's loyalty to the party was now suspect.[18]

---

[17]Correspondence, Box 3, Folders 29, 30, Carmack Papers; Smith, "The Carmack-Patterson Campaign," 58-59.

[18]*Nashville Tennessean*, 5 May 1908. See also Isaac, *Prohibition and Politics*, 113-14, 146.

Carmack also did not command support from everyone in the temperance movement. Some doubted the sincerity of his commitment and a few of the less fanatic recognized that there were issues other than prohibition. The editor of the Methodist organ, the *Christian Advocate*, wrote that because the paper was not a local journal, it had not taken a stand in the campaign. He pointed out that the race was not strictly a prohibitionist-antiprohibitionist fight. There were other important issues. Moreover, there was a time-honored tradition for a second nomination, and Patterson had given a "fairly good administration." Undoubtedly many Tennesseans agreed with the *Commercial Appeal* which observed that "Carmack and Patterson stand on the same platform. Neither of them is a teetotaler. One is just as good a temperance man as the other."[19]

Carmack's effort to unseat Governor Patterson was a hopeless cause from the beginning. Those who urged his candidacy were overly enthusiastic and overconfident about the possibility of success. The forces of temperance were also overly optimistic about their ability to deliver a sufficient number of votes for victory in 1908. Carmack was unable to obtain the endorsement of enough of the professional politicians or the leaders of local and regional factions. Few were willing to make a commitment to a losing cause. Carmack was, therefore, poorly organized and poorly funded. His campaign had to rely more on enthusiasm and hurrah. For support, he could count only on the backing of most of the leaders of the temperance movement and his own personal following.

However, the shrillness of some of his loyalists became a handicap. One supporter wrote complaining about the excessive enthusiasm of one campaign worker. "I know he is a most devout Carmack man—but don't you think he gets a little too bitter now and then?" The writer cautioned that "there is a class that can be turned by such attacks—& will help the other side out of sympathy." Some partisans were in a dilemma. A West Tennessee farmer, a long-time Carmack adherent, wrote that although he "thought Carmack had made a mistake in running this time," he would still vote for the challenger. But he considered Patterson "an able man, & good speaker . . . both are Democrats, a pity, in a family fight, a pity."[20]

---

[19]*Christian Advocate*, 10 July 1908; scrapbook newspaper clipping, Box 7, Volume 10, Carmack Papers.

[20]Jack Nelson to Carmack, 11 February 1908, Box 3, Folder 29, Carmack Papers; 26 June, 25 May, Box 4, Folder 2, Cartmell Diaries, Tennessee State Library and Archives, Nashville.

On primary election day, the Women's Christian Temperance Union staged parades in a number of cities. Women and children, dressed in white to stress the purity of womanhood, marched singing and carrying banners. There were also floats decorated with banks of Carmack's symbol, the red feather. The effort probably had little effect on the voting. As expected, Patterson won a majority of the 146 delegates. The only surprise was that Carmack did better than expected; he was defeated by only 7,000 votes. The final count gave the incumbent slightly over 85,000 to just under 79,000 for Carmack. The challenger carried East Tennessee including Knoxville and Knox County, but the governor showed strength in Chattanooga, Nashville, and Memphis, winning in Middle and West Tennessee.

The outcome of the primary was influenced by a number of factors. Patterson was an incumbent running for a second term and Tennessee traditionally rewarded successful governors with reelection. Moreover, Tennesseans, especially those in the cities, were caught up in the progressive movement that was sweeping the country. Carmack, with an image as a Bourbon conservative, was not as acceptable as Patterson. The primary was not a referendum on prohibition. It is safe to say that a majority of Tennesseans were not enthusiastic for statewide prohibition. The existing liquor laws were acceptable; most were opposed to making prohibition mandatory for the entire state.

The canvass was over, but nothing had been settled. The Democratic party was in even greater disarray. Carmack had damaged the party by entering the race, by injecting the emotional issue of prohibition, and by conducting a bitter, shrill campaign. The prohibitionists refused to accept defeat and vowed to continue their struggle to end the liquor traffic. When the Democratic party met in convention two weeks after the primary, Carmack was present and made a concerted effort to insert a plank in the platform calling for statewide prohibition. But the convention, controlled by Patterson's forces, rejected the plea and after renominating the incumbent, adopted a local option plank. Because of the split in the Democracy, the possibility of a Republican victory in November loomed. But the threat soon dissipated, in part because of dissension within the minority party and because many prohibitionist Democrats preferred not to vote Republican. On the other hand, prohibitionists made some gains in representation in the General Assembly.[21]

---

[21] Isaac, *Prohibition and Politics*, 153-57.

Carmack was deeply depressed in the weeks following the primary. He experienced bouts with illness and faced personal financial difficulties, forcing him to call upon friends for assistance.[22] In late summer, Carmack joined the Chautauqua circuit again in order to earn needed funds, but had to cancel some engagements because of illness. More important to the political environment in Tennessee than personal problems was Carmack's attitude. His political fortunes seemed to have declined even further after the second stinging defeat within two years. Always aggressive in the face of adversity, he continued the attack with greater intensity. He was even more bitter and vindictive after the gubernatorial primary; something compelled him to seek vindication. He was even more abrasive and shrill in castigating both his personal enemies and the foes of prohibition. In late August, he was given the opportunity to return to journalism, to a forum from which to continue the fight for prohibition: he was appointed editor-in-chief of the *Nashville Tennessean* by the owner, Luke Lea.

Born in 1879 into a prominent Middle Tennessee family, Luke Lea was an attorney by vocation and politician by avocation. In 1906, he was one of Patterson's allies, but the two soon parted company. In April 1907, Lea founded the *Tennessean*, a newspaper that became the state chief executive's most unrelenting press opponent. It also became the leading newspaper advocate for prohibition, refusing to accept liquor advertising and supported Carmack's bid for the governorship. There were rumors in the weeks following the primary that the defeated candidate would take over the newspaper. It is possible that prohibition leaders encouraged, if not pressured, Lea into appointing Carmack to the editorship. After all, he was an experienced journalist and the most popular figure in the antiliquor movement. How much enthusiasm Lea had for hiring Carmack can not be known nor were the terms of their agreement disclosed. It is also questionable how long the two dynamic, flamboyant, temperamental, and ambitious politicians could work in harmony. In any case, Carmack now had a forum from which to continue the crusade for prohibition, to seek vindication, and to recoup his political fortunes.

---

[22] G. T. Fitzhugh to Carmack, 7 August 1908, Box 3, Folder 32, Carmack Papers.

9

MARTYRDOM

On 31 August 1908, in a special notice, the board of directors of the *Nashville Tennessean* announced that Edward Ward Carmack had been appointed editor-in-chief of that newspaper. The statement declared that:

> Edward W. Carmack this morning becomes the editor of the Nashville Tennessean. This simple announcement embodies the fruition of the desire of thousands of Tennesseans and is pregnant with hopeful significance to the Democratic party of Tennessee. The Tennessean congratulates itself that its career has so won the confidence of the Democratic masses that, by abundant tokens, their sense of party fealty, aroused in the presence of grave party abuses and pressing public issues, has called this brilliant statesman and journalist to voice the counsels and guide the policy of a journal whose highest mission is to protect party and public from spoliation and oppression. That there has been for weeks an earnest and indeed eager desire that Mr. Carmack accept this post of responsibility, so congenial to his trained talents and so fruitful in public benefits, has been clearly manifest. The Tennessean congratulates the party and the State that its policies are to be moulded and its usefulness to be expanded by this brave and brainy son of the great commonwealth, which he has honored and loved from his youth. . . .
>
> We may add, in conclusion, that we feel certain that the press of Tennessee and the South, indeed, will congratulate The Tennessean that the profession, through it, is to be again made the possessor of the

time and talents of this gifted journalist whose younger years were devoted to its exacting and honorable duties.[1]

In his first editorial, Carmack stated that "In taking control of The Tennessean it is not necessary to make any elaborate statement as to its future policy." He had "been in full sympathy with the general conduct of the paper in the past," and he saw no reason to change those policies. "The Tennessean," he wrote, "is Democratic in politics. It is Democratic because, and only because, it believes that the principles of the Democratic party will secure the largest measure of individual liberty and the largest measure of general happiness and prosperity." He asserted that the newspaper would "lend its support to all the nominees of the Democratic party, both national and State. But it does not believe that the whole duty of a Democrat is comprehended in supporting candidates duly labeled by a party convention." A Democrat, he said, had a duty to keep the party pure and honest. A Democrat who allowed "his party made the harlot of a corrupt machine and lift no hand to save it from dishonor" was "either faithless or a coward." Carmack concluded that "in the State, as in the nation, the great issue is that presented with such force and clearness by Mr. [William Jennings] Bryan: 'Shall the People Rule?' We should answer that question in Tennessee by the overthrow of a 'dominating and merciless machine,' by giving back to the people the power it has usurped."[2]

Carmack quickly demonstrated that his journalistic talent had not been dulled in the twelve-year absence from the fourth estate. His editorials were as caustic as ever, and he was still the same aggressive crusader of old. If anything, he was even more vicious in attacking his political enemies. Once again competing publishers and editors felt the sting of his vitriolic pen. He quickly singled out for abuse "Major" E. C. Lewis, president of the Nashville *American* and an official of the Louisville and Nashville Railroad. To Carmack, the relationship of Lewis to both enterprises was tantamount to railroad ownership of the newspaper. "When a great railroad corporation owns a newspaper," he wrote, "it is for no honest or legitimate purpose. . . . It does so that it may control the sources of public knowledge" to misinform

---

[1] *Nashville Tennessean*, 31 August 1908.

[2] Ibid.

and "pervert the judgment of the people."[3] However, neither Lewis nor the *American* were Carmack's first priority. The administration of Governor Patterson was first on his agenda.

A party loyalist, Carmack always endorsed Democratic nominees regardless of how much he and they differed on issues. Although he did not bolt to the Republican nominee for governor, Carmack did not support Patterson in the general election; rather, he declared that his goal was the destruction of the governor's organization and ending its control of the party and the state. In the weeks following Carmack's take over of the *Tennessean*, Patterson and his administration were subjected to a withering attack. The editor asserted that "no democrat is bound by the platform of a convention not one of whose delegates was elected by the people. . . . No little group of federated politicians can declare their will by any sort of hocus pocus and make it the will of the people." Patterson reacted to Carmack's attack by charging the editor with treason to the party; Carmack, he said, had pledged during the primary campaign to support and work for the nominee but had reneged on his promise. The governor's observation accomplished nothing, for Carmack's offensive to bring down his most bitter personal and political enemy was in high gear.[4]

In October, Carmack began to focus on one of Patterson's close advisors and his own early benefactor and former friend, Colonel Duncan Cooper. Why he singled out Cooper is not clear; it must be assumed that he was bitter and vindictive toward his old friend. From their earliest association, despite philosophical differences, Carmack and Cooper had remained friends and political allies until Cooper joined Patterson's organization in 1906 and supported Taylor in the senatorial contest as well. Those actions precipitated a break which, according to Cooper, could have been avoided. He declared that he "tried to be Carmack's friend. Before the Senatorial Primary was held, our people [meaning the Patterson organization] went to Carmack's managers and told them that if Carmack would do the right thing we would join hands and Carmack would be nominated Senator. If Carmack had done that, he would have defeated Taylor."

---

[3]Idid.

[4]Ibid., September-October 1908, passim.

The "right thing" was for "Carmack to come out boldly for the reforms which Patterson was urging in his campaign against Governor Cox."[5] Carmack could not abandon his ally, Cox, in the middle of his senatorial bid without serious repercussions. Besides, he was not a reformer. Cooper, on the other hand, was pragmatic and more flexible, and sensing the popular mood, found it easy to board the progressive bandwagon. The break was complete by the end of the senatorial primary in 1906. Carmack blamed the Patterson forces for his defeat, and Cooper shared that blame because he was one of the governor's allies. It was questionable whether attacking Cooper was worth the effort. Although from a prominent family and well-known in Nashville and Middle Tennessee, Cooper operated behind the scenes. There was, therefore, no great political capital to be gained by abusing him. Personal satisfaction in hurting Cooper was the only thing to be gained.

Carmack had earlier made occasional sarcastic reference to Cooper. Once during the gubernatorial campaign, he described his former friend as "a little bald headed angel of Hell." In an editorial that appeared in the Memphis *News-Scimitar* in March 1908 and signed by Carmack, Cooper was identified as one of those who shared in the "political debauchery and general corruption" of the Louisville and Nashville Railroad and the Patterson machine.[6] Carmack made no mention of Cooper for several weeks after he became editor of the *Tennessean*. Then in mid-October, he identified Cooper as one of the shadowy figures lurking behind the scenes in Patterson's administration exercising an evil influence on the governor. That was the beginning of a sequence that led to tragedy. From that date on, scathing comments about Cooper became a regular feature on the editorial page. On 21 October, he identified Cooper as the real power in politics in the state and likened him to the owners and operators of one of Nashville's most disreputable dives. Two days later, Carmack again called Cooper a "little bald headed angel of hell." In the editorials, Carmack also

---

[5]Louis Brownlow to Carmack, 21 January 1908, Box 3, Folder 29, The Edward Ward Carmack Papers, Southern Historical Collection, University of North Carolina, Chapel Hill.

[6]*Nashville Tennessean*, 19 May 1908; Will Dunn Smith, "The Carmack-Patterson Campaign and Its Aftermath in Tennessee Politics," (M.A. thesis, Vanderbilt University, 1939) 83.

referred to Cooper as "Major," a suggestion that the rank of colonel was undeserved.[7]

Carmack surely gained malicious pleasure in castigating his former friend and employer and it appears that he deliberately tried to goad Cooper into rash action. Cooper was furious over the abuse, especially the reference to his bald head, and word of his anger reached Carmack. It made the editor even more vicious and shortly he had what he believed was additional reason for continuing his assault on Cooper.

Near the end of October 1906, Patterson had met with his antagonist, former Governor John I. Cox, and the two had apparently cemented an alliance. The governor probably solicited Cox's support in the general election campaign, but it was widely believed that the two had agreed to join forces to fight statewide prohibition during the upcoming session of the General Assembly. Carmack quickly observed that "there was a bridge in the tower of London, over which persons accused of high treason were compelled to pass on their way to prison. There came to be a saying that many a loyal heart has crossed the traitor's bridge. In a feeble and ridiculous sort of way the present machine in Tennessee has built itself a rickety tower and ramshackle traitor's bridge. . . . One of the earliest martyrs to make this lugubrious passage was Ex-Governor Cox." Carmack then noted that the Patterson people had once referred to Cox as a "low demagogue," "cheap John politician," "public robber," and "common crook."

> But time, the great friend of Justice and the vindicator of the just, has removed the cloud from the fair form of Governor Cox and made the purity of his motives and the nobility of his character to shine as the noonday. And so Governor Patterson and Major Cooper sent for him to come to Nashville. They made humble and profuse apologies. . . . He was received with honor into the inner councils of the elect and a solemn resolution was adopted ordering that the judgment against his integrity as a man and as a statesman be expunged from the record. This historic incident is related to show how easy it is for a man to get a reversal of judgment if the machine thinks it worth while.

Carmack concluded by suggesting that Cooper had been the one who had

---

[7]*Nashville Tennessean*, 14-30 October 1908, passim.

called Cox to Nashville and had escorted him to see the governor. He was, therefore, the one responsible for the reconciliation.[8]

Then on Sunday, 8 November, another caustic editorial appeared under the heading "Across the Muddy Chasm," a title analogous to the "Bloody Chasm" of the Civil War. Again Carmack described the name-calling between Cox and Governor Patterson, and Cooper was identified as the one who brought about the reconciliation. He wrote:

> We trust there will be no unseemly ribaldry on the part of the base and vulgar concerning the happy reunion of long-sundered hearts which was accomplished in the joyous reconciliation of His Excellency, Hon. M. R. Patterson, and His ex-Excellency, Hon. John Isaac Cox. All honor to that noble spirit, Major Duncan Brown Cooper, who wrought this happy union of congenial and confluxible spirits, separated by evil fates, though born for each other. All honor to Major Dunc, and may the blessings of the peacemaker be upon him! May he be heir to all the beatitudes, and especially to the blessings reserved for those who do hunger and thirst after righteousness!

An accompanying editorial under the title "Consent of the Governed" was a stinging attack on Patterson's machine and his ally, the "Major."[9]

Cooper was furious over the continuous abuse, and the latest editorial was the last straw. He sent word to Carmack through one intermediary, E. B. Craig, and possibly others, that "if my name appears again, the town will not be big enough to hold us both." According to one messenger, Cooper added that "one of us must die." Cooper later denied the latter part of the warning. At any rate Carmack's friends were sufficiently concerned that they persuaded him to go armed, and he borrowed a pistol. Perhaps Cooper was advised that his adversary now carried a gun, for he also borrowed a weapon, presumably for self-protection. Thus both antagonists were armed, adding to the tension, and making it more likely that the conflict would end in tragedy.[10]

---

[8]Ibid., 30 October 1908.

[9]Ibid., 8 November 1908.

[10]*Cooper v. State*, 123 Tennessee (1910) 37-231; Robert A. Lanier, "The Carmack Murder Case," *Tennessee Historical Quarterly* 40 (Fall 1981): 272-85; William Waller, ed., *Nashville, 1900-1910* (Nashville: Vanderbilt University Press, 1972) 90-101.

A more prudent man, sensing that the feud was drifting toward violent resolution, would have eased the tension by halting his attacks, but Carmack was stubborn. On Sunday night, in an "ugly mood," the editor penned his answer to Cooper's threat in a masterpiece of sarcasm. Appearing the following morning under the title "The Diplomat of the Zweibund," it was clearly an attempt to taunt Cooper. It read:

> To Major Duncan Brown Cooper, who wrought the great coalition; who achieved the harmonious confluence of incompatible elements; who welded the pewter handle to the wooden spoon; who grafted the dead bough to the living tree and made it bloom, and burgeon and bend with golden fruit; who made playmates of the lamb and the leopard and boon companions of the spider and the fly; who made soda and vinegar to dwell placidly in the same bottle, and who taught oil and water how they might agree—to Major Duncan Brown Cooper, the great diplomat of the political Zweibund, be all honor and glory forever.

An accompanying editorial, "The Knight of the Sorrowful Figure," ridiculed Governor Patterson.[11]

The editorial enraged Cooper. That morning he visited the Union Avenue office of his attorney, J. C. Bradford, an associate of his son, Robin, and "turned the air blue" with epithets in reference to Carmack. Cooper's attorney, son, daughter, Governor Patterson, and other friends, fearful that he might commit a rash act in his agitated state, sought to calm him. By early afternoon, they seemed to have succeeded, but Carmack had learned of Cooper's outburst. Cooper apparently had decided to confront his adversary and have it out; he did not inform his family and associates of his intentions.

That afternoon, Cooper received a call from Governor Patterson requesting that he come to the mansion on North Seventh Avenue to discuss closing Democratic campaign headquarters. Accompanied by Robin, Cooper set out from his son's office on foot, travelling west along Union Avenue in the direction of Seventh. On the way, they met a friend, former Davidson County sheriff, John D. Sharp, who walked along with them.

---

[11]*Nashville Tennessean*, 9 November 1908. Zweibund is translated as duel alliance. "The Knight of the Sorrowful Figure" was probably written by editorial writer J. D. Anderson. See notes, Box 2, Folder 3, James Douglas Anderson Papers, Tennessee Historical Society Collection, Tennessee State Library and Archives, Nashville.

Cooper seemed in no hurry, dallying for a time to watch excavation for the Hermitage Hotel. Upon reaching the corner of Union and Seventh, instead of turning north toward the governor's mansion, he hesitated as if he were waiting for someone. Carmack, as was his custom, had left the *Tennessean* office on the corner of Church Street and Eighth Avenue. He walked east on Church and turned north on Seventh. About half way up the block, he met an acquaintance, Mrs. Charles H. Eastman; Carmack stopped, tipped his hat, and the two exchanged pleasantries.

Cooper, at the corner of Union and Seventh, spotted Carmack, crossed the street and hurried in the direction of the editor. As he rushed up, he raised his right hand, and according to Mrs. Eastman's later testimony, declared "well here you are all right. I have the drop on you now. You dastardly coward, you cowardly scoundrel, hiding behind that woman, are you? Get out from behind that woman!" Startled, Carmack drew back, reached for his gun and, after some fumbling, got it out of his pocket. Mrs. Eastman, sensing the danger, dashed through a gate out of the way. In panic, Carmack got off two shots, both of which hit Robin, who had rushed up and jumped in front of his father; one struck his shoulder and the other passed through a sleeve. Robin, however, was able to draw his pistol and fired three times at Carmack, all hitting the target, and, according to two expert witnesses, any one could have been fatal. The editor fell, lying dead in a gutter on Seventh Avenue north within sight of the Tennessee State Capitol Building.[12]

The news of the death of the editor sent shock waves across Tennessee and the nation. People were stunned by the event; there were feelings of intense grief intermingled with shame and humiliation that such a thing could happen. Some felt a sense of rage and fury. Certainly there were those in Tennessee whose minds were sufficiently open that they could view the killing with a rational perspective. Carmack, by carrying on a highly emotional and shrill crusade against the forces of "demon run," had polarized the issue of prohibition in the minds of many people. His devoted followers were therefore willing, if not eager, to believe that the shooting was a brutal, premeditated murder—the result of a conspiracy on the part of the liquor industry. Their anger focused upon Duncan Cooper who, along with Robin

---

[12]*Cooper v. State*, 63-72; Lanier, "The Carmack Murder Case," 274-75; Waller, *Nashville, 1900-1910*, 94-97.

and surprisingly, John D. Sharp, was soon arrested and arraigned for murder and held without bond.

The mood in Nashville was reflected by an editorial writer for the *Tennessean* who privately wrote that "people more conservative than I am . . . have told me [during] the past few hours that they have never seen anything like it—the public sentiment that there is against Cooper."[13] Sentiment was so intense that the authorities were fearful that a lynch mob would develop. The *Nashville Banner* wrote that Carmack's death caused such a "bitter feeling of wrath and excitement among his personal friends and political adherents" that "it was feared that this spirit of indignation would manifest itself in some form of attempted violence."[14]

Demonstrating responsible journalism, the *Nashville Banner* headlined the story and gave a balanced account of events attendant to Carmack's death. Reflecting concern over the agitated mood in Nashville, an editorial stated that "it is not the province of a public journal to pass judgment upon a case of this kind or to seek in any way to anticipate or determine the proper course of the full and impartial administration of the law. Its wiser function and duty is to do its part in allaying public excitement, admonishing against undue and prejudicial agitation and advising calmness and patience in the interest of law and order with a view of having justice rendered by the courts."[15]

The *Nashville Tennessean*, in contrast, deliberately tried to arouse public indignation with another essay in yellow journalism. The edition on the morning following the shooting carried a large picture of Carmack; the columns were bordered in black, signifying mourning. The lead headlines and subheads read: "Senator Carmack is Shot Down in Cold Blood; Editor of Tennessean Waylaid and Shot on The Way To His Room; Sen E. W. Carmack Assassinated By Col. Duncan B. Cooper And His Son, Robin; Murder Premeditated, Deliberately Planned and Executed in Cold-Blooded Style; Had Received Threats; Coopers Fire the First Shot and Kill Him Almost Instantly."

---

[13]J. D. Anderson to J. M. Anderson, 13 November 1908, Box 9, Folder 16, Anderson Papers.

[14]*Nashville Banner*, 10 November 1908.

[15]Ibid.

The article that followed declared that "Because He dared to oppose the might of the saloons in Tennessee, Edward Ward Carmack lies cold in death, and three gaping wounds cry out for vengeance on this murderers, Col. Duncan B. Cooper and his son, Robin Cooper. The killing was murder—cold-blooded, deliberate, premeditated, with every detail planned out beforehand; murder without justification; a dastardly crime without a parallel in the annals of the state." The newspaper also accused Governor Patterson with being a part of the conspiracy and therefore an accessory to the crime.[16] It cannot be known if the publisher and the entire staff of the newspaper fully agreed with what was written, but editorial writer James Douglas Anderson observed privately that "I believe that Duncan B. Cooper ought to be hanged by the neck until he is dead, dead, dead." Moreover, "it is the province of a newspaper to call for the enforcement of the law, to prevent any future repetition of such diabolical crimes as . . . the assassination of Ed Carmack."[17]

Perhaps with slightly less intensity, a number of newspapers across the state such as the Memphis *News-Scimitar*, Knoxville *Journal and Tribune*, Jackson *Whig*, and the Knoxville *Sentinel* echoed the *Tennessean's* sentiments. A few newspapers, notably the Memphis *Commercial Appeal* and the *American*, rejected the notion that the death of Carmack was an assassination and insisted that it was a street killing resulting from a political feud. The *American's* account of Carmack's death was fair as the newspaper sought to counter the *Tennessean's* attempt inflame the public. In an editorial two days after the tragedy, the *American* declared that

> the event calls for a plain discussion of a few points, in which much should be extenuated and naught set down in malice.
>
> Numerous and varied versions of the encounter which horrified the city and State have been given publicity. It is not our purpose to try to reconcile these conflicting accounts, to sift fact from fiction, to condemn or defend. Such is the province of the courts. Nor do we come to make a Mark Antony address to stir a mob to murder by saying one thing and meaning another.

---

[16]*Nashville Tennessean*, 10 November 1908.

[17]J. D. Anderson to J. M. Anderson, 13 November 1908, Box 9, Folder 16, Anderson Papers.

> Mr. Carmack was not "waylaid" and he was not "assassinated," in any legitimate sense of these words. He met his end in a street encounter in which he had a chance to kill as well as to be killed. He was not killed because he was a prohibitionist any more than he was killed for being a white man, and the manifest effort to make him a martyr to any cause is ridiculous even though the meeting of these men resulted in a fatality.

The newspaper concluded that "the killing was the result of Mr. Carmack's peculiar style of personal journalism." It was a "deplorable" event, but "it was not wholly surprising." The *Banner*, after the one editorial the day following the killing, remained silent and avoided the controversy.[18]

Not all prohibitionists took an extreme view of the tragedy. One, a minister and former Nashville resident, wrote that Carmack's death was not "the result of a deliberate conspiracy," and "prohibition had nothing to do" with it. Carmack, he said, "was slain in a street duel, for which both were prepared. . . . The Cause of prohibition gains nothing from such misrepresentation of recorded facts by overzealous advocates," he explained.[19]

The emotional reactions to the tragedy were expressed in a variety of ways. Cobey Carmack received hundreds of telegrams and letters of condolence from across Tennessee and the nation. Events attendant to the funeral gave vent to the widespread grief. Arrangements were made to ship the body by rail to Columbia for burial. At the Nashville station, a memorial service was held in the waiting room, and the casket was carried to the train between two rows of ladies from the Women's Christian Temperance Union who tossed white carnations on the casket. At Columbia the next day, funeral services were attended by hundreds. The following Sunday, dozens of memorial services were held all across Tennessee. Speakers at the services offered the same message: they urged their listeners to greater effort to achieve an early and complete end to the liquor traffic in Tennessee. The *Banner* observed that "these manifestations of popular grief and concern over the death of a prominent citizen are exceptional in the history of the state and constitute one of the most remarkable tributes ever paid by spon-

---

[18]*Nashville American*, 11 November 1908; Hugh Walker, "Robin Cooper's Pistol Ended Carmack's Life," *The Tennessean*, 26 April 1981.

[19]Undated newspaper clipping, Box 2, Folder 14, Governor Malcolm R. Patterson Papers, Tennessee State Library and Archives, Nashville.

taneous popular expression to any man of distinction in Tennessee." The opponents of "demon rum" had a martyr.[20]

The death of Carmack stimulated the prohibitionists to feverish activity to complete the agenda established by their late leader. The campaign to end the liquor traffic in Tennessee soon reached steamroller proportions. The crusade was encouraged by a screaming press across the state, but the leader was the *Tennessean* under Luke Lea, who took over editorial control soon after Carmack's death. The newspaper's editorial effort was almost hysterical as it damned Governor Patterson and his "machine" as well as the "liquor power" which allegedly controlled the state. The WTCU, the Anti-Saloon League, and prohibitionist denominations formed lobbying groups in preparation for the upcoming legislative session. Governor Patterson and the Democratic State Executive Committee girded for battle, but when the General Assembly met in January 1909, dry Democrats entered into an alliance with Republicans and mandatory statewide prohibition seemed to be within reach.[21]

Not far from the legislative halls, another drama began on 20 January—the murder trial of Duncan and Robin Cooper and John Sharp. The trial had aspects of both a comic opera and a kangaroo court. The Coopers, who pled self-defense, could not expect a fair hearing given the inflamed atmosphere and vengeful mood in Nashville. The prosecution was headed by the colorful and dramatic courtroom lawyer, District Attorney General Jeff McCarn. He was assisted by Guston T. Fitzhugh of Memphis, a friend of Carmack's, and Job G. Garner of Lawrenceburg. The defense was led by a former criminal court judge, John M. Anderson, brother of *Tennessean* editorial writer, James Douglas Anderson, and his associates, W. H. Washington and M. H. Meeks.[22] The presiding judge, William H. Hart, was a

---

[20]Telegrams and Correspondence, Box 3, Folder 33-39, Carmack Papers; Paul E. Isaac, *Prohibition and Politics: Turbulent Decades in Tennessee, 1885-1920* (Knoxville: University of Tennessee Press, 1965) 159; *Nashville Banner*, 16 November 1908.

[21]*Nashville Tennessean*, November 1908-February 1909, passim; Isaac, *Prohibition and Politics*, 159-63.

[22]Anderson's acceptance of the case caused conflict within the family. When J. D. Anderson learned that his brother might take the Coopers's case, he wired the judge, who was then vacationing in Colorado, to try to persuade him to refuse the case. J. M. Anderson responded that he would withhold judgment until he learned the facts, but "I can't believe that it was as you seem to think." Moreover, "I have always thought that Carmack was to [sic] personal and bitter in his writings and speeches." J. D. Anderson replied that Cooper

genial and fair jurist, but he was careful to avoid giving the impression of sympathy toward the defendants. Selection of the jury took over three weeks; it was difficult to find venire men who had neither heard of the Carmack killing nor had formed an opinion about it. The chief prosecutor had one prospective juror arrested for perjury when he swore that he had no opinion. Two men were removed from the jury because they had been charged with being habitual drunkards. Throughout the trial, the *Tennessean* regularly repeated the assertion that the killing was murder, the result of a conspiracy, and the state had a clear-cut case to prove it. The newspaper also played up a rumor that the district attorney general was the target of an assassination plot.[23]

When the taking of testimony finally began, the prosecution presented a parade of witnesses. The evidence offered by most was of nominal value and often contradictory, but three were especially important to the prosecutor's case. E. B. Craig insisted that Cooper's message to Carmack had included a death threat. A newsboy testified that he had overheard Cooper say a few moments before the killing something like "we will get him." The most damaging to the Coopers was Mrs. Eastman's testimony that the defendants were the aggressors and that Carmack was only defending himself. The defense was unable to destroy the credibility of any of the prosecution witnesses. Defense witnesses included Robin Cooper, who claimed that he had acted in self-defense, while his father testified that he had had no intention of physically harming the editor; rather, he had only wanted to warn Carmack to cease the abuse or he would expose his antagonist's true personal and private character. Cooper did not elaborate nor did the defense try to explain what he meant by the latter. The only important point that the defense was able to establish was that Carmack fired first.

The jury's opinion was in agreement with the prosecution's contention that Duncan Cooper had threatened Carmack's life and that both Duncan and Robin were the aggressors. Although Sharp was acquitted of complicity, both Coopers were found guilty of second degree murder and sentenced to twenty years each in prison. The verdict was received with mixed emo-

---

had "absolutely no defense" and besides, "a lawyer's first duty is to his country, rather than a friend." J. M. Anderson to J. D. Anderson, 10 November 1908, Box 10, Folder 12; J. D. Anderson to J. M. Anderson, 13 November 1908, Box 9, Folder 16, Anderson Papers.

[23]Waller, *Nashville, 1900-1910*, 99; Lanier, "The Carmack Murder Case," 276-77; Hugh Walker, "Carmack-Cooper Trial Shook State Politics," *The Tennessean*, 3 May 1981.

tions by prohibitionists and Carmack's loyal following. Because they were bitter and out for blood, the joy over the conviction was muted somewhat because of the light sentence. "Am so disappointed that it isn't 'first degree' " wrote one, while another observed that "the verdict was not as severe as it should have been."[24]

As the drama in the courtroom unfolded, the campaign in the General Assembly to legislate statewide prohibition gathered steam. Indeed, one event seemed to complement the other. The well-organized coalition of dry Democrats and Republicans pressed two measures: one to ban the manufacture of intoxicating beverages, and the other to ban sales by extending the Four Mile Law to the entire state. Antiadministration forces also pressed for passage of a measure requiring direct popular primaries as well as changes in the state and county elections commissions. The latter measure was designed to deprive the governor's organization of effective control of election machinery. Patterson's forces put up a stiff fight; in fact, twelve administration senators fled the state to break a quorum to prevent passage. They returned when it became apparent that the bill's sponsors intended to proceed despite the lack of a quorum.

The opponents of "demon rum" applied intense pressure on legislators to enact the prohibition measures. Temperance groups crowded legislative corridors, giving public prayers, singing hymns, and heckling "wet" legislators from the galleries. Such intimidation was effective, for both prohibition measures passed easily despite the governor's opposition. After passage of the act extending the Four Mile Law, members of the WCTU held thanksgiving services at the spot were Carmack was killed and then at the *Tennessean* office. Patterson vetoed both measures, but they were overridden with votes to spare. In addition, the prohibition forces succeeded in enacting several measures designed to suppress liquor advertising, to curb solicitation to buy or sell alcohol, and to assist in enforcing antiliquor laws. Finally, a joint resolution was passed that granted permission to the recently formed Carmack Memorial Association to erect a memorial to him on the grounds of the State Capitol. Eric Lacy noted that "Carmack's ghost" was a major factor in the success of the prohibition efforts in the legislative session. When the Senate overrode Patterson's veto of the extension of the

---

[24]Ibid.; *Cooper v. State*, 63-73; Della Dortch to Cobey Carmack, 20 March 1909; Goulding Marr to Cobey Carmack, 20 March 1909, Box 3, Folder 14, Carmack Papers.

Four Mile Law, the *Tennessean* reported that a senator rose and declared: "I would to God that the immortal Carmack might open his eyes, and realize the enactment into law of that principle for which he sacrificed his life." The newspaper then noted that "at the mention of the magic name of Carmack a deathly silence pervaded the Senate Chamber and it required no far flight of imagination to picture the dead Knight of the White Banner looking from the pearly portals of heaven into the arena where vengeance was being wrought upon the traffic that claimed his life."[25]

Despite the cheers of happiness and songs of thanksgiving over the simultaneous victories in the enactment of statewide prohibition and the convictions of the Coopers, the final scenes of both dramas were yet to be played. The next act in the courtroom drama moved to the Tennessee Supreme Court which had agreed to review the case. It was argued before the high court in December 1909, and, after some apparent agonizing, the court handed down its decision in April 1910. In a three-to-two decision, the justices granted Robin Cooper a new trial on the grounds that the trial judge had erred in not giving three instructions to the jury in regard to Robin's intent as well as his right to defend himself. However, the conviction of Duncan Cooper was upheld, again by a three-to-two decision. The majority of the justices reasoned that Cooper had threatened Carmack and the latter could rightly expect bodily harm, giving Carmack a right to defend himself with force when he saw Cooper approach with his raised hand. In effect, the court held that under Tennessee law Cooper had wrongfully provoked the confrontation and was, therefore, responsible for Carmack's death, even though he had not fired a shot or even drawn his gun.

Attention shifted to the governor's mansion. It is possible, if not probable, that Governor Patterson had pardons prepared for both Coopers, for within minutes after the Supreme Court's decision was announced, he issued a pardon for Duncan Cooper. He declared that "in my opinion, neither of the defendants is guilty and they have not had a fair and impartial trial, but were convicted contrary to the law and evidence. . . . The proof showed that Robin killed the deceased and that Duncan B. Cooper did not fire a shot; without reflection upon the court it is inconceivable to my mind

---

[25]Isaac, *Prohibition and Politics*, 153-69; Eric Russell Lacy, "Tennessee Teetotalism: Social Forces and the Politics of Progressivism," *Tennessee Historical Quarterly* 24 (Fall 1965): 219-40; Walker, "Carmack-Cooper Trial."

and repugnant to every principle of justice that a man should be found guilty of murder who was not in a conspiracy to kill, and who, in fact, did not kill." Patterson was also quoted as saying that "right is right no matter what the public may think," a statement indicating that he realized the political implications of his action.[26]

The governor's action was not unexpected as prohibitionists and antiprohibition groups had long assumed that Patterson would pardon the Coopers. Many agreed with the cynical view expressed by a small-town west-state newspaper that declared soon after Carmack's death that "it is always understood that any man killing another who is attacking the railroad-whisky interests in this state will be afforded ample protection by the powers that be, and we have no doubt that Cooper's pardon is as good as written out." The state press, with the *Tennessean* leading the pack, almost unanimously denounced the pardon as a shame and a disgrace, a scandal, and an unspeakable travesty of justice. The *Tennessean* headlined the court's decision and the pardon and devoted five front-page articles to the stories. One was headlined "Hurry-up Pardon of Cooper Has No Precedent; Hundreds of Telegrams Sent Governor—Burned in Effigy." A block on the front page contained a poem by Rudyard Kipling entitled *Cleared*. The first two stanzas read:

> "Cleard," honorable gentlemen. Be thankful it's no more:
> The widow's curse is on your house, the dead are at your door.

The last read: "We are not ruled by murderers, but only by their friends." An editorial under the title "Disgraced" declared that "Honest Tennesseans hang their heads in shame when they are forced to admit they are citizens of the state of which Patterson is the Governor."[27]

Patterson, by freeing Cooper, gave his most bitter newspaper foe additional ammunition for its crusade to destroy his administration; the *Tennessean* lost no time in exploiting the issue. Patterson's pardon record was revived. For weeks, the newspaper continued to cite figures to prove that the governor had pardoned more felons than any previous chief executive,

---

[26]*Cooper v. State*, 37-231; Lanier, "The Carmack Murder Case," 272-85; Waller, *Nashville, 1900-1910*, 90-101; Walker, "Carmack-Cooper Trial."

[27]Newspaper clippings, Box 7, clipping portfolio, Volume 12, Carmack Papers.

and that his record compared unfavorably with governors from other states. The *Tennessean* asserted that Tennessee "prosecuting officers prosecute; its juries convict; and in most cases its judges impose sentences in keeping with the offenses committed." Yet felons were able to obtain pardons easily. The newspaper stated that "there had grown up in Tennessee a pardon industry" and "close friends of Governor Patterson are pocketing big fees on the pardons he grants so easily." The evidence presented by the *Tennessean* was selective, but its efforts to create a negative image of the governor were nevertheless effective.

The Cooper pardon was sensational news across the country. Although there were a few exceptions, the nation's press condemned the governor's action as a "miscarriage of justice," "disruptive of judicial processes," or "murder made no crime." The national press also condemned Patterson for excessive use of executive clemency, undoubtedly because of the *Tennessean's* emphasis on the governor's pardon record. The *Literary Digest* summarized the nation's reaction in an article entitled "Tennessee's 'Pardon Governor,' " and noted that Patterson "has few apologists." A few months later, another nationally circulated magazine published an article reflecting the widespread view of Patterson as a "high handed" political boss who pardoned excessively.[28]

The nation's opinion of Patterson was far less important than the political repercussions in the state. The pardoning of Cooper affected the Supreme Court. Rumors contended that while the tribunal was considering the Cooper case, the governor was trying to influence the decision with political pressure. When the State Democratic Executive Committee set a primary to nominate candidates for the Supreme Court, three justices—John Knight Shields, Matthew Marshall Neil, and William Dwight Beard—refused to enter, giving as their reason the governor's interference in the judicial process. It was never fully established that Patterson attempted to influence the decision, but the rumors undoubtedly embarrassed the justices. The three justices and two additional candidates entered the race for the Supreme Court as independents, and in the general election in

---

[28]Ibid.; "Tennessee's 'Pardon Governor,' " *The Literary Digest* 10 (30 April 1910): 859-60; R. E. Pritchard, "The Revolution in Tennessee," *Harper's Weekly* (26 November 1910) 9, 26.

August 1910, the independent slate, running on a "Free and untrammeled judiciary" platform, won.[29]

In the gubernatorial race, Governor Patterson declared as a candidate for reelection to a third term. When the Supreme Court overturned the compulsory direct popular primary enacted during the previous session of the General Assembly, the Democratic Executive Committee set a delegated primary for June 1910 to nominate the party candidate for governor. In a light turnout in which prohibitionists refused to vote, the governor received the regular Democratic nod. Then in August, the independent judiciary slate, with prohibitionist and Republican support, defeated the regular Democratic candidates by a large majority. To add to Patterson's woes, many of the antiprohibitionists had come to regard the governor as a liability to their cause.

Republicans nominated as gubernatorial candidate Ben Wade Hooper, an East Tennessee attorney from Newport who was a prohibitionist. It became increasingly apparent that a coalition of independent, or dry Democrats, and Republicans was forming behind him. Facing inevitable defeat in the general election in November, Patterson withdrew from the race in mid-September. He appealed to the party to unite behind a compromise candidate. The party chose the popular Senator Robert L. Taylor, a harmony candidate twice before. The regular Democracy also adopted a platform that equivocated somewhat on the issue of prohibition. However, Patterson's withdrawal came too late, for the party was now hopelessly split. Dry Democrats regarded Taylor as the administration's candidate and refused to endorse him. Independent Democrats led by Luke Lea, Edward Bushrod Stahlman, and other leaders across the state coalesced behind the Republican candidate who won handily in November. For only the second time since the Civil War, a Republican was elected governor of Tennessee.[30]

Historian Arthur S. Link observed that "Edward Ward Carmack was a more powerful factor in Tennessee politics in death than he had ever been in life" because the "political character of his assassination gave the prohibition movement exactly the impetus that it needed for successful

---

[29]Isaac, *Prohibition and Politics*, 182-94; Lacy, "Tennessee Teetotalism," 232-34; Lanier, "The Carmack Murder Case," 280-282.

[30]Ibid.; Russell L. Stockard, "The Election and First Administration of Ben W. Hooper as Governor of Tennessee," *East Tennessee Historical Society's Publications* 26 (1954): 42-51.

achievement."[31] Link might have added that in death, Carmack also brought about the downfall of Governor Patterson. But Carmack's legacy went far beyond the enactment of prohibition and the downfall of a governor. He left behind personal tragedy, turmoil, and confusion over enforcement of prohibition, a hopelessly divided Democratic party, and a climate that made it impossible for the state of Tennessee to consider, much less adopt, urgently needed progressive reforms. Few men in the history of the Volunteer State have had as much influence in death as Carmack.

---

[31] Arthur S. Link, "Democratic Politics and the Presidential Campaign of 1912 in Tennessee," *East Tennessee Historical Society's Publications* 18 (1946): 109.

10

THE LEGACY

At 11:00 A.M. on 6 June 1925, a memorial to Edward Ward Carmack was unveiled on the south lawn of the State Capitol—a full-length statue in bronze by Nancy Cox McCormack, a talented Nashville sculptor. Carmack's tribute to the South, the closing remarks of his address before the United States House of Representatives in 1898 in defense of his right to retain a seat in that body, was inscribed on the base. After more than sixteen years, the goal of the Carmack Memorial Association had reached fruition. The ceremony was solemn but colorful. The grounds were decorated with banners, penants, and flowers, bands provided music, and a large crowd that included political dignitaries, members of the Women's Christian Temperance Union, and Confederate veterans, was on hand

Publisher Luke Lea, on behalf of the association, presented the statue to the state; receiving it, ironically, was Governor Austin Peay, Malcolm Patterson's campaign manager in the gubernatorial contest in 1908. Carmack thus entered the select company of only a few illustrious Tennesseans honored with a memorial on the capitol grounds: Presidents Andrew Jackson and James Knox Polk and the boy hero of the Confederacy, Sam Davis.[1]

---

[1] *Nashville Banner*, 6 June 1925. There were several other markers on the grounds and a small memorial to Governor Neil S. Brown. A memorial to World War I hero Alvin C. York was erected later.

The dedicatory address at the unveiling ceremony was given by Guston T. Fitzhugh, a Memphis attorney, a personal and political friend to Carmack, and an associate in the prosecution of Duncan and Robin Cooper. The speaker made no attempt to identify the accomplishments of Carmack and mentioned only briefly his journalistic and political careers. Rather, appropriately perhaps, Fitzhugh extolled the virtues and character of his subject. Carmack, he declared, was brilliant, courageous, and a great man. His greatness, according to the speaker, lay in his loyalty to principle; he was loyal to his party but he placed patriotism above party. Carmack, he said, hated sham and hypocrisy; he had a reverence for tradition and the ideals of the Old South; he was a builder of character and an inspiration to struggling young men; he was an example of honesty, industry, fair dealing, love of God, and love of fellowmen. Carmack was, Fitzhugh insisted, the "knightliest of men." The speaker failed to mention the martyred editor's other traits: stubbornness, contentiousness, mental rigidity, and impatience with restraint. Fitzhugh's eulogy reinforced an image of the late journalist politician which was already well established. Shortly after Carmack's death, the *Nashville American* made a poignant prediction that the editor's "fame will endure in tradition if not in history." Carmack did indeed become a legend, and to many Tennesseans, a symbol of all the virtues in the perfect American character.[2]

Whether there was sufficient reason in the life and career of Carmack to warrant honoring his memory with a memorial in the company of such Tennessee sons as Jackson and Polk is, perhaps, a moot issue. He was in any case a remarkable figure who wielded a great deal of influence in public affairs in the state during his lifetime and for many years beyond. Carmack had a charismatic quality that attracted staunch friendships and devoted followers. As the *Nashville Banner* observed, "there was something chivalric in Senator Carmack's temperament that strengthened the warm admiration in which he was regarded. He had notably that spirit and dash, that fearless onslaught which made his warmest admirers who sought historic parallels class him as a Rupert, but he had also a kindliness of heart, urbanity of manner and strong sympathies that would have graced a gentler character."

---

[2]*Nashville American*, 11 November 1908. For Fitzhugh's complete address, see *Nashville Tennessean*, 7 June 1925; Paul Franklin Bumpus, *Carmack: The Edward Ward Carmack Story* (Franklin: Paul Franklin Bumpus, 1977) 242-51.

Carmack was an intense man "and yet it was this intenseness that drew his friends to him with" strong bonds. He was a superb writer and public speaker whose serious effort was "exalted both in thought and diction." He also "had a marked faculty for invective and ridicule. . . . His thrusts were very keen and his satire and irony often provocative, and he possessed a decided originality of expression that gave exceptional point to his satiric humor."

The *Banner* also noted that he sometimes used invective and ridicule "too freely." Because he was relentless and sometimes vindictive toward his opponents, he made bitter enemies. More important, Carmack was a crusader and a polemist. As the *Banner* suggested, he "was of an uncompromising nature; there was no half-way ground to his affections." Once he seized a cause, Carmack so polarized the issues involved that compromise or consensus in public policy was difficult, if not impossible, to achieve.³

Carmack's true place in Tennessee history was not as a symbol of virtue nor as the leader who brought about the end of the liquor traffic in the state. He was an interpreter of cultural patterns who, as a journalist and politician, both reinforced established values, beliefs, and norms, and brought about social change by setting the issues on the social agenda. Carmack was a product of an era when brutal newspaper attacks were common. It was an age when print journalism monopolized the news media but competition within the medium was intense. He was typical of the dynamic and aggressive journalists of the nineteenth and early twentieth centuries who became popular political leaders, a breed that died with the advent of the electronic media and with changes in the structure and organization of print journalism. He was the most prominent Tennessee editor of his day and certainly one of the most outstanding produced in the Volunteer State.

As a journalist and a political leader, Carmack was an eloquent spokesman for the more conservative values and beliefs. As much as anyone of his generation, he perpetuated the romantic myths of the Old South and glorified the Southern ethos. Whereas he contributed to establishing the myth of the Lost Cause, he was one of those who helped bring about the final reconciliation between the North and the South. Carmack was a leader in the running battle against the threat to the established social, political, and economic patterns by the agrarian radicals of the late nineteenth cen-

---

³*Nashville Banner*, 9 November 1908.

tury. He led in setting the agenda for free and unlimited coinage of silver. The free-silver crusade failed but Carmack used the issue to win a seat in Congress.

The most significant issue championed by Carmack was prohibition. He had ridiculed the movement early in his editorial career, but after his defeat in the senatorial contest in 1906, he seized the liquor issue and quickly became the unquestioned leader in the crusade for prohibition. After Patterson's victory in the gubernatorial primary in 1908, Carmack returned to journalism to continue the fight against "demon rum" and was shrill in his editorial attacks on both his political opponents and the opponents of prohibition. Indeed, it seems that Carmack deliberately tried to taunt his enemies into violent retaliation. His death was the catalyst that hastened legislation to end the liquor traffic in Tennessee. However, the harshness of his crusade, the nature of his death, and his martyrdom left a legacy of personal tragedy for those around him.

Carmack left a widow with a ten-year-old son, Edward Ward Carmack, Jr. Obsessed with public issues and his role in public affairs, the elder Carmack had not been concerned with wealth or the accumulation of material goods. He had no estate and Cobey Carmack was left penniless. However, she was hardly destitute, for relatives on both sides of the family were able to provide at least the minimum of material needs. Moreover, Carmack's friends, as well as some of his opponents, were prepared to come to his widow's assistance. Early in 1909, most of the Tennessee delegation to Congress joined a movement to secure for her the appointment as postmistress at Columbia. Although she desired the position, Cobey Carmack tried to avoid the appearance of seeking the job. She wanted it to seem that the appointment was made to honor the memory of her late husband. However, Lemuel Phillips Padgett, congressman from the seventh district, the district in which Columbia was located, apparently had already committed to another individual, and he blocked Cobey's appointment. Even Carmack's widow could not avoid controversy. Cobey did receive the position four years later, when President Thomas Woodrow Wilson bypassed the patronage logjam and made her postmistress by direct appointment.[4]

---

[4]Correspondence, Box 3, Folder 41-42, The Edward Ward Carmack Papers, Southern Historical Collection, University of North Carolina, Chapel Hill.

Ned Carmack, Jr., spent his life in the shadow of the tragedy of his father's death. Like his elder, Ned was brilliant and eloquent in both the written and spoken word. He became an attorney, a journalist, and a politician, but he was never able to match the senior Carmack's success. As a young man, Ned was a trifle wild, something of a playboy, and once in college was disciplined for academic reasons. What prominence he achieved in public life was based on the magic name of Carmack rather than talent. In 1942, he came close to success when he ran for the Democratic senatorial nomination against Senator Tom Stewart. The deciding factor was the large vote that turned out for the lackluster incumbent by the Shelby County political machine of Edward Hull Crump. Ned Carmack tried again for the Senate in 1946, but was swamped by the venerable old Senator Kenneth McKellar. In his later years, Ned became something of a recluse with a reputation as an eccentric, subcumbing to a dependency upon alcohol.[5]

Carmack's death haunted the Cooper family. Duncan Cooper was pardoned and the prosecution, for various reasons, eventually dropped the charges against Robin. Nevertheless, the stigma of allegedly having committed an "assassination" remained. In 1919, Robin Cooper disappeared mysteriously and his murdered body was found a few days later. Twenty-one-year-old Ned Carmack was a suspect, but his alibi convinced the authorities that he had had nothing to do with it. Nonetheless, because the police were never able to locate the guilty party or parties, there were those who believed that young Carmack had avenged his father's killing. Moreover, when Duncan Cooper died in 1922 of natural causes, some assumed that Ned was responsible. A legend developed that young Carmack climbed through the window and suffocated the helpless old man with a pillow. In his later years, Ned Carmack, Jr., took pleasure in subtly encouraging the belief that he had been responsible for the deaths of both Duncan and Robin Cooper.[6]

The prohibition crusade and the circumstances surrounding Carmack's death also plagued Governor Patterson. Whether Carmack's campaign to destroy the governor and his organization would have been successful under normal circumstances can never be known, but the editor's death and the subsequent newspaper campaign against Patterson were

---

[5]Hugh Walker, "Ned Carmack Claimed Revenge," *The Tennessean*, 10 May 1981.

[6]Ibid.

certainly factors in his ultimate political demise. Patterson became one of Tennessee's most maligned governors with an undeserved image of villainy that obscured a reasonably successful progressive administration and forced him to withdraw from the governor's race in 1910. In 1913, he was embarrassed when found intoxicated in a raid on a house of prostitution in Nashville. Shortly thereafter, he gave up liquor, converted to prohibition, and became a paid lecturer for the Anti-Saloon League. He tried a political comeback in 1932 when he ran for the Democratic gubernatorial nomination with, ironically, the support of Luke Lea's organization. He came in a poor third in a three-way race.[7]

The satisfaction felt by the opponents of "demon run" in achieving statewide prohibition soon turned to frustration. Enforcement, especially in the cities, proved to be difficult as evasions of the law were flagrant and widespread. For several years, enforcement was the chief issue and from time to time, the General Assembly enacted legislation aimed at bringing about compliance. In 1915, for example, the legislature provided for the ouster of public officials who failed to enforce the liquor statutes, but the measure was no more effective than other acts. The ratification of the Eighteenth Amendment to the United States Constitution in 1919, which provided for the end of the liquor traffic nationwide, had no significant impact in the Volunteer State. In the 1920s, Tennessee was one of the nation's leading producers of "moonshine" whisky. The nation gave up its noble experiment in 1933 by repealing the Eighteenth Amendment and within a few years, Tennessee also abandoned its efforts to achieve complete prohibition, legalizing beer and providing for local option on other liquors. Although most rural counties chose to remain dry, the cities gradually became wet once again. Thus, within thirty years all of the efforts of Carmack and the prohibitionists were nullified. Carmack's crusade and martyrdom had come to naught.[8]

The prohibition movement and Carmack's martyrdom caused confusion and turmoil in Tennessee. The nationally circulated *Independent* observed in 1910 that:

---

[7]Paul E. Isaac, *Prohibition and Politics: Turbulent Decades in Tennessee 1885-1920* (Knoxville: University of Tennessee Press, 1965) 220n.

[8]Ibid.; Eric Russell Lacy, "Tennessee Teetotalism: Social Forces and the Politics of Progressivism," *Tennessee Historical Quarterly* 24 (Fall 1965): 229-40.

To the outside world Tennessee doubtless seems a State gone mad. She has for the last five years been the victim of nearly every imaginable political hysteria. The results have been far-reaching and deplorable. Business and social life have been disorganized. Families and churches have been disrupted, while government has become a mockery. Every branch of government has been prostituted by one faction or another to the uses of partisan politics. The law has become a jest and municipal governments and judicial officers have actually been elected for the express purpose of nullifying statutes. A candid view of the future inspires little hope for immediate improvement.[9]

The editorial expressed a view of Tennessee that was undoubtedly biased by the *Tennessean*'s vituperative campaign against Governor Patterson, but the *Independent*'s interpretation of conditions in the Volunteer State was only slightly exaggerated. Tennessee was indeed in turmoil and the Democratic party was split asunder. In 1910 independent prohibitionist Democrats joined Republicans in a fusionist movement to elect Ben W. Hooper governor. The legislative session of 1911 was one of intense conflict between the minority regulars and the fusionists, but the insurgents were able to elect one of their own, Luke Lea, to the Senate to replace James B. Frazier. The fusionist alliance held firm again in 1912 and Hooper was returned to the governor's office. By 1914, the regulars had accepted prohibition and a semblance of unity returned. The Democracy elected governors in 1914, 1916, and 1918. As the party remained preoccupied with the liquor issue, other vital problems were ignored, resulting in prohibition becoming synonymous with progressive reform in Tennessee.

In the first decade of the twentieth century, the nation was swept by the progressive reform movement. Although progressivism did not lend itself to an easy definition, the movement was largely urban and middle class and was led by reformers who were concerned with such issues as corruption in politics, concentration of wealth, and a wide variety of social problems. Early on, Tennessee, no less than other states, was caught in the mood of the times, and the drive for social and political reforms was especially strong in the state's urban centers. Various groups in Tennessee worked for women's suffrage, to improve education, and to conserve natural resources.

---

[9]"Politics of Hysteria in Tennessee," *Independent* (22 September 1910): 263-64.

Many urged that business enterprise, especially companies providing public services, be regulated by expanding the power and increasing the responsibilities of the Railroad Commission which had been established in 1897. Others insisted that Tennessee's most critical problem in need of remedy was an outdated constitution that propagated an inadequate revenue system and an inefficient and wasteful state government.

By the first administration of Malcolm Patterson, various groups were openly espousing progressivism and policymakers were beginning to listen to the reformers. The progressives, according to George Brown Tindall, were "the successors and heirs of the Bourbons, who preserved tradition under the rubric of reform." Carmack, philosophically a Bourbon conservative, was unable to reconcile tradition with innovation; he was no reformer and, therefore, not in tune with the times. He was especially opposed to a more paternalistic government, a requirement implicit in many of the progressive demands. Voting patterns in the senatorial primary in 1906 indicate that his image as a conservative may have been an important factor in his defeat by Robert L. Taylor. Similar patterns in 1908 suggest that his lack of commitment to progressivism militated against him in the gubernatorial contest with Patterson.[10]

Carmack was, however, a progressive on two issues: disfranchising blacks and prohibition. Many Southern progressives advocated depriving blacks of the vote and segregating them socially as a means of purifying politics, while to others "prohibition became the sum of progressivism." Carmack was an advocate of disfranchisement of the blacks, but he was unable to generate enough enthusiasm in Tennessee to achieve the goal by statute. On the liquor question, he was less concerned with it as a moral issue than as a means to defeat his personal and political enemies, and he, more than any single individual, made the whisky issue the sum of progressivism in Tennessee. So while neighboring states enacted labor reforms, workman's compensation laws, election reform and tax reform, improved public health and education, and provided for corporate regulation, Tennessee was primarily involved in attempts to stamp out the liquor traffic. Although minor

---

[10]William D. Miller, *Memphis During the Progressive Era, 1900-1917* (Memphis: Memphis State University Press, 1957); J. M. Shahan, "The Rhetoric of Reform: The 1906 Gubernatorial Race in Tennessee," *Tennessee Historical Quarterly* 35 (Spring 1976): 65; George Brown Tindall, *The Persistent Tradition in New South Politics* (Baton Rouge: Louisiana State University Press, 1975) 1-23.

progress was achieved in some areas, education for example, reform was virtually ignored after 1909.

Business regulation was debated, but it was not until 1919 that the power and jurisdiction of the Railroad Commission was significantly increased. Proposed election reforms were ignored for many years. Not until 1923 and Austin Peay's business-progressive administration were these concerns effectively addressed. Thus, because of Carmack's shrill crusade for prohibition, the circumstances of his death, and his martyrdom, the editor-politician promoted divisiveness in Tennessee, draining the state of its energies and diverting its enthusiasm from other reforms.[11]

Edward Ward Carmack was a brilliant journalist who set issues on the social agenda. He became a symbol of virtue in character and success in a moral crusade, but he also left a legacy of tragedy, bitterness, hatred, political upheaval, and distracted Tennessee from attempting to cope with a host of social, economic, and political problems in the early twentieth century.

---

[11]Jack Temple Kirby, *Darkness at the Dawning: Race and Reform in the Progressive South* (Philadelphia: J. B. Lippincott Company, 1972); Dewey W. Grantham, *The Regional Imagination: The South and Recent American History* (Nashville: Vanderbilt University Press, 1979) 77-106; George Brown Tindall, *The Emergence of the New South, 1913-1945*, Vol. 10, *A History of the South*, ed. Wendell Holmes Stephenson and E. Merton Coulter (Baton Rouge: Louisiana State University Press, 1967) 18; Wallace McClure, "Governmental Reorganization, A Consitutional Need in Tennessee," *Tennessee Historical Magazine* 2 (1916): 89-97; Franklin O. Rouse, "The Historical Background of Tennessee's Administrative Reorganization Act of 1923," *East Tennessee Historical Society's Publications* 8 (1936): 104-20.

PICTORIAL ARCHIVES

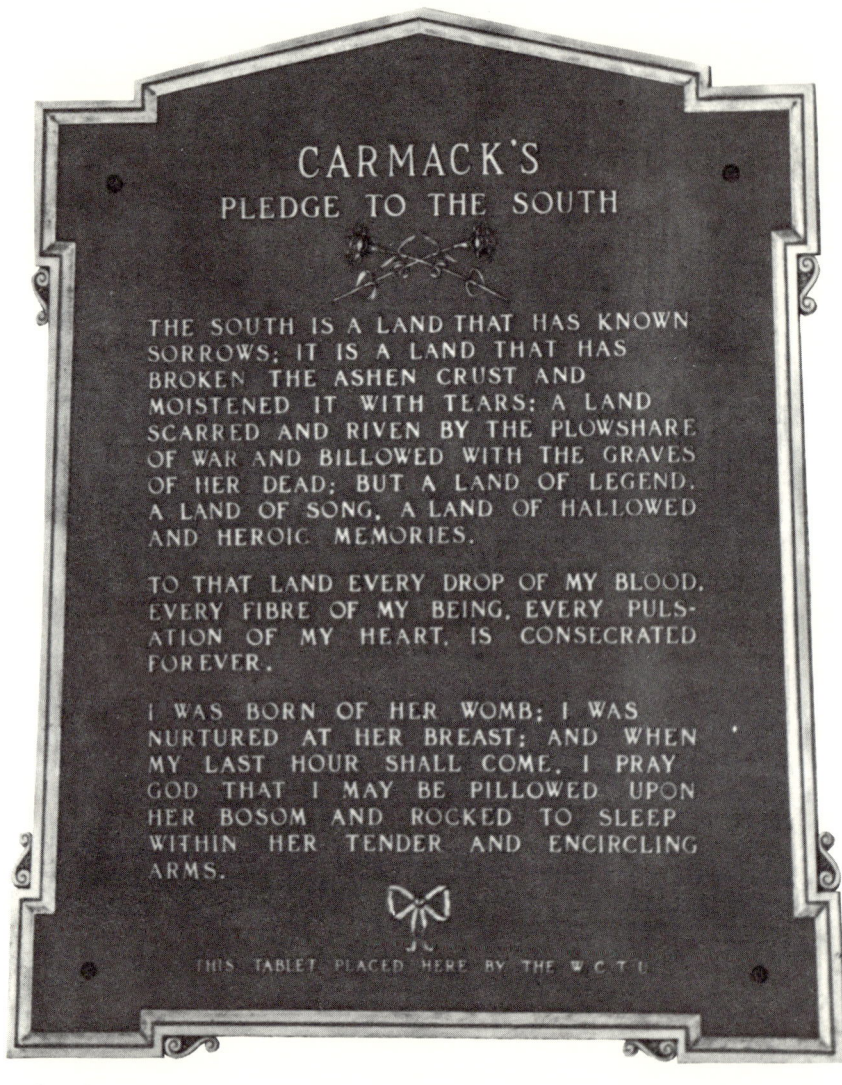

Edward Ward Carmack's "Pledge to the South" engraved on a plaque at the base of his statue on the grounds of the State Capitol in Nashville.

Senator Edward Ward Carmack (Tennessee State Library and Archives, Nashville)

Senator Carmack and his son in the front yard of their home in Columbia, Tennessee. This picture appeared in Harper's Weekly, 29 June 1907. (Library, University of North Carolina, Chapel Hill)

Portrait of Edward Ward Carmack (date unknown)

Colonel Duncan Brown Cooper (Tennessee State Library and Archives)

Senator William Brimage Bate (Tennessee State Library and Archives)

Senator Isham Green Harris (Tennessee State Library and Archives)

Senator Robert Love Taylor (Tennessee State Library and Archives)

Governor Malcolm Rice Patterson (Tennessee State Library and Archives)

Governor Benton McMillin (Tennessee State Library and Archives)

Senator James Beriah Frazier (Tennessee State Library and Archives)

The Dunnington family home in Columbia, Tennessee, where Cobey Dunnington Carmack lived after her husband's death. The building now houses a funeral parlor and mortuary.

Portrait of Edward Ward Carmack in 1902 (The Tennessean)

Front page of the Nashville Tennessean, 10 November 1908.

View of the statue of Edward Ward Carmack, facing south on the south lawn of the State Capitol in Nashville.

BIBLIOGRAPHICAL ESSAY

It would be superfluous and pedantic to list every source examined in research for this book, or for that matter all cited in the notes. Many sources were consulted and a great deal proved to be redundant, or of little or no value. The following is a selected bibliography containing the principal sources that contributed significantly to the narrative.

MANUSCRIPTS

The most pertinent information came from manuscript collections. Most valuable was, of course, the Edward Ward Carmack Papers in the Southern Historical Collection, University of North Carolina Library, Chapel Hill. Although the collection contains a large volume of correspondence received, there are numerous copies of Carmack's letters and writings as well as documents. The collection also contains a large number of newspaper clippings in both scrapbooks and portfolios. Another collection of Carmack's papers is in the Tennessee State Library and Archives in Nashville, the Edward Ward Carmack Correspondence, but it contains only two items. The Franc M. Carmack Diaries, Southern Historical Collection, University of North Carolina, Chapel Hill, are valuable for information on Carmack's father and ancestors.

Several collections of papers of political leaders and prominent individuals bear on Carmack and his period. A rewarding collection is the James Douglas Anderson Papers, Tennessee Historical Society Collection, Tennessee State Library and Archives. Anderson was a writer, journalist, and a Carmack loyalist who served with him as an editorial writer. The Duncan Brown Cooper Papers, Tennessee State Library and Archives, has a few useful items but reveals little about Cooper and his family. The papers of Tennessee's governors are on deposit in the Tennessee State Library and Archives. Although generally disappointing, the papers of Governors Robert L. Taylor, Benton McMillin, James B. Frazier, John I. Cox, and Malcolm R. Patterson contain a few items relative to Carmack and provide some insights into the era. A few letters in the Jones Family Papers, Tennessee State Library and Archives, the correspondence of a prominent Bolivar, Tennessee, family, relate to the subject, and the Robert H. Cartmell Diaries in the same depository contain interesting observations on Carmack and the times by a Madison County farmer.

NEWSPAPERS AND MAGAZINES

Newspapers, most of which are on microfilm in the Tennessee State Library and Archives, constitute an important source of information on Carmack and his times. The journals he edited—the *Nashville Democrat*, March-November 1888, the *Nashville American*, 1888-1892, the Memphis *Commercial*, 1892-1894, the Memphis *Commercial Appeal*, 1894-1895, and the *Nashville Tennessean*, August-November 1908—reveal Carmack's journalistic and editorial style. Many issues of the short-lived *Democrat* and the first few months of Carmack's tenure on the *Commercial* are missing. Carmack began his career in journalism in Columbia, Tennessee, in the mid-1880s as an editor or editorial writer. Unfortunately, there are no extant copies of his early journalistic efforts. There are, however, occasional references to Carmack in surviving copies of the Columbia *Herald* and Columbia *Herald and Mail*, as well as to Webb's school, Cobey Dunnington and her family, and Duncan Cooper. Beyond Carmack's tenure as an editor, the *Nashville American*, 1886-1910, the *Commercial Appeal*, 1895-1910, and the *Nashville Tennessean*, 1908-1910, were examined selectively as were the Memphis *Appeal-Avalanche*, 1892-1894, and the *Nashville Banner*, 1888-1910. Perusal of two small-town newspapers, the *Shelbyville Gazette*, 1898-1906, and the *Manchester Times*, 1902-1906, was profitable.

The newspaper clipping collection in the Carmack Papers was a rich source of information because items came from a wide range of journals: small-town weeklies and major dailies in Tennessee as well as papers beyond the state. Selective runs were made in the *New York Times*, 1897-1910, the *Washington Post*, 1898-1910, the New York *Daily Tribune*, 1902-1908, and the Louisville *Courier-Journal*, 1888-1910. Two denominational newspapers in Tennessee, the *Baptist and Reflector*, 1906-1908, and the *Christian Advocate*, 1898-1908, were examined selectively. Nationally circulated magazines occasionally mentioned Carmack and social and political conditions in Tennessee. Selective examination of *Harper's Weekly*, the *Independent*, *The Literary Digest*, and *The Review of Reviews* between 1900 and 1910 produced several useful articles.

PUBLIC DOCUMENTS

Carmack's speeches, remarks, and voting record in Congress are in the *Congressional Record*, 55th-59th Congress, 1897-1907. The detailed state Supreme Court review of the Cooper-Sharp murder trial is in *Cooper v. State*, 123 Tennessee (1910) 37-231.

BOOKS, ARTICLES, and THESES

There are any number of brief biographical sketches of Edward Ward Carmack and all are strongly sympathetic, superficial, and repetitious of detail. A chapter in Kenneth McKellar, *Tennessee Senators As Seen By One of Their Successors* (Kingsport: Southern Publishers, Inc., 1942), concerns Carmack. Although biased and containing errors of fact, McKellar's volume is useful for sketches of the lives of other United States senators of the Carmack era. A short sketch of Carmack's life is in Paul Franklin Bumpus, *Carmack: The Edward Ward Carmack Story* (Franklin: Paul Franklin Bumpus, 1977). It is a valuable collection of the editor's speeches and editorials. The life and death of Carmack and the murder trial are traced in a series of articles by Hugh Walker in the *The Tennessean*, 19, 26 April, 3, 10, 24 May 1981. The latter two are useful for details on the lingering effects of Carmack's death and the murder trial of Duncan and Robin Cooper and Ned Carmack, Jr.

Two biographies, Robert E. Hooper, *Crying in the Wilderness: A Biography of David Lipscomb* (Nashville: David Lipscomb College, 1979), and Laurence McMillin, *The Schoolmaker: Shawney Webb and the Bell Buckle Story* (Chapel Hill: University of North Carolina Press, 1971), bear on Carmack's family and youth. A good description of the political environment in Memphis in the 1890s and Carmack as an editor in that city is in Thomas Harrison Baker, *The Memphis Commerical Appeal: The History of a Southern Newspaper* (Baton Rouge: Louisiana State University Press, 1971). Clyde J. Faries, "Carmack vs. Patterson: The Genesis of a Political Feud," *Tennessee Historical Quarterly* 38 (Fall 1979): 334-47, examines the 1896 congressional race. A good analysis of the Carmack murder trial is in Robert H. Lanier, "The Carmack Murder Case," *Tennessee Historical Quarterly* 40 (Fall 1981): 272-85.

There is a wealth of interpretive material on Tennessee in the post-Reconstruction era. Two are especially important: the older Daniel Merritt Robison, *Bob Taylor and the Agrarian Revolt in Tennessee* (Chapel Hill: University of North Carolina Press, 1935), and Roger L. Hart, *Redeemers, Bourbons and Populists: Tennessee, 1865-1900* (Baton Rouge: Louisiana State University Press, 1975); the latter provides an incisive revisionist treatment. East Tennessee Republicans are described in Gordon B. McKinney, *Southern Mountain Republicans, 1865-1900: Politics and the Appalachian Community* (Chapel Hill: University of North Carolina Press, 1978).

The history of the prohibition movement in Tennessee is adequately traced by Paul E. Isaac, *Prohibition and Politics: Turbulent Decades in Tennessee, 1885-1920* (Knoxville: University of Tennessee Press, 1965). A good short treatment is Eric Russell Lacy, "Tennessee Teetotalism: Social Forces and the Politics of Progressivism," *Tennessee Historical Quarterly* 24 (Fall 1965): 219-40. Except for prohibition, there is a dearth of scholarly literature on the Progressive era in Tennessee. J. M. Shahan, "Reform and Politics in Tennessee: 1906-1914" (Ph.D. dissertation, Vanderbilt University), is an interpretative study of the era. William D. Miller, *Memphis During the Progressive Era, 1900-1917* (Memphis: Memphis State University Press, 1957), is a study of only one city; election battles are discussed in J. M. Shahan, "The Rhetoric of Reform: The 1906 Gubernatorial Race in Tennessee," *Tennessee Historical Quarterly* 35 (Spring 1976): 65-82, and in Arthur S. Link, "Democratic Politics and the Presidential Campaign of 1912 in Tennessee," *East Tennessee Historical Society's Publications* 18 (1946): 107-30; and blacks in the Progressive era are covered in Lester C. Lamon, *Black Tennesseans, 1900-1930* (Knoxville: University of Tennessee Press, 1977).

Several broader studies are invaluable for achieving an understanding of the Carmack era. These include C. Vann Woodward, *Origins of the New South, 1877-1913*, Vol. 9, *A History of the South*, ed. Wendell Holmes Stephenson and E. Merton Coulter (Baton Rouge: Louisiana State University Press, 1967); Charles R. Wilson, *Baptised in Blood: Religion of the Lost Cause, 1865-1920* (Athens: University of Georgia Press, 1980); Thomas L. Connelly, *The Marble Man: Robert E. Lee and His Image in American Society* (New York: Knopf, 1977); Jack Temple Kirby, *Darkness at the Dawning: Race and Reform in the Progressive South* (Philadelphia: J. B. Lippincott Co., 1972); Dewey Grantham, *The Regional Imagination: The South and Recent American History* (Nashville: Vanderbilt University Press, 1979); George Brown Tindall, *The Emergence of the New South, 1913-1945*, Vol. 10, *A History of the South*, ed. Stephenson and Coulter; and Tindall, *The Persistent Tradition in New South Politics* (Baton Rouge: Louisiana State University Press, 1975).

There are a number of works on Tennessee in the late nineteenth and early twentieth centuries of varying value that provide some insight into the Carmack era: Clyde L. Ball, "The Public Career of Colonel A. S. Colyar, 1870-1877," *Tennessee Historical Quarterly* 12 (March, June, September 1953): 23-47, 106-28, 213-38; Sarah McCanless Howell, "The Editorials of Arthur S. Colyar, Nashville Prophet of the New South," *Tennessee Historical Quarterly* 27 (Fall 1968): 262-76; William Waller, ed., *Nashville in the 1890s* (Nashville: Vanderbilt University Press, 1970); J. A. Sharp, "The Entrance of the Farmer's Alliance into Tennessee Politics," *East Tennessee Historical Society's Publications* 9 (1937): 77-92; Sharp, "The Farmer's Alliance and the People's Party in Tennessee," *East Tennessee Historical Society's Publications* 10 (1938): 91-113;

Verton M. Queener, "The East Tennessee Republicans As A Minority Party, 1870-1896," *East Tennessee Historical Society's Publications* 15 (1943): 49-73; Queener, "The East Tennessee Republicans in State and Nation, 1870-1900," *Tennessee Historical Quarterly* 2 (1943): 99-128; William Waller, ed., *Nashville: 1900-1910* (Nashville: Vanderbilt University Press, 1972); Queener, "The East Tennessee Republican Party, 1900-1914," *East Tennessee Historical Society's Publications* 22 (1950): 94-127; Russell L. Stockard, "The Election and First Administration of Ben W. Hooper As Governor of Tennessee," *East Tennessee Historical Society's Publications* 26 (1954): 38-59; Stockard, "The Election and Second Administration of Governor B. W. Hooper of Tennessee as Reflected in the State Press," *East Tennessee Historical Society's Publications* 32 (1960): 51-71;

J. Winfield Qualls, "Fusion Victory and the Tennessee Senatorship, 1910-1911," *West Tennessee Historical Society Papers* 15 (1961): 79-92; Wallace

McClure, "Governmental Reorganization, A Consitutional Need in Tennessee," *Tennessee Historical Magazine* 2 (1916): 89-97; Franklin O. Rouse, "The Historical Background of Tennessee's Administrative Reorganization Act of 1923," *East Tennessee Historical Society's Publications* 8 (1936): 104-20; Andrew David Holt, *The Struggle for a System of Public Schools in Tennessee, 1903-1936* (New York: Bureau of Publications, Teachers College, Columbia University, 1938); Maury Klein, *History of the Louisville and Nashville Railroad* (New York: The Macmillan Company, 1972); and Thomas D. Clark, *The Southern Country Editor* (Indianapolis and New York: The Bobbs-Merrill Company, 1948).

Carmack was the subject of several unpublished theses. They are shallow works, except one: Will Dunn Smith, "The Carmack-Patterson Campaign and Its Aftermath in Tennessee Politics" (M.A. thesis, Vanderbilt University, 1939), is useful for tracing the events of the debates between Carmack and Patterson in the gubernatorial campaign of 1908.

INDEX

Agrarian revolt, 38-47, 66, 105
Agricultural Wheel, 39
Allen, "Private" John, 74, 78, 80-81
Anderson, James Douglas, 148, 150
Anderson, John M., 150
Anti-Imperialist League, 92
Anti-Saloon League, 123, 133, 135, 150, 164
Armistead, George Harrison, 114, 116, 117, 129
Baptist and Reflector, 124
Bate, William Brimage, 64, 82-83, 102, 105-108, 110-11
"Black and Tan" Republicans, 75
Blair bill, 21, 22, 24
Bledsoe Female Academy, 6
Bonfort's Wine and Spirit Circular, 134
Bourbon "regular" Democrats, 18, 24-25, 39, 41, 52-53
Bourbonism. See Bourbon "regular" Democrats
Brownsville, Texas, affair, 99-100, 102
Bryan, William Jennings, 71, 75, 78, 140
"Buchanan Democrats," 63
Buchanan, John Price, 39, 40, 41, 43, 44, 46-47, 63-64, 65

Campbellite Church. See Christian Church

Carmack, Agnes (sister), 6
Carmack, Cornelius (great-great grandfather), 4-5
Carmack, Cornelius (grandfather), 4, 5, 6
Carmack, Edward Ward (uncle), 5
Carmack, Edward Ward: education, 2, 10-11; personality, 3; ancestry, 4-5; birth, 6; childhood, 9; admitted to the bar, 12; in Tennessee General Assembly, 12; editorial writer in Columbia, 13; marriage, 13-14; as a Bourbon "regular" Democrat, 20, 24, 26, 51-52, 88; appointed editorial writer for the *Daily American*, 14, 17; appointed editor of the *Nashville Democrat*, 24; friendship with Duncan Cooper, 20, 35, 48; feud with Arthur S. Colyar, 25-31; appointed editor of the *Daily American*, 33, 35; on sectional conflict, 36-37; on the Old South, 37; on the Lost Cause, 37, 101; on Confederate veterans, 37-38; on the agrarian revolt, 39-42; editorial attacks on John H. McDowell, 43-47, 63-64; appointed editor Memphis *Commercial*, 48; aligns with "old families" in Memphis, 51-52; editorial attacks on Judge DuBose, 53-61; editorial feud with W. A. Collier, 54-61; aborted duel with W. A. Collier, 59-60; appointed editor of the *Commercial Appeal*,

61; editorial debate with Henry Watterson, 62-63; on monetary policy, 69-70; conflict with *Commercial Appeal* board of directors, 71-72; resigns as editor of the *Commercial Appeal*, 71-72; 1896 congressional race, 72-76; election to Congress challenged, 76-80; defends seat in Congress, 79-80; election to the Senate, 83-85; as an orator, 87-88, 100-101; on war with Spain, 89-90; on imperialism, 89-96; on Cuba, 90-91; on the Philippines, 91-95; on the Panama Canal, 95-96; on race and race relations, 96-100; "Lecture on Character," 102; the "snap caucus," 108-109; challenged by Robert L. Taylor (1906), 109; 1906 senatorial contest, 109-13; governor's race (1906), 115-18; urged to enter 1908 governor's race, 120-22; on prohibition, 124-28; 1908 governor's race, 128-37; appointed editor of the *Tennessean*, 138-39; break with Duncan Cooper, 141-42; editorial attack on Duncan Cooper, 142-45; death, 146; statue, 159; legacy, 160-67

Carmack, Edward Ward, Jr., 14, 15, 162, 163

Carmack, Elizabeth Cobey Dunnington, 13, 14, 75-77, 119, 149, 162

Carmack, Elvira Kate Holding, 5-11

Carmack, Francis "Franc" McMillin, 5-8

Carmack, Joseph (great uncle), 5

Carmack Memorial Association, 152

Carmack, Nancy Agnes Smith (paternal grandmother), 4-5

Carmack, Samuel Cornelius (brother), 6

Charleston *News and Courier*, 62

Chicago *Tribune*, 36

Christian Advocate, 136

Christian Church, 6, 8

Cleveland, Grover, 24, 63-64, 70, 73, 92

Collier, William A., 31, 49, 63; editorial debate with Carmack, 52-61; loses the *Appeal-Avalanche*, 61

Columbia *Herald and Mail*, 13

Colyar, Arthur St. Clair, 20, 24, 32; background, 22-23; editor of the *Daily American*, 22-23; conflict with Carmack, 25-31

Confederate monuments, 100-101

Confederate veterans, 36, 37, 38, 100-101

Cooper, Duncan Brown, 22, 35, 48, 147, 148, 155, 160, 163; acquires the *Daily American* (1886), 18, 19; background, 19-20; acquires the *Daily American* (1888), 32; in 1906 senatorial contest, 141-42; abused editorially, 142-45; death of Carmack, 145-46; tried for murder, 150-52; pardoned by Governor Patterson, 153-54

Cooper, Robin, 145-46, 147, 148, 150, 151, 153, 160, 163

Cox, John Isaac, 108, 110-11, 115, 117-18, 142-44

Craig, E. B., 120, 144, 151

Crawford, West J., 60, 61, 71, 72

Culleoka Institute, 1-3, 10, 12

David Lipscomb College, 8

Democratic party, 17-20, 39, 165. See also Bourbon "regular" Democrats

Dibrell, George Gibbs, 112

DuBose, Judge Julius J., 53-56, 58, 61

Dunnington, Elizabeth Cobey. See Elizabeth Cobey Dunnington Carmack

Dunnington, Ellen Ewing, 14

Dunnington, Frank Cobey, 13

Eastman, Mrs. Charles H., 146, 151

Eighteenth Amendment to the Constitution, 164

Euclid Hill Academy, 5, 10

Evans, Henry Clay, 66-67, 135

Farmer's Alliance, 39-47, 64-66. See also agrarian revolt and Populist party

Fitzhugh, Guston T., 150, 160

Folk, Edgar E., 124, 134

"Force bill," 37, 40

"Four Mile Law," 123-24, 133, 152-53

Franklin College, 5, 6, 8

Frazier, James Beriah, 105, 107-108, 110-11, 115-16, 118, 165

Grosvenor, Charles Henry, 77, 78, 79

Harper's Weekly, 87, 102

Harris, Isham Green, 18, 31, 70, 73-74, 81, 82, 88

Harrison, Joshua, 2, 3

Hepburn-Dolliver bill, 126

Hepburn Rate bill, 88

Holding, Elvira Kate. See Elvira Kate Holding Carmack

INDEX

Holly Springs, Mississippi, 59, 60
Hooper, Ben Wade, 156, 165

Independent, 99
Indianola, Mississippi, incident, 99
Jacinto, Mississippi, 5-9
Jackson *Whig*, 148
Journalism, history of, xiv-xvi
Journalism in Tennessee, xiv-xvi
Joy, Charles, 73, 81
Keating, John McLeod, 31
Knoxville *Journal and Tribune*, 148
Knoxville *Sentinel*, 148

"Law and Order League," 53
Lea, Luke, 128, 138, 150, 156, 159, 164-65
"Lecture on Character," 102
Lewis, E. C., 140, 141
Lipscomb, David, 8-9, 11, 119
Lipscomb, Granville, 9
Lost Cause, 37, 101, 161
Louisville *Courier-Journal*, xvi, 27, 62
Louisville and Nashville Railroad, xv, 120, 132, 140, 142
Lyceum Bureau, 102

McCarn, Jeff, 150-51
McCormack, Nancy Cox, 159
McDowell, John Henry, 43-47, 64
McKellar, Kenneth Douglas, 72, 76, 84-85, 163
McKinley, William, 76, 90, 91-92
McMillin, Benton, 82-85, 105, 106, 107, 108-109, 112, 116
McMillin family, 4
Marshall Gazette, 112-13
Maury Democrat, 13
Memphis charter revision, 132
Memphis *Appeal*, 31, 49
Memphis *Appeal-Avalanche*, 41, 49, 50, 52, 54-56, 60, 61
Memphis *Avalanche*, 49
Memphis *Commercial Appeal*, 61-67, 71, 72-73, 75, 92, 109, 136, 148
Memphis *Daily Commercial*, 41, 47-49, 50-65
Memphis *Evening Scimitar*, 61
Memphis *News-Scimitar*, 148
Minerva College, 6
Model License League, 133

Money issue, 69-70
Moore, William Robert, 36
Morning Jacksonian, 130

Nashville *American*, 120, 140-41, 148-49
Nashville *Banner*, 24, 41, 121, 147, 149, 160-61
Nashville Bible College, 8
Nashville *Daily American*, xv, xvii, 13, 17-33, 35-49, 63
Nashville Democrat, xvi, 24-33, 35
Nashville *Evening and Sunday Morning Herald*, 35, 41, 43
Nashville *Tennessean*, 128, 138-42, 146-48, 150, 152-55
Nashville *Union*, 17, 20, 21, 23, 24
Nashville *Union and American*, 13, 17
"New residents" of Memphis, 52
New South creed, 18, 23, 52
New York Times, 93, 103

"Old families" of Memphis, 51-52, 53, 54
Old South myth, 37, 161

Panama Canal, 95-96
Patterson, Josiah, 39, 40n.6, 73-74, 85; 1896 congressional race, 75; contests 1896 election, 76-81
Patterson, Malcolm Rice "Ham," 85, 115-18, 120-21, 138, 141, 143-45, 148, 150, 152, 157, 159, 162-66; 1908 governor's race, 128-37; pardons Duncan Cooper, 153-54; pardon record, 154-55; 1910 elections, 155-56
Peay, Austin, 129, 159, 167
Pendleton Act, 133
People's party. *See* Populist party
Philippine Islands, 90-95
Platt Amendment, 90
Populist party, 63, 65-66, 69. *See also* agrarian revolt
Progressive movement, 165-66
Prohibition, 137-38; prohibition movement, 123-26; in 1906 senatorial contest, 126-28; in 1908 governor's race, 131, 132-36; enactment of statewide law, 152-53; failure of, 164
Prohibition party, 125, 134

Railroad Commission, 166-67
Republican party, 17-18, 24-25, 66, 137, 156

Roosevelt, Theodore, 92, 94-96, 99, 102, 119
St. Louis *Globe-Democrat*, 31, 36
Sensational journalism, xv
Sharp, John D., 145, 147, 150
Shelbyville Gazette, 106, 107
Sherman Silver Purchase Act, 69-70, 73
"Sky blue" Democrats, 13, 19
Smith, Nancy Agnes. *See* Nancy Agnes Smith Carmack
"Snap caucus," 108-13
Snodgrass, D. L., 83, 85, 109
Social Darwinism, 100
"Southern Sound Money Convention," 70-71
Stahlman, Edward Bushrod, 24, 28, 31, 156
State debt, 19
Stephenson family, 4
Stratton, B. M., 54, 55, 60-61

Taylor, Alfred Alexander, 21
Taylor, Robert Love, 23-24, 39, 75, 81, 82-84, 105-108, 115-16, 120, 126-29, 141, 156, 166; elected governor (1886), 21; on the Blair bill, 21-22; 1906 senatorial contest, 109-13

Teller Amendment, 89, 90
Temperance movement. *See* prohibition
Tennessee Coal, Iron, and Railroad Company, 23, 26, 30
Tennessee Supreme Court, 153-56
The Olympian, 98
Tollett "Good Roads Bill," 124
Turley, Thomas Battle, 76, 82-84
Turney, Peter, 63, 66-67

Vendome Theater, 112

Washington, Booker T., 99
Washington Post, 80, 88, 102, 113-14
Watterson, Henry, xvi, 27, 62
Webb, John, 10-11, 11n.13
Webb, William Robert "Sawney," 1, 1n.1, 2, 3, 10-11
Webb's school, 1-3, 1n.1, 10-11
Weekly Toiler, 43, 65
Whig industrialists, 18, 19
Women's Christian Temperance Union, 123, 133, 137, 149, 150, 152, 159

"Yellow journalism," xv